BLOODGAMES
The Story of the Vaughans,
a Southern Family and Its Neighbors

Terry Vaughan

HERITAGE BOOKS
2009

HERITAGE BOOKS

AN IMPRINT OF HERITAGE BOOKS, INC.

Books, CDs, and more—Worldwide

For our listing of thousands of titles see our website
at
www.HeritageBooks.com

Published 2009 by
HERITAGE BOOKS, INC.
Publishing Division
100 Railroad Ave. #104
Westminster, Maryland 21157

International Standard Book Numbers
Paperbound: 978-0-7884-0944-8
Clothbound: 978-0-7884-8245-8

This volume concerns itself with a branch of the Vaughan Family. Although several branches of Vaughans have been subject to treatises, this branch seems to be little known and even less written about.

The volume began as a sketch of one family, but soon outgrew its pants. The impetus for the expansion lies partly in the natural demand of the material for expression--in the words of the Yokums, no man is an Ireland--and partly because during the compilation I developed a strong interest in the local history and historical research in general.

In an effort to keep a flow to the work, while at the same time presenting as much material as possible to researchers, I have adopted the technique of putting digressions in sidebars. Hopefully the result is a work that is entertaining as well as of utility. I humbly accept my work as a success if it serves only as a resource for a few researchers struggling in their quest for information. I hope it is of assistance to you, Dear Reader.

Associated families receiving rather extensive treatment are Andersons, Bradfords, Brunsons, Clarks, Duboses, Friersons, Harrisons, Jameses, Joneses, Moores, Rees', Reynolds, Singletons, Smiths, Spanns, Sumters, Watieses and Wilsons. Other well-known families were often in the subject areas, but I have written less about them because much is already in print on these others (such as Canteys, Caperses, Millers, etc.) or they were not central to the direction of my research. I hope you are not offended. Also I doubt not that many may know more of the families than I. I offer only the statement of the sporty knuckler who said, as he wiped the blood from his nose: "We is outclassed."

My dates are sometimes at variance with other researchers. One must choose. I chose wherever possible to use primary sources, such as grave markers in the case of birth dates, death dates, etc. Often I give both dates when conflicting dates appear, leaving the reader to choose according to the source he prefers. I have also tried to indicate where I had doubts about my source or if I were unsure of my conclusions (or those of others) from the evidence of the given source.

My sources are primarily census records, various probate court records, obituaries, military records (primarily from the U. S. Archives), grave markers, family Bibles, local newspapers and other published works. Years ago, when I was studying at the University of South Carolina, I on occasion took the bus to Sumter and, with notebook in hand, jotted names down from courthouse records. I have not always been able to cite the document for each fact gleaned and to do so would probably be overly tedious, but I have done so if it seemed important. I have tried to follow the rule of providing enough information for the reader to check for himself and have included abstracts in an appendix at the end. A bibliography of sources is also included. Bracketed information indicates I am the supplier. An instance for using brackets would be to correct an error in spelling or omitted information by a censustaker or court official.

Many people assisted in bringing this work into existence. Certain of these I would like to mention in particular. My grandmother, Eva Wright Vaughan's, prodigious memory was of paramount importance. Sadly, she passed away in 1989 at the age of ninety-nine. Her sister, Annie Lizzie Dubberly, now also deceased, was of great help. Both of these ladies were able to recall events of nine decades past, supplied word-of-mouth testimonials and the initial motivation for the project. My father,

Miles L. Vaughan, Sr., related events of the second decade of this century. My uncle, James Douglas Vaughan, seems to have been the initial undertaker of this project. From him it passed to my brother Miles L. Vaughan, Jr., who supplied me with core material from which I proceeded. During research I made the acquaintance of Lynn A. Weber of Burbank, California. Pat, as she is known, was working on parallel lines and supplied much information, particularly copies of the "Vaughan Bible."

A special thanks to Mrs. F. Russell Galbreath of New Smyrna Beach, Florida, from whose files I received much information. Her information came in large part from Raymond Dick and Miss Jenny Dargan, deceased cousin and daughter, respectively, of Major John Dargan, cited later; J. Nelson Frierson, cited in text; her own researches; and information from a professional genealogist working on similar lines, now deceased, Mrs. Eugene Stanley of Savannah, Georgia.

Thanks to Mrs. Clara Mae Jacobs of the South Caroliniana Library in Columbia and the many other helpful employees there. My compliments to the employees of the South Carolina Archives research room for their assistance. In Sumter I received help from Miss Margaret McElveen and Mrs. Myrtis Osteen, members of the Sumter County Historical Society. Much information on the Friersons came from Mary Chesnut Phillips Britton, descendant of both Vaughans and Friersons. Mrs. Peggy Norris of Sumter furnished information on many members of the Bradford Family. Verna Fitzpatrick of Dunwoody, Georgia, provided much information on the line of Henry Jackson Vaughan. I also owe a lot to Linda Crawford. Thanks to the staff of the Orange County Public Library, especially the genealogy reading room staff, Elizabeth Ward, Katharine Cooper, Mercedes Stephens, Eleanor Crawford, Carol Festit and Michael

Hopkins to name a few specific people who helped.

In the latter stages of this work I drew extensively from material in the genealogical library of the Church of Jesus Christ of the Latter Day Saints, especially the International Genealogical Index microfiche. I would like to thank Joan Adkins Lindsey, Ed and Mildred Campbell, Jo Ann Fults, Rosemarie Forrest, Henry Danner, Rosa Campbell, Bob Jessup, Carol King, Virginia Macfie, Emma Minshew, Ethel Porter, Providencia Rosado, Rhonda Watson, Peggy Willard, Wilma Woodruff and Jean Workman of Orlando.

We are indebted to the W. P. A. for the work they did many years ago, transcribing records in the courthouses for filing in archives. The researcher must exercise care, however, for errors did creep in. For instance a name such as John I. Moore appears often in a certain time and place; then suddenly appears a John J. Moore, who promptly disappears from the records. Some things the researcher should not accept unquestioningly. "I" and "J" often seem to transform themselves; script S often became an "L" in typing; "f's" became "s's"; double s, written much like the German estzet, becomes "B"; and a certain script H has been known to become an "L". I also received the help of Ruth McCleskey, who is credited mostly in the text. I hope I have given credit where it is due and sufficiently alerted the reader to major pitfalls.

Terry Vaughan
Winter Park, Florida
September 4, 1991

In the past five years I have received additional assistance in gathering information for this volume. I therefore acknowledge these

contributors: Mrs. Nolan Stewart Vaughan of
Yazoo City, Mississippi; Susan (Vaughan) Edge,
daughter of Aubrey Vaughan, of Vaughan,
Mississippi; Marguerite (Mrs. Fred) Marchman
of New Port Richey, Florida; Arlina Moss of
Punta Gorda, Florida; Thomas A Dorrough of
Friendswood, Texas; and William A. Vaughan of
Canton, Mississippi.

My brother Robert E. Vaughan, currently of
Grand Junction, Colorado was of immeasurable
help in formatting the final document for
publication.

I had most difficulty in getting information on
living or recently living members of the target
families   This perversity of nature results
from the fact that there are not as many
written records on them and it is difficult to
carry on enough correspondence to get a lot of
material for such a work. For that reason--and
because I look upon this work as a resource
book--I have included several pages at the end
that can be used by any who so desire to
continue their own tree.

Terry Vaughan
8052 Striped Marlin Way,
Orlando, Florida 32822
May 22,1996

INTRODUCTION: MIGRATIONS

Do you like a mystery? This volume begins with a mystery. Perhaps you feel a genealogical work should solve mysteries rather than create them. Yet an exciting facet of genealogical study is that one mystery leads to another, so that no matter how many you solve another is waiting in the wings.

Our initial mystery: Who was the father of Henry, Noel and Naomi Vaughan? In 1772 the Vaughan Family arrived in Sumter County, South Carolina, then known as Claremont District of Craven County. They had come from Northampton County, North Carolina, where they are known to have resided from at least as early as 1749. They used the name Vaughan, but were the three Vaughans by blood? In his will Vincent Vaughan speaks of Henry, Noel and Naomi in different terms from his other four children. The three removed to South Carolina. In his will Vincent had referred to Henry, Noel and Naomi as Claders, also calling Noel Huckens and Hutchen. The other four did not remove to South Carolina (notwithstanding the fact that a John Vaughan left a will naming his wife Ginea in Sumter in 1800, since a North Carolina will proves Vincent's John died in North Carolina long before 1800). We will address this mystery in detail as we study Vincent a few pages hence.

Let's trace the movements of the descendants of these Vaughans. Henry had five sons and two daughters. Most of this generation remained in South Carolina. Two sons did leave the state. Vincent, son of Henry, had moved to Alabama by 1817, but was deceased by 1819, per legal documents. John Bradford Vaughan moved to the Gulf Coast, apparently about 1810 or 1811. He commuted between Jackson County, Mississippi, and Mobile. Censuses locate John B. in Jackson

County in 1830 and Mobile in 1840. John's children also appear in the censuses of the areas. A third generation member of Henry's line, also named Henry, removed to Yazoo County, Mississippi, about 1836 and remained there until his death, leaving many descendants in the area.

Noel Vaughan had three sons and one daughter. All but one of the sons remained in South Carolina. That son, William Vaughan, Jr., left for Alabama--about 1832 it seems--sojourning for a year or two in Troup County, Georgia. William seemed to be spurred to migration by the opening of the Creek Indian lands, like those also in Yazoo, Mississippi, where his cousin had located. Economic factors probably had also exerted an influence, the economy of South Carolina having become depressed.

In the fourth generation, a son of Noel, Jr., James Vaughan removed to McLennan County, Texas, and several later generations found Texas an attractive destination.

The Vaughan name has almost disappeared from Sumter County. Many descendants of female members of the family remain in names such as Frierson, Dargan, Rees, Reynolds and others.

In the text I have given a letter/number designation to members to help the reader keep track. Males are given a number corresponding to birth order, as best I could determine, in the family. Females likewise receive a letter according to birth order. The total number of letters and digits indicate the generation of descent from Vincent and Frances Vaughan. For example, 1a1 would be the eldest son of a first daughter. Where ages or order were not available, coding was done on the order most likely from existing information. As we shall see, Vincent's #1 designation may be honorary.

TABLE OF CONTENTS

In the Beginning: Toeing the Line

This treatise concerns a certain Vaughan Family, which emerges under that name in 1749 in Northampton County, North Carolina. In that year Vincent Vaughan died, leaving a will naming his wife and seven children: John, Margaret, wife of Peter Breathen, Vincent, Sarah, Henry Clader, Noel Huckens and Naomy Vaughan Clader. An abstract of this will may be found in James Robert Bent Hathaway's Register of North Carolina, vol. I, page 497. The original is in the North Carolina Archives in Raleigh. The deponent signed as Vinson, Vinson and Vincent seeming to be used rather interchangeably for this individual.

The naming of the last three children as Clader (or Clador) and Huckens (or Hutchen), together with the wording of the will and some later documents, has led to speculation that these three might have been stepchildren to Vincent. Henry, Naomi and Noel were definitely children of Frances (Waddill) Vaughan.

First, the wording of the will: Vincent's will provided bequeaths of property to the first four children, but the last three were to receive only the future issue of a slave "loaned to his wife during her widowhood." Secondly, a deed of gift from Noel Waddill to his sister, Frances Johnson's, children does not name the other four. Frances had married William Johnson after Vincent's death. Noel's deed, listed in Book B, page 228 of Sumter County Conveyances, states Noel is a resident of New Kent County, Virginia, and names as Frances' children Naomi Sones (changed to Jones by erasure), Henry Clader and Noel Hutchens Clader. The deed was dated 12 March 1761, but not recorded until 25 April 1805. Thus Naomi had married Sones by 1761. The failure of the document to mention the other Vaughan children surely means these others were not her children. Noel's bequeath to Naomi and her

1

children was "one Negro girl Sal and her
increase, in possession of William Johnson of
Northampton County, North Carolina; to Henry
Clader and Noel Hutchens Clader, two negro
slaves, Pat and her child Judith, in possession
of said William Johnson." To Frances he gave
use of Pat "during her [Frances'] natural
life." Consideration was love and affection.
The document was signed by Noel Waddill and
witnessed by John Waddill, Jr., William Irby
and (by her mark) Hannah Waddill. The document
was proven before J. Edwards, Pub. Reg., by
William Irby.

The third item pertinent to the parentage of
these three Vaughans is the will of a Vinson
Vaughan, dated 10 December 1764, from
Northampton County (Will Book One, Will 84,
page 127). Son of Vinson of the 1749 will, the
junior Vinson names in his will sisters Sarah
Crump and Margaret Hazelwood [the former Mrs.
Breathen]. He also left bequeaths to John
Vaughan's children, although not specifically
saying John was a brother. The conspicuous
point is that the three Vaughans above are not
mentioned.

To previous researcher, Mrs. Eugene Stanley,
this meant these three were stepchildren to
Vincent, having been born to a Mr. Clador, a
Mr. Hutchens or both. This might be true, but
perhaps Vinson just had less affection for his
half siblings. As for the elder Vinson's will,
it was not uncommon for a parent to give
tangible bequeaths to his older children, while
a trust or future accrual from same were put
into the custody of a widow for minor children
to possess later or reap the benefits thereof.

This researcher has been unable to locate any
Clader, Clador, Claytor, Clardy, Hutchings,
Hutchen or Huckens (or phonetic equivalent of
the same) in any North Carolina/Virginia record
who could qualify as an earlier husband of
Frances Waddill. The three children at issue
were probably minors in 1749. Otherwise they
lived to very advanced ages; Noel did not die
until 1829.

Both Frances and Vincent came from New Kent County, Virginia. Vestry lists there treat of Vincent Vaughan, contractor, builder and sawyer by profession. This Vincent was likely a father or kinsman to the subject of this vignette, for the Vincent of vestry records would have been much older than Frances. For information on this Vincent see the Vestry Book of St. Peter's Parish and also Virginia Genealogist, vol. II, page 95. The Vestry Book states Vincent was a sawyer on pages 75, 85, 94 and 105, this reference placing him as doing sawyer work in the first decade of the 1700's. If the same as the Vincent who died in 1749, he would have been well established professionally even before Frances' birth. Still, it was not uncommon for young widows to marry men much older than themselves, for an established husband could better provide for their children--likewise, the older man needed a young wife to manage the household. Vermeille Galbreath believes Vincent was the son of a John Vaughan, a migrant to America. Many Vaughans were in the New Kent County area and three appear on quit rent rolls for the county. Frances was born on 2 May 1706 (Vestry Book, page 407), daughter of William Waddill, a member and vestryman of St. Peter's Church. This church had as members such historically prominent personages as Custises, Lewises, Meriwethers, Dandridges and Parkes. Galbreath believes William Waddill's father was also a migrant to America.

In Northampton County the elder Vincent's name appears in several deed transactions, mostly as a witness;. These transactions involved other Vaughans and sometimes Hollands. Vaughans and Hollands appear in an Upper Parish Vestry of the early 1740's for Nansemond County, Virginia, perhaps this is only a coincidence. Appendix XII covers the above deeds.

Frances remained in North Carolina after marrying William Johnson. Henry, Noel and Naomi removed to South Carolina in 1772. The year of migration is confirmed in an

application for Revolutionary pension by
William Vaughan, Sr., eldest son of the above
Henry. In the application he stated he was
born in 1764 and removed to Craven County
[Sumter], South Carolina, in 1772.
Corroboration is provided by deed in
Northampton County wherein Henry Vaughan
conveys property--acquired from William Spence
in 1763 (Deed Book 3, page 266)--to William
Love of Brunswick County, Virginia, on 26
November 1772 (Deed Book 5, pages 279-281).
Incidentally Brunswick County was just across
the line from Northampton County. In a
document of 9 June 1787, Noel Vaughan and his
wife attested, along with thirteen others, that
"they knew Amy Cornet and her mother Margaret
to be free people" and formerly of Northampton
County, North Carolina, near the Roanoke River.

Thus, whether natural children of Vincent or
not, Henry and Noel (and possibly Naomi before
her marriage to Sones) were bearing the name of
Vaughan when they removed to South Carolina,
Henry using that name when he bought land in
1763 from Mr. Spence. Mrs. Stanley and Mrs.
Galbreath feel the name was adopted by the
three out of love for their "stepfather."

Naomi's obituary in the <u>Camden</u> <u>Gazette</u> <u>and</u>
<u>Mercantile</u> <u>Advertiser</u> of 12 August 1819 states
she was born in Brunswick County, Virginia.
The obituary indicates by her age that she was
born about 1736. Since Brunswick County is
directly above Northampton County and indeed in
Virginia, Naomi could have been born in either
county. Unless well versed in the local
geography, one might be uncertain of the state
of one's birth. The Roanoke Rapids area
reached into both states and, if legal business
were conducted in one state, documents might be
filed there, even if both parties resided in
the other. Possibly a person near the line
might go from one state to the other several
times in the course of his daily tasks. A
person might put the county of one state with
the name of the other state in a deposition: in
his pension application previously mentioned,
William Vaughan, Sr., states he was born in

Northampton County, Virginia. We know this is not correct as that county in Virginia is on its Atlantic neck. We cannot know for sure, if he was born in Brunswick County, Virginia, or Northampton County, North Carolina. The uncertainty, however, surely places the site on the border of the states. William Vaughan, Jr., eldest son of Noel Vaughan, named Virginia as his place of birth in several censuses. Born in 1772, probably before the Vaughans departed for South Carolina, he was likely born about the same place as William, Sr.

Another Vincent Vaughan lived in Granville County, North Carolina. He stated in depositions that he came from Northampton County and earlier from New Kent County, Virginia. Several other Vincents are known and Appendix XII discusses them. A John Vaughan who died in Sumter in 1800 seems to be of no relationship to the 1772 emigrants. A courthouse fire of 1800 destroyed most of the records relating to this John. The will of the younger Vincent Vaughan (see page 1) makes it clear his brother John had died by that date.

A Caravan to Craven

Naomi Vaughan (1a)

Naomi Vaughan, daughter of Frances and daughter or step-daughter to Vincent Vaughan, was born about 1736, according to her obituary. Naomi married first a Mr. Sones or Jones. According to Noel Waddill's deed of 1761 she had married and had children by that year. J and S were written in much the same way around the turn of the 18th century and, since we cannot hear the pronunciation of the name, we cannot know the original pronunciation and whether the name changed. After the first decade of the 1800's we no longer see the name Sones, but many references to a Henry or William Jones appear in Sumter records. By Sones Naomi had two children: Hall (1a1) and Mary (1aa).

Hall (nickname for Henry) had two sons and one daughter: Henry, Jr. (1a11), William (1a12) and Mary (1a1a), who married Dempsey Tyner. Sumter County Deed Records (Book A, page 319) records the sale of four slaves by John Bradford Vaughan to William Jones. The names of these two grandsons of Naomi coincide with the Joneses we spoke of in the previous paragraph.

Mary, Naomi's daughter, married on 17 July 1790 James Bates. Four children are known: Martha (1aaa), born in 1791, who married James Gay, Jehu (1aa1), Hariet (1aab), born in 1799 or early 1800 and John (1aa2), born in 1806 or early 1807. An item from the Camden Equity Journal serves as a source of information on the last two children and on Martha Gibson, mentioned below: on 19 February 1816 James Gibson petitioned to be guardian of Harriet and John Bates aged 16 and 9, respectively. The wording of the petition indicates Martha's half-sister Mary was deceased. Perhaps James' wife Martha was also deceased, since the petition was in his name only; more likely he was the only one required to petition, although both he and Martha presented an earlier

petition to the court, which will be mentioned later.

Naomi married secondly William Hampton. According to Mrs. Eugene Stanley (South Carolina Historical and Genealogical Magazine, vol. 69, page 218) Naomi was a widow and the marriage, the second for both, was about 1780 in North Carolina or Virginia. Hampton had a daughter from a previous marriage. Aley Hampton married Edward Micheson of Caldwell County, Kentucky. They had two children: Rebecca Stephens Micheson, who married Jonathan Styles, and Nancy, who married on 29 July 1813 Lewis Martin. By Hampton Naomi had two or three other children: Patsy (1ab), Martha (?) (1ac), and Elizabeth (1ad).

Mrs. Sally Dwight of New York City states that Martha and Patsy are one and the same. This researcher has found reference to both in the same document; still they could be one and the same. Documents show that Patsy predeceased her mother.

Martha married first Joseph Sylvester, son of Asberry Sylvester. They had five children: William Asberry (1ac1), Sarah Anne (1aca), both of whom died young; Joseph H. (1ac2); Mary Jerusha (1acb); and Frances E. (1acc). Martha married secondly James Gibson, son of Phineas Gibson, by whom she had seven children as best can be determined. Martha and her second husband petitioned the court for the executors (James Sylvester and James Bates) to partition her first husband's estate. Sylvester was Joseph's brother and Bates was Martha's half-sister's husband. This petition was heard on 12 February 1815 by Judge Thomas Waties. The petition above (of 1816) was heard by Judge deSaussure and indicates James Bates must have died in the interim, so that the two younger Bates children were orphans. The two court petitions cited came from South Carolina Magazine of Ancestral Research.

Elizabeth married Mason Spears, by whom she had six children: Elizabeth (1ada), who married

Atkinson; Austin (1ad1); Alaof (1adb); Richard
Hampton (1ad2); Martha Greniry (1adc); and
Theodore Mason (1ad3). Mrs. Dwight feels that
Elizabeth was identical with Aley and thus
Hampton's daughter by his first wife. This
seems unlikely, since she would thus have
returned from Kentucky, married Mr. Spears and
moved to Mississippi. Mr. Spears was
administrating William Hampton's estate in 1805
and was himself deceased in 1811. Page 312 of
Conveyance Book EE of Sumter County shows that
Elizabeth had moved to Amite County by December
1817 and the 1820 census for that county lists
her as a head of household, as was her son
Austin.

By 1850 Joseph Sylvester was living in Gadsden
County, Florida. His wife was Violet Winslow
Wilson Davidson. The census of that year lists
their children as Sarah (1ac2a), Isabella
(1ac2b), Joseph (1ac21), Emma (1ac2c), James
(1ac22), Augusta (1ac2d), William (1ac23), Mary
(1ac2e) and Rebecca (1ac2f).

Mary J. married John M. W. Davidson, a doctor
of Gadsden County who was also active in the
county's educational system. He was an elder
in the First Presbyterian Church there. He had
five sons who served in the Confederate forces:
Lt. Col. R. M. Davidson; Maj. Joseph S. M.
Davidson; Capt. William M. Davidson; Dr. John
E. A. Davidson; and Edgar Lee Davidson. There
are indications some of the Davidsons and/or
Sylvesters later moved to Ocala. For extensive
information on these two families see Miles K.
Womack's Gadsden: A Florida County in Word and
Pictures and David A. Avant, Jr.'s Illustrated
Index of J. Randall Stanley's History of
Gadsden County, 1948 (L'Avant Studios,
Tallahassee, 1985). In the latter work Avant
has pulled together papers compiled by Stanley
but never published. According to Stanley the
Davidson and Sylvester Families descended from
Major John Davidson of Rural Hill, North
Carolina, a signer of the famous Mecklenburg
Declaration of Independence. Dr. J. M. W.
Davidson and his sister Violet (Davidson)

Sylvester, who settled in Gadsden County with their families in 1828, were his grandchildren.

Naomi died on 24 July 1819. Her obituary states she was born in Brunswick County, Virginia. William Hampton died in February of 1805. He left no will, but there are estate papers. William's brother Richard had a will probated in 1796 in which William was a witness, William Vaughan, Jr., another.

Much of the foregoing derives from Sumter County wills. Abstracts follow:

The will of Naomi Hampton, probated in 1819, names her daughters Martha Gibson and Elizabeth Spears; her grandchildren Joseph H. and Mary Sylvester, William and Henry Jones, Jr., Mary (Polly) Tyner, Jehu Bates and John Bates, and Martha Gay; her brother Noel Vaughan; her niece Elizabeth DuBose; and nephew William, son of Noel.

The will of Joseph Sylvester names his wife Martha; mother Martha West; and children Joseph H., Mary J., and Frances E. Sylvester. This will was probated in 1812 and executed by Joseph's brother James.

The will of Asberry Sylvester names his wife Martha; sons Joseph, James, Manson, Demarcus and John; daughters Sarah, wife of Col. John Moore, and Mary; mother-in-law, Mrs. Watkins. This will was dated in 1807 with James Gibson witnessing.

The will of Mason Spears names his wife Elizabeth; his sons Austin, Richard Hampton and Theodore Mason; daughters Alaof and Martha Greniry Spears and Elizabeth Atkinson. This will was probated in 1811 and executed by Littleton Atkinson, Austin Spears and Jeremiah Pitts.

Dr. John Matthew Winslow Davidson, 1801-1879, moved to Quincy in 1828 from Mecklinburg County, North Carolina. With his wife, Mary Jarusha Sylvester Davidson, he opened a school for the children of Quincy and the surrounding area in addition to serving as a dedicated physician in Gadsden County.

Dr. J. M. W. Davidson was on the board of elders of Old Philadelphia Presbyterian Church in Quincy about 1838. Letters of Andrew Jackson indicate that Reverend Davidson attended a friend of Jackson's, Dr. Bronaugh, in 1821 or 1822. In 1854 Davidson was a commission member of a committee for locating the site for a West Florida Seminary. A John Davidson was also a Republican senator from Gadsden County in 1868. He also served as a county judge (Florida Historical Quarterly, 10/1964, page 128).

HENRY VAUGHAN, SR. (11)

Henry Vaughan, Sr. was the son of Frances
Vaughan and either son or step-son to Vincent.
He appears to have been the older of the two
brothers who migrated to South Carolina. Henry
married Frances Elizabeth Bradford. According
to her great-grandson, Maj. John W. Dargan, she
came to South Carolina with an only brother
Richard and was a descendant of John Rolfe and
Pocahontas. At least part of this story is
probably true, but it is unlikely she came with
an only brother. Many Bradfords seem to have
come to South Carolina at the same time as
Henry and his wife. Families often migrated en
masse in those days for protection, especially
against Indian attacks. William, Nathaniel,
John and Celia Bradford all signed the 1787
document concerning Amy Cornet stating they
came to South Carolina in 1772 and other
Bradfords were likely in the train. A will of
a Thomas Bradford of North Carolina, dated 23
May 1761 in Northampton County, names the
decedent's children: William, Henry, Thomas,
Nathaniel, Richard, Edith, Sarah and Elizabeth.
This was probably Elizabeth's family, but also
a Thomas Bradford, with wife Mary, left a will
of 22 March 1785 in Granville County, North
Carolina, naming children Benjamin, David,
Ephraim, Philemon, Thomas, Edith, Elizabeth,
Mary, Sarah and Sealy, many of whom were born
in Northampton County (see IGI for dates and
places of birth) and a John Bradford of
Northampton (who married Rebecca Pace and left
children John, Nathaniel, Richard and three
unnamed sons) is known. For this last Bradford
Family the IGI gives birth dates and places and
a self-published work by Frieda Reid Turner,
entitled The Pace Family, 1607-1750 and
published in 1993, has some information. More
will be said concerning the origins of the
Bradfords in Appendix XII and other Appendices.

Henry died in 1809 and his wife followed him
six years later in 1815. In a deposition
Henry's son William states his family arrived
in South Carolina in 1772. A deed in

Northampton County records shows that in that year Henry sold to William Love property acquired in 1763 from William Spence. Henry received a grant from South Carolina for the material he supplied to the Continental Army during the Revolutionary War. See State Grant Book for dates of 31 May and 15 July 1784. In 1778 and 1779 he had served as petit juror for the area east of the Wateree River. Henry lived on Green Swamp, land he later bequeathed to his heirs.

Children of Henry and Elizabeth were William, Sr. (111), born 22 May 1764, married Alice Cook, granddaughter of Ann Clark, and died 21 September 1857; Henry, Jr. (112), born 13 September 1767, married Mary Margaret Anderson and died 5 March 1814; Frances (11a), born in 1778, married John Reynolds and died 6 June 1857; Elizabeth (11b), married firstly to Amos DuBose and later Samuel Dwyer, and died in November of 1822; Vincent (113), who married Elizabeth _____ and died about 1819; John Bradford (114), married firstly to Sarah Singleton and later to [Daughdrill--probably Winnie]; and Richard (115).

The 1761 will of Thomas Bradford was executed by Mary his wife, also named in the will, and his son Nathaniel. The will also named neighbors Richard Span and John Richardson, whose lands Thomas' abutted and whose names are also prominent in the Sumter area shortly after this time.

WILLIAM VAUGHAN, SR. (111)

William Vaughan, Sr. was born on 22 May 1764.
This date is given in his own testimony, so we
choose it over the 1765 listed on the
daguerreotype mentioned later. William was of
the impression he was born in Northampton
County, Virginia; however, existing documents
clearly show the area of his birth. He meant
Northampton County, North Carolina; perhaps
just across the border in Virginia. Most
documents pertaining to the family were
recorded in Northampton County, but the family
lived so near the border, he could have been
born in Brunswick County, Virginia. His aunt
Naomi was considered to have been born there.
William was designated as senior because his
cousin, son of Noel Vaughan, was about 8 years
his junior. The practice of giving the moniker
of senior and junior to same-named persons when
not father and son in bygone days has caused
much woe to researchers.

Early in life William joined the army of
General Marion, serving in John Malone's
Company of Horry's, later Richard Richardson's,
Regiment. On 10 February 1790 William married
Alice, granddaughter of Ann Clark. According
to Major John Dargan's sketches (passed through
Raymond Dick), Alice was born 24 July 1774,
daughter of Samuel and Alice Cook. William was
co-executor of the will of Henry Vaughan, Sr.
Until about 1817 his brother Vincent was co-
executor, but in that year was discharged of
that duty, presumably because he had relocated
to Alabama, although other reasons we will
treat later may have played a part. William
was also executor of the estate of his mother
Frances E. Vaughan.

For his early service William drew a pension
and received bounty land. Papers pertaining to
the pension are included in this sketch.
William was a member of the States Rights and
Free Trade Party, according to the 8 September
1832 issue of the Sumter Gazette.

Children of William and Alice were Kiturah
(111a), born in 1790. married to Samuel J.
Bradford and died 9 June 1855; Emily E.
(111b), born 20 October 1797, married John Milton
Dargan and died 17 May 1865; James Alexander
(1111); John Horace (1112), born 5 September
1801, married Victoria A. Dargan and died in
1832; Alice (111c), married Benjamin Mitchell;
Leonora C. (111d), married Samuel C. Mitchell;
Mary Henrietta (111e), born in 1811, married
Timothy Lee Jones and died 30 December 1831;
Martha E. (111f); and Frances M. (111g), who
married Hugh G. Cassells.

William's obituary appeared in the Sumter
Watchman of 23 September 1857: "Death of a
Revolutionary Soldier--The last surviving
soldier of our Revolutionary struggles,
resident in Sumter County has passed away!
William Vaughan is no more! Who cannot drop a
tear upon the departure of this noble son of
the glorious past?

"Mr. Vaughan was born in May 1764 and had
therefore reached his ninety-fourth year. He
joined the army in his 16th year, and was with
Marion and Sumter in several of their most
severe engagements. He was married to the
bereaved wife who now survives him on the 10th
of Feb., 1790. They had therefore lived
together as husband and wife for a period of
near 68 years.

"Few more generous and brave men than William
Vaughan have ever lived. Although infirm and
tottering under the weight of his many years, a
bare allusion to the stirring scenes of the
past would cause his dim eye to flash with an
almost unnatural brightness, while the sound of
fife and drum seemed to inspire within his
bosom all the fires of patriotism that burned
so brilliantly there during the days of his
youth. It is said that his hatred for the
tories was proverbial, and that the mention of
them in his presence, even during the last days
of his life, would draw from him some
expression of his feelings toward them.

"He died at the residence of his daughter, Mrs. Dargan, about 4 miles from this place, on Monday [22nd] morning last. Resquiescat en pace."

William was buried in the Dargan family cemetery on the home place near Stateburg.

The Frierson Family of Sumter has an old daguerreotype, in a case lined in red plush, of William Vaughan. It had passed down from the generation of Henry's children and for years was known only to be of "Uncle Bill." The daguerreotype was taken 7 December 1855. The notation on the daguerreotype states William was born 22 May 1765 in Northampton County, Virginia, an error clarified above.

William's granddaughter, Elizabeth Alice Brunson, related to Mr. Dick that "the old man swore something terrible and insisted that his name be spelled Vaughan."

William was witness to the wills of Robert Stamper, dated 26 January 1803, and Richard Hampton, dated 28 November 1796.

Following are copies of two certificates of pension for William and his widow and the narrative of his deposition for a Revolutionary War pension.

William Vaughan

File Designation W11691--Revolutionary War

6378

South Carolina

(Alis Vaughan,

widow of William Vaughan,

SC

who served in the Revolutionar

war, as a Private of Cavalry

Inscribed on the Roll at the ra
of 83 dollars 33,
cents per annum, to commenc
on the ~~21 February 1853~~, 21
September 1857

Certificate of Pension issue
22d, day of April 18
and sent to

James Taylor
Sumter SC

Recorded on Roll of Pensioners under
February 3, 1853, Page 346. Vol. 4.

William Vaughan

Certificate of Pension issued 24 day of Jan '34

I. *South Carolina* 23.437

William Vaughan —

of *Sumter,* in the State of *So. Cao:*
who was a *Pr Cao* in the commanded
by Captain — — of the *Reg?* — commanded
by *Col. Richardson* in the *So. Cao:* —
line for *2 months* —

Inscribed on the Roll of *So. Carolina*
at the rate of *83* — Dollars *33* — Cents per annum.
to commence on the 4th day of *March, 1831.*

Certificate of Pension issued the *24th* day of *Jan: 34* —
and sent *J. S. Wilder* —
Sumterville — So Ca

Arrears to the 4th of *Sept 1833* — 208.32
Semi-ant. allowance ending *June 34* — 41.67
$2 49 99

{ Revolutionary Claim }
{ Act June 7, 1832. }

Recorded by *Nath Rice* **Clerk.**
Book *E* **Vol.** *6* **Page** *52*

The following is a transcript of William's
pension application:

Declaration to obtain the benefit of the Act of
Congress passed June 7th 1832.--

The State of South Carolina)
Sumter District   )
County of Claremont   )

On this 30th day of October in the year of our
lord one thousand eight hundred and thirty two,
Personally appeared in open court, before B. J.
Earle in the court of Commonpleas Sessions now
sitting William Vaughan, a resident of the
county, District and State aforesaid, now in
his sixty ninth year, who being first duly
sworn, according to Law, doth on his oath make
the following declaration, in order to obtain
the benefit of the Act of Congress passed June
7th 1832. I was born in Northampton County
Virginia, on the twenty second day of May
seventeen hundred and sixty four and in the
year one thousand seven hundred and seventy two
removed to Craven County So. Carolina--I was
living in that part of Craven County, which is
now called Claremont, when I entered the
service of the Country--and since the
revolution, I have to this time resided in
Claremont county, District and State aforesaid.
In the summer of the year seventeen hundred and
eighty after the fall of Charleston, I joined
Genl. Marion as a volunteer on the South side
of the Santee, near Murray's Ferry. The
captain of my company was John Malone--The
Colonel of the Regiment was at the first period
of my service Peter Horry--afterwards Richard
Richardson, was engaged in may skirmishes
during the whole of the war. I was present at
the taking of Fort Motte--Genl Marion
commanded--assisted by Col Lee--A short time
afterwards, I was at the siege of Fort Watson,
under the command of Marion, assisted as well
as deponent recollects by Col Lee. I do not
recollect the month--but the year was seventeen
hundred and eighty one and the weather was

warm. I was engaged in the Battle of Eutaw--
under the command of Marion, (The troops of
Marion were placed in front with orders to fire
twelve rounds. The American Forces were
commanded by Greene--The Principal cavalry
officers were Washington and Lee. Marion's men
had joined Gen'l Greene at Miss Thompson's
Plantation in Orangeburgh District, and marched
with the regular army to Eutaw. I was also
present at the Battle of Quinby Bridge--Marion
and Lee were there--I took share in the siege
of Georgetown--in three days the British
evacuated the place. I do not recollect of
serving with the regular army at any other time
except the Battle of Eutaw--Col Lee of the
Continentals was sometimes with Marion. I do
not recollect of taking any discharge from the
service--very few discharges if any were taken.
I have never received one cent for my services
and I hereby relinquish every claim whatever to
a pension or annuity except the present one and
do declare that my name is not on the pension
roll of the agency of any State whatever.

Sworn and subscribed the day and year
aforesaid.
B.Earle presiding Judge   xWilliam Vaughan
of common pleas Sessions in open Court at
Sumter Courthouse.

State of South Carolina, Sumter District.
I Obadiah Spears, a soldier of the Revolution
residing in Claremont County, District and
State aforesaid, do hereby certify that the
above Deponent with myself and about twenty
others joined Marion about June, seventeen
hundred and eighty. The deponent and myself
were frequently in the same mess--I know him to
have been in the service of his country under
Marion, until the close of the war or near
about that time. I recollect him very well at
Fort Motte--Fort Watson--Quinby Bridge and
Georgetown. he was quite young. Sworn and
subscribed on the 30th day of October in the
year of our Lord one thousand eight hundred and
thirty two
B. J. Earle presiding Judge   xObadiah Spears
in open court

State of South Carolina)   The Revd. Henry D.
)   Green appears and
Sumter District   )   makes oath that he
is personally acquainted with the deponent Wm.
Vaughan--that he is a respectable man and
entitled to credit and that he is generally
believed to have been in the service of his
country during the Revolutionary War.
B. J. Earle presiding Judge   H. D. Green
as aforesaid in open Court

And the said Court do hereby declare this
opinion after the investigation of this matter,
and after putting the interrogatories
prescribed by the War Department, that the
above named applicant was a revolutionary
soldier, and served as he states. And the
court further certifies that it appears to them
that Obadiah Spears who signed the preceding
certificate is a Revolutionary Soldier--and
that H. D. Green is a Clergyman both residing
in Sumter District--are credible persons and
their statements entitled to full credit.
                B. J. Earle
                presiding Judge
                in open Court

I, Ths. J. Wilder Clerk of the Court of Common
Pleas do hereby certify that the foregoing
contains the proceedings of the said Court in
the Matter of the application of Wm. Vaughan
for a pension
In testimony whereof I have hereunto set my
hand and seal of office this 31st day of
October 1832--
                        Th. J. Wilder
                        CCPs

South Carolina)
Sumter District) To amend former declarations
made in pursuance of the Pension Act of June
7th 1832 Wm. Vaughan appears and on being sworn
deposesth (sic) as follows--That he with
several of his neighbors in or about the
commencement of October in the year of our Lord
one thousand seven hundred (repaired?) from the
neighborhood of what is now Stateburg to the
forces under Genl Marion on the South Side of

Santee River. The deponent did not join the army under Marion for any specified term of service or any particular engagement--The deponent was in his seventeenth year and the house of his father was within a mile and a half of the main road between Charleston and Camden--This road was frequently traversed by the British and there being also many tories in the vicinity of his fathers dwelling--it was frequently visited by both the British and the tories--thus rendering it impossible for the deponent to return home and leaving him the only alternative of remaining continually with an embodied force. The deponent therefore remained under the command of Marion and in active service until about the first of June in the year of our Lord one thousand seven hundred and eighty two. The only terms of his engagement was the period of the expulsion of the British from the Country. When that was effected he intended to quit the service and not before.--No mention was even made to him of enlisting or volunteering for any specified length of time and he never thought of quitting the service until discharged in June in the manner stated on his second declaration--His officers were those stated in his previous declaration--as before stated the Regiment was commanded by Peter Horry and Richard Richardson. Major Benson was killed in a skirmish with the British on Widow Tedyman's land on Wontot Swamp east of Cooper River in which skirmish the deponent was engaged. I was present at siege of Forts Watson and Motte. Marion commanded the forces at both places--Col Lee commanded the cavalry--I was engaged in the battles of Biggen Church and Quinby Bridge where Sumter being the Senior officer took command--I was also at the Battle of Eutaw still under the command of Genl Marion--The Regiment commanded by Col Richard Richardson-- Marion's men were placed in the front lines with orders to fire twelve rounds we obliqued to the Right still firing on the enemy's flank- -In my former declaration I have stated the circumstances of my service after the Battle of Eutaw until my joining the corps of Cavalry under Col Maham but still attached to the

brigade under Marion--I was dismissed in time
as before stated--never having absented myself
from service for one year and eight months more
than two or three days at a time and then with
the permission of my commanding officer and
never having slept a single night under my
father's roof--The deponent served during the
whole period as a private. The troops under
Marion embodied by competent authority--In the
partisan warfare waged by Genl Marion his men
were never in garrison but always in the field
nor was the deponent employed in any civil
pursuit during the one year and eight months he
was at his country's service--The deponent is
unable to answer the sixth question more
satisfactorily than by stating that he received
no written discharge because as he believes
none or very few written discharges were given
at that by Genl Marion or his officers--The
deponent does not regard himself as a member of
the militia but as one who volunteered for an
indefinite period of time or as long as his
services were required.
        x Wm. Vaughan
Sworn before me
this Decr 2d 1833
John Hemphill
        Q. U.

South Carolina)
Sumter District)   I Thomas J. Wilder Clerk of
the Court of General Sessions & Common Pleas
for said district do hereby certify that John
Hemphill, before whom the above depositions
were taken is acting Justice of Quorum for said
district & legally authorized to administer
oaths
Given under my hand & seal of Said Court this
9th day of December AD 1833

Accounts of the actions mentioned in the above
testimony are summarized below with quotes and
abstracts from Encyclopedia of the American
Revolution, Mark M. Boatner III, David McKay
Co., Inc., New York, @1974, 3rd printing 01/76.
Accounts are from pages 711, 384 and 377,
respectively.

On the morning of 14 April 1780, about 3 A. M.,
the British made contact with the Revolutionary
guard and routed the Continental Cavalry posted
in front of Biggins Bridge. Tarleton was
reinforced by two regiments under Lt. Col.
Webster and thus the line of communications to
Charleston was cut. The disaster was
considered a result of faulty tactics by Huger.
He not only failed to employ observation
parties to detect Tarleton's presence, but also
failed to use foot soldiers to guard the bridge
when they would have served better than
cavalry.

Action at Fort Motte took place on 12 May 1781.
The fort was strategically located where the
Congaree and the Wateree join to form the
Santee and was a principal depot on the British
line of communications between Charleston and
the interior. The large mansion of the widow
Mrs. Rebecca Motte had been strongly fortified
by a stockade, ditch, and abatis, and was held
by British Lt. McPherson with 150 infantry and
a small detachment of dragoons. After their
maneuvers against Watson [also a battle of the
Southern Campaign] Lee and Marion reached Fort
Motte on 8 May and started regular approaches.
A surrender summons sent on the 10th was
refused. That evening the rebels received
information that Rawdon was retreating toward
Fort Motte from Camden; beacon fires the
morning and evening of the 11th encouraged the
defenders and told the attackers they would
have to take the place quickly or abandon the
operation. Lee conceived the idea of setting
fire to the Motte mansion by firing flaming
arrows onto the shingle roof, which was dry
after a period of sunny weather. When Mrs.
Motte was informed that this decision had
reluctantly been made, she not only accepted
the fact but produced a fine East Indian bow
and bundle of arrows. (Mrs. Motte had been
living at a nearby farmhouse from which Lee and
Marion directed the siege). The morning of the
12th, Dr. Irvine of Lee's cavalry advanced with
a flag to inform McPherson that Rawdon was not
yet across the Santee and request his
surrender. The British commander again

refused. By noon the rebel trench was within range and Pvt. Nathan Savage of Marion's Brig. dropped two "African Arrows" onto the roof. When enemy soldiers went to the attic to knock off the burning shingles they were driven away by artillery. A white flag appeared, the fire was extinguished, and the garrison surrendered at 1 P. M.

"By invitation of Mrs. Motte," says Lossing happily, "both the victorious and captive officers partook of a sumptuous dinner from her table. . ." Greene arrived the day of the surrender, having been worried about completing this operation before Rawdon could intervene; he returned to his camp after ordering Lee to take Ft. Granby and Marion to take Georgetown.

Marion lost two men in the siege, Lt. Cruger and Sgt. McDonald; there were no other men killed on either side. The prisoners were paroled, and the officers joined Rawdon at Nelson's Ferry on the Santee.

Action at Fort Granby, South Carolina took place on 15 May 1781. The British post, near modern Columbia, was held by 352 men under a Md. Tory, Maj. Andrew Maxwell. The garrison included 60 German mercenaries; the rest were Tories, presumably of Maxwell's Prince of Wales Regt. Although this was a strong post, Henry Lee knew that Maxwell was not noted either for courage or military proficiency and that he had devoted most of his energies to collecting plunder. Lee left Ft. Motte on 13 May and the next night emplaced a 6-pd. gun within 600 yards of the fortified frame building known as "Fort Granby." When the fog cleared the next morning, Lee fired the cannon and his Legion infantry moved forward to deliver a musket fire on Maxwell's pickets. When summoned to surrender, Maxwell agreed to do so if he and his men could keep their plunder, and if the garrison (including tories) could withdraw to Charleston as prisoners of war until exchanged. Knowing that Rawdon might arrive at any moment to save the fort, Lee agreed with the condition

that all horses fit for public service be surrendered. Maxwell's mercenaries, who were mounted, objected, and negotiations were suspended. When Lee received word from Capt. Armstrong, who had been screening in the direction of Camden with a small cavalry force, that Rawdon was across the Santee at Nelson's Ferry and was approaching Ft. Motte, Lee agreed to Maxwell's terms. The capitulation was signed before noon of the 15th, and Maxwell moved off with two wagons full of his personal plunder. Without the loss of a man--on either side--the rebels gained possession of an important post along with a considerable supply of ammunition, some salt and liquor, two cannon, and the garrison's weapons.

Lee's good sense in handling this situation is expressed in Napoleon's Maxim 46: "The keys of a fortress are well worth the freedom of the garrison."

SUMMARY OF WILLIAM VAUGHAN'S ACCOUNT

Joined on south side of Santee at Murray's Ferry, one of the battles in Greene's Southern Campaigns. Joined in summer of 1780.

Captain of the company was John Malone, company part of Marion's forces.

Colonel of regiment was Peter Horry and later Richard Richardson.

Present at fall of Ft. Motte, where commanders were Marion and Col. Lee.

Present at siege of Ft. Watson, Lee & Marion again commanding.

Present at the Battle of Eutaw with Greene's forces, joined by Marion near Miss Thompson's Plantation in Orangeburg, Washington & Lee assisting with cavalry forces.

Present at the Battles of Quinby (Bridge) and Biggins Church; Sumter commanded at Quinby, assisted by Marion and Lee; all three were in joint command at Biggin's Church.

Joined corps of cavalry under Col. Maham after Battle of Eutaw and was attached to Marion's Brigade.

Participated in the siege of Georgetown.

KITURAH VAUGHAN (111A)

Kiturah, also known as Kitsy according to Major Dargan, was born in 1790, daughter and eldest child of William, Sr., and Alice Vaughan. She married Samuel J. Bradford, who Dargan states was a cousin.

Kiturah died on 9 June 1855. It is not known by this writer in what manner husband and wife were cousins. Another section treats the Bradfords, but we have not been able to place Samuel in the relationship scheme.

Four children came of this marriage: John F. (111a1); William M. (111a2); Frances M. (111aa), who married Benton Qualls; and Placidia (111ab), who married James Cannon.

EMILY E. VAUGHAN (111b)

Emily was the second child of William , Sr.,
and Alice Vaughan. She was born on 20 October
1797 and in 1819 or 1820 married John Milton
Dargan, son of John M. and Mary Dargan. The
Dargans of Sumter seem to have descended from
John Milton's parents, his father being the
noted Capt. John Dargan who received a royal
land grant in 1756 and died in 1765 or 1766
(Deed Book N-4, pages 226-231, of Charleston
records). The John Dargan named as brother to
Rev. Timothy Dargan on page 103 of Rambles in
the Pee Dee Basin (Bibliography) was father to
John M., whose estate papers in Sumter date to
1818. Captain John Dargan of the French and
Indian War was the son of Timothy Dargan, who
appears to have been the forebear in the state.

John and Emily had nine children. The eldest
was Leonora A. (111ba), born 10 September 1821,
who married Amos A. Nettles and died on 11 May
1848. Amos was the youngest son of Jesse and
Ann (Stroud) Nettles.
This was Amos' second
marriage and after
Leonora's death Amos
married Mary S. Wilder
on 17 December 1848
according to the Sumter
Banner of 20 December
of that year.

Other children of John
and Emily E. Dargan
were Martha (111bb),
born 30 January 1824
and married to Hardy
Scarborough; Mary A.
(111bc), born 13 April
1825, married to Samuel
J. Bradford, widower of
Kiturah (Vaughan), and
died 4 April 1875; John
(111bl), born 23
December 1826, who
attained the rank of

The large Nettles
Family had been in the
Sumter area since at
least the 1740's.
Amos, who was born on
7 March 1801, had as
brothers and sisters
Josiah, born 29 July
1770; Winnie, who
was born 29 March
1773; Jesse, born 10
August 1775; Elizabeth
who married Mr.
Atkins, born 1
February 1778; Anna,
who married Mr.
McKellar, born 22 May
1779; Hezekiah, born
11 April 1782; Martha,
who married Mr.
Rogers, born 17 April
1784; Temperance, who

major in the army, married Jane McCoy in Sumter on 19 April 1860, and died 20 March 1889; Frances Elizabeth (111bd), born 13 September 1828 and died unmarried on 21 May 1867; Emma Alice (111be), born 3 February 1830 and died May 1854; Amanda Kiturah (111bf), born 9 July 1832 and died 12 December 1834; Robert James (111b2), born 10 May 1838, married to Frances McCoy, sister of Jane, and died 20 February 1873; and Sara Strother (111bg), born 12 March 1840 and died sometime early in 1900.

The estate of the elder John Dargan was administrated by his wife Mary. Bundle 33, Package 3 of the Sumter County Probate Records shows that she went bond on 16 February 1818 with William Vaughan and Ben Gerald. This is the only document the package contains. On 25 April 1831 Ordinary William Potts appointed a Middleton Dargan to an appraisal commission in an estate settlement. The inventory was held 28 April 1831, as attested to by John M. Dargan. It seems the court was unsure whether the M. stood

married Mr. Holladay born 21 April 1788; John, born 30 March 1790; Harvey, born about 1792; Elsie (Elcey), who married Mr. Pack, born 2 September 1794; Joseph Marley, born 30 November 1796; Tabitha, born 27 July 1799; and Mary, birth date unknown.

Many of these Nettleses are found in deed and other legal records of the Sumter area. Hezekiah was especially active in the community and brother John was a court clerk in 1827.

Much of this information comes from Jesse Nettles' estate settlement and will found in Roll 74, Package 10 of Sumter Proceedings. In Mary Brunson's (wife of Isaac Brunson) will of 1838, she names Amos Nettles as a brother-in-law. Hezekiah married Susan White. One of their sons, Joseph Hezekiah, was born on 17 March 1827. Jesse Nettles, Jr. left a will of 1837 naming sons William and John and daughters Hariet, Sophronia, Huldah and Caroline.

The elder Jesse

for Middleton or Milton. The name may thus have been corrupted. There was Middleton in the Bradford Family, one closely allied with the Dargans.

Emily died, according to her son, for which see below, on 17 May 1865 at the age of 67 years, 5 months and 15 days. Her husband left a will, dated 8 June 1847 and recorded 23 August 1847. It was witnessed by Robert D. Bradford.

Much of the above information comes from records compiled by Major John William Dargan, oldest son of John and Emily. This information was conveyed by his cousin, Raymond Dick, and his daughter Jennie to Mrs. Vermeille H. Galbreath, from whom this writer got it. Major Dargan listed his own offspring: an unnamed daughter (111b1a), born and died 14 February 1861; Milton (111b11), born 22 February 1862, who married in Dallas, Texas, Effie Rauch; John W., Jr. (111b12), born 6 December 1864 and died unmarried 14 May 1891; Shelby (111b13), born 10 March 1867 and died 2

Nettles' will recorded 21 February 1825 names also as heirs grandchildren Ann, James D. W. and Jesse I. McKellar. The elder Jesse Nettles was born in then Craven County on 4 June 1745, son of Solomon and Elizabeth Nettles. Jesse had brothers and sisters Jacob, born 15 September 1741; John and Mary, twins, born 4 December 1747; Marley, born 21 May 1751 (?); Elijah, born 18 January 1752; Mourning, born 3 May 1754; Isham, born 3 May 1758 and Martha, born 29 January 1759 (?). At this time there was also a William Nettles in Craven County. He married Mary Mathis and was of such an age he could have been a nephew or (much) younger brother of Solomon. Children of William and Mary (Mathis) Nettles were Israel, born 26 December 1768; William, born 5 February 1772; Elizabeth, born 10 June 1775; Joseph K., born 3 June 1778 and married in 1804 to Abigail S.; Samuel, born 20 August 1780; James, born 20 August

February 1868; Leon (111b14), born 11 September 1868 and married in Dallas, Texas, Ina Dixon; and Jennie (111b1b), born on 17 October about 1870. Jennie was living in Atlanta in 1962 and her exact year of birth was a secret with her, as she felt no one should know her exact age.

Robert James Dargan's descendants are not known to this writer, but two of his grandchildren resident in Sumter were named Blanding.

There is some confusion regarding the children of John and Emily Dargan. Major Dargan's account lists Mary as Mary Alia (Alice?), but probate records name Emma as Emma Alice. It is doubtful there were two Alices in the family at the same time. Probate records indicate Emma married Samuel M. Dinkins, but Major Dargan says she married Mr. Stith. Major Dargan says Sara Strother married Mr. Richardson, but

1784; and John G. R. Nettles, born 16 March 1786. James apparently married Natala, daughter of Richard Bradford, Jr., according to the latter's will. Possibly William, Sr. had been married earlier to Amy Alexander; Sumter County records show on 23 August 1766 the birth of Mary Nettles to William and Amy (Alexander) Nettles. Deed Book AA, page 45, for Sumter County concerns lands of Thomas Sumter, originally granted to William Nettles on 10 October 1769. There was also a Joseph Nettles, about the same age as the above William, Sr., who married Elizabeth Perdue and, on 10 August 1776, had a son by her. One of John B. Miller's daughters, Elizabeth, was the deceased wife of John Nettles by the time of Miller's will in 1851. He could have been any of three of the above John Nettleses.

probate records indicate Sara married Stith. The 1850 Sumter County census clears this up by showing Wm. H. Stith and Emma A. Stith living with Emily Dargan and married within the year. (The Elizabeth Alice Vaughan listed as a household member was probably Elizabeth A., the

daughter of John Horace. She would have been 18 in 1850.) By 1870 a William B. (V?) Stith was in Major Dargan's household and could have been the W. Vaughan Stith, known to have been born to Emma Alice and William H. Stith.

Major Dargan also traced his mother Emily's Vaughan ancestors in a compile. It has many errors, however, and should not be used without corroboration from other sources.

The large Darlington Dargan Family descended from Rev. Timothy Dargan and his son, Timothy Dargan, Esq., with some possibly descending from a Jeremiah or William Dargan, known to have been associated with the Congaree Baptist Church by 1772 or earlier.

JAMES ALEXANDER VAUGHAN (1111)

James Alexander was the first son of William, Sr. and Alice Vaughan. The 1830 Sumter County census lists him as a one-person household with two slaves. Most of what we know of him is from the Sumter Gazette. Issues of 5 November 1831, 12 May and 8 September 1832, and 13 July 1833 list him as a member of the States Rights and Free Trade Party. Occasionally he served as a committee member to that party. Issues of 3 March, 7 April, 6 October and 3 November 1832; 2 and 16 February and 2 March 1833 of the Gazette establish that James was a captain and later lieutenant colonel in the 2nd Bn., 20th Regiment of the South Carolina Militia. He served as Adjutant and Judge Advocate. According to the Camden Journal of 11 December 1829 James had attained the rank of lieutenant by December of that year. By 24 July 1830 he was a captain. The Southern Whig of 8 March 1832 also names him as a military man. The Gazette of 13 October 1832 has James on the postal overdue letter list. James probably moved to Richland County in connection with his military duties; his name appears there in newspaper notices of the 1830's.

James died unmarried some time before 1840.

JOHN HORACE VAUGHAN (1112)

John Horace was the second son of William, Sr. and Alice Vaughan. He was born 15 September 1801. On 30 March 1825 he married Victoria A. Dargan, daughter of John M. and Mary Dargan. John Horace was killed in 1832 by Thomas Magee, who, according to the 20 April 1833 issue of the Sumter Gazette, was convicted of manslaughter. The 6 October issue of that newspaper also carries a reference to the incident.

As a result of John's death and subsequent settlement of estate, Victoria was involved in several land transactions. Deeds in the Sumter courthouse, dated 3 August 1830 and 17 December 1833, pertain to land transactions involving Victoria. The Sumter Gazette of 8 October 1831 carries notice of an overdue letter at the post office for Victoria.

Children of John H. and Victoria were Mary Theodosia (1112a), who married Edward Henry Mellingchamp, and Elizabeth Alice (1112b), born 6 February 1831, married on 21 June 1857 to John T. Brunson and died in Georgia in 1904.

Mellingchamp was an acting Lieut. Sergeant in the Confederate Army. Children of the Brunsons were Claudia (1112ba), born 26 November 1866, married in Charleston on 27 November 1885 to William Edward Dick, and died 28 June 1889 and Alice (1112bb), who married William H. Zemp of Camden. Zemp was the son of Dr. Francis Leslie and Abathiah (Capers) Zemp. See Historic Camden, pages 364-5, for an account of the Zemp heritage. Alice was probably the mother of the girl who married John G. Lige of Charleston and, as Raymond Dick relates in a narrative, was "like a sister to me."

The only child of Claudia and William Dick was Raymond Dick (1112ba1), born on 27 March 1887 in Sumter. It is through this Dick that much of this material has come. Mr. Dick's mother died a couple of years after his birth and he

was raised by his grandmother Brunson. He
attended Clemson for three years. Later he
moved to Idaho, then on to the state of
Washington. After the Zemps moved to Los
Angeles in 1910, Mr. Dick joined them in 1911,
where he met and married Mary Badger. Mrs.
Dick died in 1952 in Glendale. Mr. and Mrs.
Dick are known to have had one son (1112ball),
born in 1918, who in turn had three sons, aged
10, 7 and 2 in 1961. The Dr. George W. Dick
who owned Acton Plantation between 1902 and
1906, at which time he sold it to Col. John J.
Dargan, may have been related to these Dicks.
Col. Dargan was a newspaper editor for some
time in the late 1800's and was of the Dargan
Family of Darlington.

After his death, John Horace's widow Victoria
married Timothy Lee Jones, widower of John's
sister, Mary Henrietta.

ALICE D. VAUGHAN (111c)

Alice was the daughter of William, Sr. and
Alice Vaughan. She married Benjamin Mitchell,
son of Stephen Mitchell. Stephen Mitchell's
will was dated 24 August 1820 and recorded on
15 September of that year. The will names
Benjamin and Samuel Clark Mitchell (who married
Alice's sister Leonora). Other children of
Stephen and Abigail Mitchell were James,
Stephen, Daniel Clark, Abigail and Unisey
Mitchell and Susannah Tisdale, wife of
Christopher Tisdale.

Alice's share of her mother's estate was
divided among her children William L. (111c1)
and a daughter (111ca), not named in the
documents. This unnamed daughter had married
William F. Deschamps, by whom she had two
children: Elizabeth Alice (111caa) and William
W. (111ca1).

LEONORA COOK VAUGHAN (111d)

Leonora, daughter of William, Sr. and Alice Vaughan, married Samuel C. Mitchell. She died without issue, having been born in late 1809 or early 1810. Her Approximate birthdate comes from her obituary, which appears in the Sumter Banner of 28 May 1851: "Mrs. Leonora Cook Mitchell, died in Sumter District, May 20, 1851, in the 42nd year of her age. She was a member of the Methodist Episcopal Church. Having no children . . ."

Leonora's middle name of Cook tends to corroborate by implication Jennie Dargan's statement that Alice was the daughter of Samuel and Alice Cook.

Samuel Clark Mitchell was the son of Stephen and Abigail Mitchell and brother of Benjamin Mitchell, who married Alice, Leonora's sister.

MARY HENRIETTA VAUGHAN (111e)

Mary Henrietta, fifth daughter of William, Sr.
and Alice Vaughan, was born in 1811. She
married Timothy Lee Jones, son of Mary Jones.
Papers relating to the estate of Mary Jones are
found in Bundle 53, Package 1 of Sumter Estate
Settlements. The proceedings mention Timothy's
siblings, but not his father, as is often done
in the estate settlements of widows.

Mary Henrietta died on 30 December 1831,
probably childless. Quoted in part is her
obituary from the **Sumter Gazette** of 7 January
1832: "Departed this life on the 30th ult,
Mrs. Mary Henrietta Jones, consort of Timothy
Lee Jones, and a daughter of William Vaughan,
Sr. of this district, aged 20 years.

"Could the sympathies . . ."

Timothy Lee Jones later married Victoria A.
Vaughan, widow of John Horace Vaughan.

MARTHA E. VAUGHAN (111f)

In a family of mostly daughters Martha was yet
another, probably the sixth, born to William,
Sr. and Alice Vaughan. It seems an irony that
this zealous patriot should have raised up so
many women, when we get the impression that he
would have revelled in a troop of little
soldiers.

We know of Martha's existence only from deed
records pertaining to William Vaughan's estate
settlement. This writer has been unable to
find any other information on Martha in extant
records.

41

FRANCES M. VAUGHAN (111g)

Frances, the last child of William, Sr. and
Alice Vaughan, was born on 21 December 1814.
On 7 February 1833 she married Hugh Gamble
Cassels, son of Henry and Agnes Cassels.

Children of Frances and Hugh were James Hugh
(111g1), born on 27 June 1834; William Benjamin
(111g2), born 14 August 1836; Leonora Suzanna
(111ga), born 5 June 1838; Agnes (111gb), born
in 1841; Theodore (111g3), born about 1843;
Samuel (111g4), born in July 1846; John
(111g5); Martha (111gc); and Robert Franklin
(111g6), born 17 June 1852, married 15 March
1877 and died 11 December 1931.

One source says that Hugh was born on 9 May
1808. Hugh's mother Agnes was probably a
Gamble before marriage. Many Gambles lived in
Sumter County, the two appearing most often in
legal documents being John and James Gamble.
Estate proceedings in the estates of both James
and Catherine Gamble name Agnes Reardon Gamble,
probably identical with the subject of this
item.

Frances died on 27 March 1882 and Hugh followed
her in January of 1890. They are buried in
Antioch Cemetery in Island Grove, Florida.

HENRY VAUGHAN, JR. (112)

Henry Vaughan, Jr. was born on 13 September 1767. He was born in North Carolina and arrived in South Carolina with his parents in the caravan of 1772. Henry married on 3 March 1795 Mary Margaret Anderson. Margaret, as she was known, was the daughter of John Anderson, Sr. and his wife Margaret and was born on 12 February 1779.

Henry lived for many years at his estate, Cherry Vale Plantation. He inherited much of his father's estate, but had also purchased the tract on which he built the plantation in 1794 from Thomas Darrington. [Darrington's will was probated in Sumter County on 28 July 1800, but was also recorded in Clarke County, Alabama on 5 January 1836.] Cherry Vale was begun almost immediately after the purchase of the lot and the original tract was increased with the purchase of adjacent lands. After Henry's death the plantation passed to his son, Henry III, and later to the latter's brother-in-law, John James Frierson, when Henry III caught "Mississippi Fever." Cherry Vale stayed in the Frierson Family until it was sold to a Sumter realtor by J. Nelson Frierson, great-grandson of John James. After passing to another realtor three years later, in 1956, the house was destroyed in a fire. According to statements made by Hubert G. Osteen and Mark Reynolds in the early 1950's to Sallie Anderson and conveyed by Claude Neuffer, the Sumter Highway from the junction of the Columbia and Camden Highways to Stateburg had long been called "Vaughan Road."

Henry died in an epidemic which also took the life of his daughter Mary Margaret. He died on 5 March 1814, about 6 o'clock in the afternoon according to testimony of Dr. Andrew Silliman in open court at Ordinary. This date is the one that should be taken as accurate, because there is disparity between dates found on his headstone and in family Bibles and the date given above. Court proceedings were rather

lengthy in settlement of the estate, because a
deathbed will was produced after the death,
which was, however, undated, unwitnessed and
unsigned. In spite of testimony of the
attending physician, Dr. Andrew Silliman, and
John Heriot the court, rightfully I think,
decided to go by the will of 04/01/1811. That
will had been duly witnessed and the court
seemed unsure what Mr. Vaughan was trying to
accomplish with his attempt to make another
will in the hectic final moments of his life.
A reading of the court proceedings seems to
underscore the confusion, although the terms
expressed in the latter will do not differ a
great deal from the earlier one. Shadrick
Brown made deposition as witness to the 1811
will. The appraisal of personal property of
the estate was just under $40,000. If notes
and landed property are included, Henry must
have had quite an estate.

At this point I might point out that it must
have been especially difficult to execute
settlement of Henry's estate, because his wife
survived him, only one of his children was of
majority, one had died only about a month
previously, and his own father's estate was
still unsettled. His mother did not die until
1815 and his father's estate was particularly
troublesome to settle because the will had only
two witnesses. J. Nelson Frierson was of the
opinion that a contest in the settlement of the
elder Henry's will arose because the other
children felt their father had settled special
benefits upon one of the sons, Vincent, during
his lifetime. Frierson was of the belief that
Henry, Sr. had lived with Vincent for some
period, although I have been unable to find
corroboration of that contention. At any rate,
the estate seems not to have been settled until
after the death of Elizabeth and the lack of a
third signature as witness to the will was the
legal basis for halting proceedings on it.

Henry's widow survived him until 13 June 1832,
dying at the age of 53 years, 1 month,
according to the Sumter Gazette of 18 June 1832
(53 years, 4 months, according to South

Carolina Historical *and* Genealogical Magazine,
Vol. 30, page 56, which lists inscriptions from
Holy Cross Church Cemetery).

Children of Henry and Mary Margaret were Julia
Finetta (112a), born 20 April 1796, married to
John James Frierson and died 10 April 1880;
Mary Margaret (112b), born 25 December 1797 and
died 1 February 1814; Henry III (1121), born 31
March 1800, married Emma M. Rees and died about
1870; John Anderson (1122), born 8 March 1803
and died 6 November 1821; and Vermelle M.
(112c), born 28 June 1809, married first to
Frederick Wentworth Rees and, after his death,
John Singleton Bradford, and died 6 September
1887. Vermelle's birthdate is sometimes given
as 28 June 1804, but this does not fit with
some of the legal documents and this writer
believes the 1809 date is the right one and
that the 1804 date comes from the similarity
between the 9 and the 4 on some of the old worn
tombstones.

Many of the members of this family are buried
at the Church of the Holy Cross in Stateburg,
including Henry, Jr. Anne King Gregorie notes
in her History of Sumter County that the First
Baptist Church of Sumter obtained its lot from
the settlement of the estate of Henry Vaughan,
Jr.

Below is an article from the Sumter paper on
Cherry Vale

History Of Cherry Vale, Destroyed By Fire, Told

Facts and figures concerning the history of Cherry Vale, historic plantation home near Sumter destroyed by fire Sunday, were made available to The News and Courier yesterday by J. Nelson Frierson, dean emeritus of the University of South Carolina Law School, who now resides in Charleston.

Frierson's records date to the late 18th century: and encompass every major transaction in the old home's life. Many of his records are original; several are photostated copies.

According to these files, the tract of land on which the plantation home stood was deeded Henry Vaughan Jr. in 1794 by a Thomas Darrington. The area of this original tract was 100 acres, but Vaughan later continued to add large tracts surrounding the site.

Vaughan's father, incidentally, had come to Sumter County prior to the Revolutionary War from Northampton, Va. William Vaughan, elder brother of Henry Vaughan Jr., at the time of his death in 1858, was the last surviving Revolutionary War soldier in Sumter County.

The back portion of the home was apparently begun almost immediately after the purchase of the tract. Though records of the construction and completion dates of the portion are lost, Frierson has knowledge that Vaughan's daughter and his great-grandmother, Julia Finetta Vaughan, was born in the rear section of the home in 1796.

Henry Vaughan Jr. died in 1814. In the ensuing division of his estate, the plantation home passed to his son Henry Vaughan III. In 1836, imbued with what Frierson calls "the Mississippi fever," the son left Sumter County for adventure and riches in the Delta State.

John James Frierson, who had married Vaughan's sister Julia in 1817, then bought the plantation from Vaughan. In 1839, on the death of Frierson, the plantation passed to his elder son, John N. Frierson, grandfather of the retired law school dean here.

It was John N. Frierson who added onto the rear portion of the home the beautifully designed "main section." It was completed by 1844, the year in which Frierson took his bride, the former Catherine K. Converse, daughter of a Protestant Episcopal minister in Statesburg, to live in the historic home.

The home remained in the possession of the Frierson family until 1953 at which time it was sold by its joint owners, including J Nelson Frierson, to a Sumter realtor.

Frierson yesterday said he understood the plantation had been sold since its purchase in 1953, but was uncertain of the buyer.

A photograph of the complete plantation home prior to its destruction appears in Wallace's "History of South Carolina," Volume III, page 79.

JULIA FINETTA VAUGHAN (112a)

Julia Finetta, sometimes cited as Finetta Julia, was the first-born of Henry and Mary Margaret Vaughan. Born 20 April 1796 at Cherry Vale, she married on 1 May 1817 John James Frierson, Rev. Mr. Roberts performing. Born on 23 June 1792 in Clarendon County, John James was the son of Major John and Ann (Bannister) Frierson. Research on this parentage was difficult as it was indicated to me that the major had married Polly or Rachel Davis, and from other quarters a Rachel McDonald. The John Frierson who married Polly Walne Davis in 1775 seems to have remained in Charleston and John Greer Frierson, who married Rachel McDonald, was not the major. A Rachel Davis had married Willis McDonald in Richland County and John Greer does not name his wife as mother of his children in his will of 1842; perhaps he may have married her later in life. The 1800 Sumter County census shows Major Frierson living next door to John Bannister, likely the father of his wife. Major Frierson passed away in 1825 and his son died on 15 November 1839. Julia survived her husband until 10 April 1880 [1882 per SCHGM, Vol. 30, page 56].

Children of Mr. and Mrs. Frierson reaching majority were John Napoleon (112a1), born 21 February 1818, who married on 2 May 1844 Katharine Kellogg Converse and died 19 February 1882 [1887 per Family Puzzlers]; and James Julian (112a2), born 19 January 1832, married to Mary Chesnut Grant and died 1 August 1880 [1890 per Family Puzzlers]. Mary died on 12 June 1907.

John's wife, Katharine Converse, was the daughter of Rev. Augustus L. and Mary A. (Kellogg) Converse. Katharine was born on 3 July 1827 and died 7 October 1899. There were eight children of this union: Augustus (112a11), born 21 June 1845 and died a prisoner of war at Pt. Lookout, Maryland on 29 July 1864; Mary Kellogg (112a1a), born 14 July 1846 and married to John Reed; Henry Vaughan

(112a12), born 3 December 1847 and died 10
January 1848; James Julian (112a13), born 9
June 1849, married on 29 May 1872 to Elizabeth
Nelson and died 16 February 1890; Julia Finetta
(112a1b), born 9 June 1850, married to Dr. W.
W. Anderson on 6 December 1871 and died 5 May
1899; Katharine Converse (112a1c), born 8
August 1851 and died 5 April 1884; John Temple
(112a14), born 4 January 1853, married on 29
December 1875 to Elizabeth Vanderhorst Murray
and died 1 February 1914; and Clara Converse
(112a1d), born 29 June 1864, married on 10
October 1888 to James Reynolds and died 2 July
1948. James Reynolds, who died in 1895 at 27
years of age and is buried in the Holy Cross
Cemetery, may have been identical to the
husband of the above-named Clara, but he could
also have been a son of Julia and Marcus
Reynolds (see compile on Vermelle Vaughan).

James Julian married on 28 April 1856 [29 April
per Family Puzzlers] Mary Grant, also known as
Minnie, daughter of William Joshua and Harriet
Serena Grant and granddaughter of James Chesnut
of Camden. Their children were Mary Chesnut
(112a2a), born 23 March 1857, married 19
October _____ to Samuel Lang and died 25 August
1901; William Grant (112a21), born 13 April
1858 and died 2 August 1933; and Julia Vaughan
(112a2b), born 7 May 1859, married to Wilson
Waties Rees, Jr., about 1895 and died without
issue on 12 March 1944. Mr. Rees was the son
of W. W. Rees and Frances Caroline Mayrant.
The younger Rees was born in 1857. The elder
Rees was born on 20 March 1831, married Miss
Mayrant on 29 April 1851 and died on 29
September 1864. The senior Mr. Rees was the
son of Colonel Orlando Savage Rees of Stateburg
and Catherine Waties, daughter of Judge Thomas
and Mary Ann (Glover) Waties.

Judge Waties was born in 1760 and had spent
several years of his youth with relatives in
Kent County, England. He came to Sumter from
Georgetown, South Carolina. A more detailed
account of his background may be found in C.
H. Neuffer's Names (XIV, page 26). See also
South Carolina Genealogies (Bibliography),

Vol. IV, for a history of the Waties Family.
Colonel Rees was born on 19 August 1796 and
died on 9 April 1852. He was the son of
William and Mary (James) Rees. His wife
Catherine, whom he married on 6 April 1819,
was born on 12 October 1796 and died 22 June
1855.

The Friersons were a large and influential
family in Sumter County and retained their
position over many years. They seem to have
moved into the Stateburg area with John
James' marriage to Julia Finetta Vaughan.
Many Friersons are buried in the cemetery of
the Church of the Holy Cross in Stateburg.
The family furnished several large landowners
and a prominent Sumter lawyer. J. Nelson
Frierson, son of James Julian (112a13) and
Elizabeth Frierson, was for many years
president of the University of South Carolina
Law School. James Nelson was born on 6
February 1874 and married, on 19 February
1901, Louise Dwight Mazyck. Their daughter
Louise Mazyck, born 23 May 1903, married
Richard L. Kerr, Jr., and lived at last word
in the old Charleston family home at 7 Gibbes
St. For a complete downline of John Napoleon
Frierson see The Friersons of Stateburg
(Bibliography).

An account in Neuffer's Names (XIII, pages
32-33) states that John James Frierson's
widow "Miss Lizzie" raised eight children.
The only Frierson this writer can find, who
married an Elizabeth and had James in his
name, was James Julian (112a13), who married
Elizabeth Nelson and had eight children to
survive infancy. Neuffer's information came
by way of Sallie Anderson, who states she was
a niece of "Miss Lizzie." I think Sallie
must have been Sarah Blanding Anderson,
daughter of Julia Finetta (Frierson)
Anderson, the latter a sister to James Julian
and wife of Dr. W. W. Anderson.

Writing in the 1800's, William Frierson
Fulton gives a history of one family of South
Carolina Friersons. This family counted for
its American forebear one William Frierson
who came to America about 1730 from Northern
Ireland, the Friersons having removed to that
country from Scotland some 60 years earlier.
This William of County Downs, Ireland,
settled in Williamsburg. Fulton, in his
Family Record and War Reminiscences (see
Bibliography), traces the descendants of this
branch in part through three generations
until one son in the fourth generation
removes to the area of Mt. Zion near
Columbia, Tennessee. He also briefly relates
information regarding William Frierson, Jr.,
one of the sons of the original settler. The
younger William was a captain in the
Revolution and led a company at King's
Mountain. He was also great-great-
grandfather to Fulton. If anyone wants to
know more on this line the current author can
provide a little help. From other sources we
can trace William's descendants from his
children John, James, William, Robert, Thomas
and Agnes through two more generations still
seated in Williamsburg (some sources say
Georgetown, but I think only the records were
held in Georgetown). It is difficult to
place these Friersons. Records show up in
Georgetown and Charleston. Part of the
difficulty lies in the practice during the
royal period of keeping records in
Charleston. Many of those who show up in
Charleston have names and demographic
information similar to inhabitants of Sumter
(about which we will say more later). While
removal is a possibility, we know that in
many instances duplicate records were kept.
The same is true for Williamsburg and
Georgetown. In those early days, when people
were few and business was transacted in few
places, people often appeared in places quite
foreign to their residences and, depending on
the nature of one's business, appeared in the
legal records of that area. It would seem
that, although William Frierson Fulton's
ancestors may have arrived in Williamsburg in

1730, there was an earlier group, possibly
kin to the later arrivals. A William
Frierson was born to Aaron and Mary Frierson
in Williamsburg in 1711, the parents having
surely been there prior to 1711, and there
were John Friersons in Williamsburg as early
as 1717.

The Friersons that settled in the Sumter area
seem originally to have come to the Clarendon
section of the district. There they settled
among the Davises, Gordons, Chandlers,
Coopers, McDonalds, Conyerses, Gambles,
Casselses, McIntoshes and others. At the
same time Major John Frierson was in the
Clarendon area, a John Greer Frierson and a
third John Frierson lived there too. The
line is not too clear: John Greer's father
was George and George's father was James.
Birth records for George appear in both
Clarendon (St. Mark's) and Williamsburg
Parishes; it is likely this James is the son
of William of Ireland. The third John
Frierson married Aley Dickey and they had
several children, one of whom was Aaron
Taylor Frierson. Aaron Friersons are
mentioned in a will of John Frierson of 1760
in Charleston and as a relative of a John
Frierson of Williamsburg in 1739, so that
once again threads seem to come together. An
Absalem Frierson is mentioned as a relative
of Mr. and Mrs James Frierson of Williamsburg
in 1749 and an Absolem Frierson appears in a
will of James Frierson of 6 May 1777 listed
in both Charleston and St. Marks Parish. So
it seems all of these Friersons are going to
tie together and spring from one or two
branches of the Williamsburg area. [Thus I
have hopefully somewhat clarified the
background of the South Carolina Friersons.
I feel compelled to apologize, for
undoubtedly many who read these words have a
fuller view of the mosaic. The space here
was much too small to trace all the down
lines. For those interested in further
research I recommend John L. Frierson Jr.'s
The Friersons of Stateburg and a work I have
never seen--but hope to one day--

In this branch of the family were many
plantations. Julia Finetta's brother, Henry
III, sold Cherry Vale to John James Frierson
when Vaughan went to Mississippi. The deed
for sale, made in January of 1836, can be
found in Sumter Equity Records (Roll 23, New
Series). John James once had another
plantation known as Bluefield. According to
Neuffer it was purchased from either William
Vaughan or John M. Dargan. In the same
article Neuffer mentions a William G.
Frierson, a James Frierson Rees and a Mary
Chesnut Lang. These were children of James
and Mary Grant Frierson in the above caption.
A granddaughter of Mrs. Lang, Mary Chesnut
Phillips Britton, yet lives in Sumter.

Another plantation owned in earlier
generations was the Wyboo Plantation, owned
by the Friersons. Many writers have
speculated upon the curious name. Perhaps it
was named after the earlier North Carolina
plantation Wadboo. Wyboo was at one time in
the possession of Major John Frierson.
According to Neuffer Major Frierson was the
son of a James Frierson (XVII, page 31) and
acquired the land through James Frierson,
Sr.'s will of 1780, said lands having been
acquired as early as 1765.

Two other estates of the Friersons were Rural
Plains, estate of John Napoleon Frierson,
which he willed to his widow, Katherine
Converse, it passing in 1887 to their
daughter, Julia Anderson, and Eureka, estate
of James Julian Frierson, which passed to his
widow, Elizabeth Frierson.

Sumter District was home to a large family of
Rees'. One of these families usually spelled
their name Reese. Joseph Reese emigrated to
the Sumter area from Duck Creek, Kent County,
Pennsylvania according to **South Carolina**

Baptists (Bibliography).   He married first
Ann Reynolds and, after her death, Sarah
_____.   He came to Congaree in 1745 where Evan
Reese had 250 acres of land in 1747.   A
memorial of 1767 speaks of 100 acres east of
the Pee Dee River, originally conveyed in
1750 to Daniel Rees and in 1759 to Joseph
Rees.   Mr. Reese was a founding Baptist
minister in the area, but was soon called to
the Charleston circuit.   His place was taken
by Richard Furman, perhaps the most renowned
clergyman in South Carolina.   Children of
Joseph Reese were Catherine Wells, Joseph
Reese, Jesse Reese, Mary Arthur, Timothy
Reese, Ann Tucker and John Altum Reese.
David Reese gave six acres of his property
for use of public buildings of Salem County
according to page 38 of Revill's **Sumter
District** (Bibliography).

Most of the other Rees' in Sumter District
spelled their name without the final e.   All
we have been able to identify were related to
one another.   William Rees, who married Mary
James, daughter of Sherwood James, is
generally spoken of as the patriarch of this
branch of Rees'   According to Sallie
Anderson, quoting conversation with Miss Mayo
Rees in Neuffer (XIV, page 26), the William
Rees now subject came to Stateburg in 1760
from Virginia.   According to Thomas Stubbs in
the same source (I, page 2:2), he began
acquiring land in the High Hills area as
early as 1762.   In Sumter Estate Settlements
(Bundle 81, Package 3) we find the will of a
Mary Rees, who was the mother of William.
This we know from comparison of her heirs to
their known relationship to other Rees'.
There was also a John Rees who left an estate
in Camden District of St. Marks Parish,
inventoried on 1 May 1782 and not forwarded
to Sumter District when that district was
formed.   From   names   of   appraisers,
administrator and date of death he could well
have been the real patriarch of the family.
At any rate brothers and sisters, children of
Mary Rees were Huberd Rees, who served early
on as sheriff of the district, Edwin Rees,

Isham Rees, Hugh Rees, Scarborough Rees, the
aforementioned William Rees, Elizabeth
Rogers, Mary Gayle, Jane Rembert, Edith
Williams and Anna Lee.

William Rees had sons William J. and Orlando
Savage Rees and a daughter Maria Penelope
Rees. William J. Rees had a son Frederick
Wentworth. William J.'s will, recorded 22
June 1850, lists his granddaughters Julia
Reynolds and Margaret Rees, this, along with
what we know of Vermelle Vaughan, serving as
proof Wentworth was his son. William J.'s
will also mentions nephews Wilson and William
J. Rees, his brother Orlando S. Rees, friends
E. M. Anderson and Vermelle Bradford, and
great-grandson William W. Reynolds. It is
unclear why he did not feel it proper to call
Vermelle a daughter, but perhaps it was due
to her remarriage after the death of his son.
His mention of William W. Reynolds is the
only indication to this writer that Julia
Vaughan and Marcus Reynolds had a son of that
name. William J. Rees also mentions his home
of Oakley in his will.

William J. Rees, son of Orlando S. Rees,
sometimes referred to as Jr., left a will,
recorded 30 July 1852. In it he mentions his
uncle William J. Rees, so it was probably
written before the latter's death. William
J., Jr. gives gifts to his mother and father
in his will, so it was surely made before his
father's death on 9 April 1852. He also
mentions Wilson W. Rees and E. M. Anderson
and his god-daughter, Catherine Waties, in
the will. Wilson was his brother and Edward
McKenzie Anderson was a cousin of William
Wallace Anderson. The great-grandson of
William J. Rees, Sr. married Elizabeth Waties
Anderson, daughter of William Anderson.
Catherine Waties was surely related in some
way to William J., Jr.'s mother. William J.,
Jr. married Maria Ford, but she must have
predeceased him.

Orlando S. Rees, as earlier stated, married
Catherine Waties. Her brother's will,

recorded 18 July 1823, names Orlando Rees as a friend. Besides what is here written, the reader can find much on the children and later descendants of Col. Rees in South Carolina Genealogies, Vol III, pages 104-105.

Maria Penelope Rees married, on 11 May 1813, John Mayrant, Jr. Maria was born in Sumter District in 1791 and died 9 March 1849. She is buried in Jackson, Mississippi. Her husband was the son of John and Isabella (Norvell) Mayrant and removed from South Carolina to Alabama and later Mississippi. He died in New Orleans on 25 June 1848 and is buried in Jackson, Mississippi. Their children were Isabella Norville, born in 1819, Francis, born in 1828, Mary, birth date unknown, and Sarah Huger Mayrant, born in 1834, who married General Wirt Adams. (See compile on Henry Vaughan III and his sons for more on Adams.) Mary (James) Rees mentions Maria P. and grandchildren Sarah Huger and Frances Maria [Francis?] Mayrant in her will, recorded 4 September 1838. The biographies of these persons can also be seen in South Carolina Genealogies (Vol. III, pages 102-103.

A General Orlando Rees lived for some years in the Sumter area. He later migrated to central Florida, where it is said the village of Orlando, now a large city, took its name from him. He was about the same age as William Rees, but William was Orlando Savage's father and we cannot say how the General was related to Col. Orlando Rees. He would seem to be an uncle, but none of William's brothers were so named. A cousin perhaps? Huberd, the sheriff, also mentioned as a steward of the Stateburg Jockey Club in the City Gazette of 7 October 1790, had a son, John Whitehead Rees. Edwin had daughters Sarah and Elizabeth; Isham had a daughter Sarah; and Hugh had sons Hugh and Benjamin. None are named Orlando, but there may have been others. In Orlando the road that runs next to the now-closed naval base is General Rees Rd., also named in honor of

the South Carolina worthy. The will of James Spann, Sr., written in 1827, was witnessed by an Orlando L. Rees, which this writer suspects to be a transcription error. The script L. and S. were often mistaken for one another by the transcriber.

Henry Vaughan III married an Emma Rees. She was surely related to these Rees, but, once again, the writer is at a loss to say in which manner. Many of these Rees' appear in the royal land grants for South Carolina in Craven County as well as a couple not heretofore encountered. We find Daniel and Joseph without the final e in their Rees(e). Royal grants in the grant books name Benjamin Rees (1772), Daniel Rees (1752), Hugh (1775), John (1770, 1771, 1772), Isom/Isham (1769), Joseph (1769, 1772), Peter (1771, 1774), Richard (1765) and William (1762, 1767, 1769). Other information on the Rees' can be found in volumes of memorials for South Carolina and in deeds recorded in Charleston before the county courts were formed for retention of this material. Although further treatment is considered beyond the scope of this treatise, the writer can state that he has been unable to add anything to the genesis or relationships in this family from information in these last two sources.

PETITION FOR PENSION OF JULIA FINETTA FRIERSON

No 25745
Act of March 9, 1878.

WAR OF 1812.
15927

Julia F. Frierson
Stateburg S. C.
Wid. of
John J. Frierson
Lieut. Capt. James Bennett
S. C. Mil.
Died Nov. 15 1829

Received June 17 1878
Claimant
Stateburg Sumpter Co
S. C.
Attorney.

June 18/78. Hon. D. W. Aiken
"26" J. H. C.

June 20/78
3d Aud. service
J. A. L.

Oct. 29/78 - 3d Auditor ... Jan. 5/78 returned for service ... calling attention to report of service of J. Richbourg in his B. L. ... Game Co.

Oct. 29/78 Claimt cares Richardson & Richardson Status.

Nov. 16/79. Hon. D. W. Aiken ... of C. status.

FILE DESIGNATION: WO 25745 (1812)

JULIA FINETTA FRIERSON PENSION CERTIFICATE
OF 22 JAN 1879
FOR SERVICE OF JOHN JAMES FRIERSON
WAR OF 1812

No. 15,924

1719 may 25. Shit & J. Nelson Frierson — E

WAR OF 1812.

Act of March 9, 1878.

WIDOWS' PENSION.

South Carolina

Julia F. Frierson

widow of

John J. Frierson

Rank Ensign

Company Capt J Bennett.

Regiment

S C Mil.

New Orleans Agency.

Rate per month—Eight dollars.

Commencing March 9, 1878.

Certificate dated Jany. 22. 79.
and sent to Pension Agent.
5 Feby 79.

Van Newell, Clerk.

JULIA FINETTA FRIERSON
5 JUL 1878 AND 19 DEC 1878
PENSION APPLICATION AUDIT REPORTS

No. 25,745 (1)

№ 25745

Treasury Department,

THIRD AUDITOR'S OFFICE.

December 19, 1878.

Respectfully returned to the Commissioner of Pensions with the information that John J. Frierson, Ensign, in Captain James Bennett's Company of South Carolina Militia, War of 1812, is Mustered present with his Company from 11th of October to 28th of November 1814 and from 28th November 1814 to 28th of February 1815. Joseph Richbourg, is Mustered present for the afforementioned dates, was discharged as Corporal March 7th 1815.

Deputy Auditor.

Treasury Department,

THIRD AUDITOR'S OFFICE,

July 5 , 1878.

Respectfully returned to the Commissioner of Pensions with the information that the rolls of Capt. James Bennett's Company of S.C. Militia show that Ensign John J. Frierson served from (Oct.) 11, 1814, to for 6 mos, 181 . Length of service not given — No Regt. Roll

Deputy Auditor.

JULIA FINETTA'S CLAIM OF WIDOW

U.

WAR OF 1812.

CLAIM OF WIDOW FOR SERVICE PENSION,

Under the provisions of Sections 4736 to 4740, (inclusive,) Revised Statutes, and the Act of March 9th, 1878.

N. B.—All the blank spaces in this form must be carefully filled up in accordance with the instructions on the back hereof; and from the best information possessed, or obtainable, by the applicant.

State of *South Carolina* } ss:
County of *Sumter*

On this *Eleventh* day of *June* A. D. one thousand eight hundred and *Seventy Eight*, personally appeared before me *Eugraw Richard Adair* within and for the county and State aforesaid, (1) *Julia Finetta Furciva* aged *12* years, a resident of *Sumter County*, in the State of *South Carolina*, who, being duly sworn according to law, declares that she is the widow of (2) *John Lewis Furciva* deceased, who was the identical (3) *John Lewis Furciva* served under the name of (4) *Furciva adjutant Clais* as a (5) *Lieutenant* in the company commanded by Captain *James Bennett*, in the Regiment of commanded by *Adam McCullen (Colonel)*, in the war of 1812; that her said husband (6) *Volunteer* in *Alexander's branch*, in said State, on or about the day of *October* A. D. 1814, for the term of *six years* and continued in actual service in said war for the term of *three months and twenty da* and whose services terminated, by reason of *an honorable discharge* at, on the day of *February*, A. D. 1815.

She further states that the following is a full description of her said husband at the time of his enlistment, viz:

She further states that she was married to *John Lewis Furciva* at the city or town of *New Station*, in the county of *Sumter*, and in the State of *South Carolina*, on the *Final* day of *May*, A. D. 1811, by one (10) *Probate*, who was a (11) *Probate Minister of the M. E. C.*; and that her name before her said marriage was *Julia Finetta Laughter*; and she further states that (12)

and that her said husband (13) *John Lewis Furciva*, died at the State of *South Carolina*, on the *fifteenth* day of *December*, A. D., and that she has not again married; and she further declares that the following have been the places of residence of

She makes this declaration for the purpose of obtaining the pension to which she may be entitled under Sections 4736 to 4740, (inclusive,) Revised Statutes, and the Act of March 9th, 1878, and hereby appoints, of, her true and lawful attorney, to prosecute her claim; and she further declares that she has heretofore made *no* application for (15)

and that her residence is No. _____ _____ street, city or town) of _____
county of _____, State of _____ and that her post-office address is
_____ _____ _____

ATTEST:

_____ _____

Also personally appeared _Warren H. Burgess_ aged _66_ years, residing
at _near Statesburg_ in _Sumter_ county _South Carolina_ and _Willis Vaughn_
_____ aged _70_ years, residing at _near Statesburg_ in said county
_____ in said State _____ persons whom I certify to be respectable and entitled to credit, and who,
being by me duly sworn, say that they have known the said _Julia Fenella Trueson_ for
_45_ years and for _60_ years, respectively; that they were present and saw her sign her name (or make
her mark) to the foregoing declaration; that they have every reason to believe, from the appearance of said claimant
and their acquaintance with her, that she is the identical person she represents herself to be; and they further say that
they are able to identify her as the person who was the wife of the identical (16) _____ _____
who rendered the service alleged in the above application (in the company of Captain _____ _____
in the regiment of _____ in the war of _1812_)—by the following
named facts and circumstances, viz: (17) _____

and that they have no interest in the prosecution of this claim.

_____ _____

Sworn to and subscribed before me this _Eleventh_ day of _June_, A.D.
1878; and I hereby certify that the contents of the above declaration, &c., were fully made known and explained to
the applicant and witnesses before swearing, including the words _____ erased,
and the words _____ added; and that I have no interest, direct or indirect, in
the prosecution of this claim.

_____ Notary Public

WIDOW'S BRIEF

Claim No. *25.745*
Act of *Mar. 9, 78*
Cert. No. *15927*

SERVICE PENSION,
War of 1812.

Original Cert.
Reopened from
Act of ....

WIDOW'S BRIEF.

Julia R. Frierson ...., widow of

John J. Frierson ....

Rank: *Ensign*
Captain *James Renault*
Regiment: *Mil.*
State: *S.C.*

Post Office: *Statesburg*, County of *Sumter*, State of *S.C.*
Attorney: *Claimant* .... P.O.: *as above*
.... County, State of .... Fee .... Contract

Application filed *June 17*, 18*78*.

Alleged service. *Volunteered as a ... in transmission ... S.C. in Oct. 1814 in Capt. James Renault's Co. S.C. Mil. & was discharged in Feb. 1815.*

Record evidence of service. *Sick report dated Dec. 5, 1873 shows that John Frierson Ensign in Capt. ... Co. ... Mil. ... was in 2 ...*

Parol evidence of service. *commenced ... with said company ... Feb 11 to Mar 28, 1815 & from Mar 28, 1814 to Feb 22, 1815.*

Length of service. *152 days ... subsequent to Feb 17, 1815*

Proof of identity. *examining witness, ... required. Identity by a ... service is verified by ...*

Proof of loyalty.

Admitted *January 6*, 18*79*, to a pension of **EIGHT DOLLARS** per month
from *Mar 9, 1878* the date of *act*.

No pension previously applied for

Alex. R. Spell
Pension Searcher.

N.O. Bounty Land claim *issued*
Bounty Land Searcher.

Examiner.

APPROVED *January 16, 1879*
W. J. Eaton
Reviewer. (OVER.)

62

State of South Carolina)
County of Sumter   )
                        I George W. Reardon
Clerk of the Court of Common Pleas in & for the
Said County and State do hereby certify that
the Role of the Notary Public for said County
and said State is kept in my Office: That
Guignard Richardson before whom the foregoing
[p. 82] Affidavit is taken is a Notary Public
in & for said County and State duly appointed
and qualified according to law, and full faith
and credit is due to his Official Certificate
as such Notary Public; and that Notary Public
are authorized by the laws of said State to
administer oaths for general purpose.

Given under my hand and Official seal this the
thirteenth day of June A. D. 1878.

                        George W. Reardon

                        C. C. P.

State of South Carolina)
County of Clarendon   )
                        Personally appeared Joseph Richbourgh
and Dover Frierson persons residing in the
County of Clarendon in Said State well known to
me and whom I certify to be respectable and
entitled to credit, and who being duly Sworn by
me depose and Say as follows--that is to say,
the Said Joseph Richbourgh for himself alone
deposeth and sayeth--That he is eighty-eight
years of age--that he is well acquainted with
the late John James Frierson who at the time of
his death and for many years previous thereto
resided near Statesburgh in the County of
Sumter in Said State and with his widow Julia
Finetta Frierson (who as his widow is an
applicant for a pension under the Act of
Congress approved March 9th 1878--That this
deponent was a soldier in the War of 1812
between the United States and Great Britain--
That he volunteered on or about the 19th day of
October 1814 for Six months--That he served
until the later part of February 1815 when
peace was declared, a period of over five

months--That this deponent knows the fact of his own personal knowledge that the Said John James Frierson volunteered in the service of The United States for the Said War of 1812 at the same time and place this deponent did--that the volunteering took place at a place called "The Old Muster Ground" in Clarendon County then a part of Sumter District in Said State-- That the said John James Frierson volunteered to serve the United States in the War of 1812-- for Six months--that he Served as third Lieutenant in the Company Commanded by Captain James Bennett in the Regiment of which Adam McWillie was Colonel and the Brigade of which Pinckney was General--That he served from the time he volunteered in October 1814 until the later part of February 1815 when peace was declared and he was honorably discharged

That the Said John James Frierson owned a valuable Plantation with a large number of slaves thereon on the Santee River in Clarendon County aforesaid not far from the residence of this deponent- That he was in the habit of visiting said Plantation Several times a year and was often accompanied in Said visits by the Said Julia Finetta Frierson his wife- That this deponent often Saw and conversed with them during their Said visits and in that way this deponent had every opportunity of becoming well-acquainted as well with the said Julia Finetta Frierson as with the Said John James Frierson- That they were persons of wealth and culture and of the highest social position and though this deponent was not present at their marriage he can safely affirm and depose that they were husband and wife and were so recognized-treated and received into society by the whole community in which they lived and by their acquaintances everywhere.

And this deponent further says that the said John James Frierson departed this life at his residence aforesaid in or about the year 1839 that he left him surviving his said widow and their two sons- John N. Frierson and James Frierson and that the said John James Frierson

was never married except to the said Julia
Finetta Frierson.

And deponent further sayeth that he has no
interest direct or indirect in the prosecution
of the claim for a pension under the Act
approved March 9th 1878 of the said Julia
Finetta Frierson.

And the said Dover Frierson for himself alone
deposeth and sayeth that he is about seventy-
eight years of age- that from his earliest
recollection and until he was emancipated
during or at the close of the late Civil War he
was the slave of the said John James Frierson
during his lifetime and from and after his
death, of James Julian Frierson one of the two
sons of the said John James Frierson: and that
he and this deponent resided on the plantation
of the said John James Frierson on Santee River
in Clarendon County in said State- that he
knows that the said John James Frierson
volunteered in the service of the United States
during the War with Great Britain of 1812- that
he volunteered in Clarendon County then a part
of Sumter District in said State- That this
deponent was the Body Servant of the said John
James Frierson during the whole time that he
was in the Service of the United States, and
knows that he volunteered some time in October
1814 and served as lieutenant in a company
commanded by captain James Bennett and a
Regiment commanded by Col-Adam McWillie- that
he served until the later part of February 1815
where on Peace being declared he was honorably
discharged

That this deponent served on said Plantation of
the said John James Frierson in the capacity of
Ostler and House Servant that he was well and
as intimately acquainted as a servant could be
with the said John James Frierson his wife the
said Julia Finetta Frierson and their two sons
John Frierson and James Julian Frierson: that
they the said John James Frierson and Julia
Finetta Frierson were married in the year 1817
near Statesburgh in Sumter District (now Sumter
County in said State at the residence of the

Father of the Said Julia Finetta Frierson-:
that the said Julia Finetta Frierson was the
first and only wife of the said John James
Frierson- that he resided until his death near
Statesburgh in Sumter District-now Sumter
County aforesaid and that he died at his
residence in the year 1839- leaving his wife
and his two sons above named surviving and that
this deponent has no interest whatever direct
or indirect in the prosecution of the claim of
the said Julia Finetta Frierson to a Pension
under the Act of Congress approved March 9th
1878
Attest-   Joseph Richbourg
                         his
Robert Thompson Dover x Frierson
Isaac Bagnal   mark

Sworn to and subscribed before me this twenty-
seventh day of May A. D. 1878- and I do hereby
certify that the contents of the above
deposition were fully made known and explained
to the witnesses above named befor (sic)
Swearing them and that I have no interest-
direct of indirect in the prosecution of the
claim in said depositions mentioned- (the word
"Sons" in the Affidavit of Dover Frierson being
first underlined)
                         G. Allen Huggins
                         Trial Justice

The State of South Carolina)
County of Clarendon   )
                I William Barfield Clerk of the
Court of Common Pleas and General Sessions in
and for the said County and State do hereby
certify that the roll of Trial Justices in and
for said County is keeped in my office- that
Trial Justices have full power, jurisdiction
and authority under the Laws of the said State
to administer oaths and take depositions of
witnesses- that G. Allen Huggins Esquire whose
certificate under his hand immediately precedes
this very certificate was at the date thereof a
Trial Justice in and for the County of
Clarendon aforesaid- That all due faith and
credit should be given to his certificate- That
Trial Justices have no Official Seals and that

the certificate aforesaid of the said Joseph
Richbourg and Dover Frierson is in due form and
by the proper officer.

> Given under my hand and official
> Seal at Manning in the County of
> Clarendon in said State this
> twenty-seventh day of May in the
> year of our Lord one thousand
> eight hundred and seventy-eight.
>> W. A. Barfield
>>> Clerk of the Court
>>> of Common Pleas and
>>> General Sessions

MARY MARGARET VAUGHAN (112b)

Mary Margaret was born on 25 December 1797, second daughter to Henry and Mary Margaret Vaughan. According to her tombstone she died on 1 February 1814. A notice in the Charleston _____ of 8 March 1814 states she died on the first ult., which also means the 1st of the previous month. Thus we have corroborating dates. Incidentally, first inst. would have meant in the parlance of the day, the first day of the current month of March. Her death was the result of an epidemic, which also claimed her father the following fifth of March.

MISSISSIPPI FEVER

HENRY VAUGHAN III (1121)

Henry III was the only son of Henry, Jr., and
Margaret Vaughan to survive his youth. He was
born on 31 March 1800 at Cherry Vale according
to the family Bible. His marker in the Vaughan
Cemetery in Mississippi gives the date of 3
March. Possibly the second digit is worn off
the marker. Henry attended the University of
South Carolina in 1816 as a member of the
Junior Class. Later he attended Yale
University as a graduate student in the Law
School. Yazoo: Its Legends and Legacies states
Henry was a graduate of Harvard Law School, but
this writer believes the statement is in error.
Henry returned to Sumter after his schooling
and became a businessman, lawyer and landowner.
He formed a close association with John Blount
Miller, a well-known resident there. Henry
remained in Sumter until about 1835 or 1836,
when he caught "Mississippi Fever." Various
sources give the year of his relocation as
early as 1830 (Yazoo County Story, page 68,
which states he moved from Charleston) to as
late as 1844 (Yazoo: Its Legends and Legacies);
however, the many deed records in Sumter County
indicate preparations were being made in 1835-
36 and military records of Charles B. Vaughan
(11213), showing he was born in Attala County,
Mississippi in 1837 would indicate the move
actually took place in that year. Henry still
had a letter in the post office in Attala
County in 1839. A notice from the Sumter
Gazette and Constitutional Advocate of October
1832 (copy p. 72) indicates Henry was unloading
his property in anticipation of a move at that
early date. The family of John Anderson came
with Henry to Mississippi. Since Henry's son
James B. (11215) married a daughter of John
Anderson in Mississippi, this would have been a
relative of Henry's mother (rather than his
maternal grandfather). An obituary of Henry's

69

friend, John B. Miller, is carried 4 November 1851 in the Sumter Banner.

While in Sumter Henry was Commissioner of Buildings. In the militia he rose to the rank of major. The Sumter Gazette (10 September, 5 & 12 November, 10 December 1831; 17, 24, & 31 March; 7 & 14 April, 12 May, 6 October and 3 November 1832) traces his rise in Claremont Troop, Sixth Cavalry Regiment of the South Carolina Militia. Henry was a vestryman for Claremont Episcopal Church (Gazette: 4 May 1833) and served on the commission to establish the Stateburg Post Office (Gazette: 27 July & 3 August 1833). He was a steward for the Stateburg Jockey and Turf Club (Gazette: 10 & 17 December 1831). The Gazette of 5 January 1833 carries a notice from Henry concerning a runaway slave.

On 8 March 1827 Henry married Emma M. Rees. Emma was born on 1 January 1810 and died on 16 March 1881.

An interesting account concerning Henry appears in Gregorie's History of Sumter County: An odd suit in chancery, growing out of a card game and involving a race horse, was brought in 1827 by William H. James, J. G. Frierson, Henry Vaughan, William Myers, and Matthew H. Moore. James set forth in his bill that in 1825 he had played cards with Myers and lost $750, which he had payed [sic] by a note payable to Frierson. Frierson explained this by the statement that he had bet with Myers and won $750 of the money lost by James, of which he had relinquished $200 and accepted a note from James for $500. Before the note matured, it was endorsed by Vaughan and transferred by Frierson to Moore in payment for a racehorse. Moore then brought suit. James, "acting from a false notion of Honour," confessed judgement, and Moore proceeded to sell James' property to satisfy the judgement. James, alleging fraud and collusion in the card game, then appealed to the court of chancery to cancel all proceedings. As the allegation of cheating was not sustained, the question for the chancellor

to decide was whether the court could give relief to James after he had confessed judgement in a court of law. In handing down his decree, Chancellor de Saussure summarized the laws which made gambling debts uncollectible, thus proving the note was void. He therefore ordered a perpetual injunction to restrain the defendant from enforcing the judgement at law against James.

The Camden Journal of 30 August 1828 carries a notice of a reception for Stephen D. Miller, State Senator from Sumter [and brother of John B.], with Henry serving on the reception committee.

BELOW IS A COPY OF HENRY'S SALE NOTICE
FOR CHERRY VALE AND OTHER PROPERTIES
AND ONE VIEW OF CHERRY VALE

LAND FOR SALE.—The ...
subscriber offers for sale the following
Lands in Sumter District—

The plantation on which ... ...
containing 2,500 acres, five m..., ...
from Stateburg, and on both sides of the
road to Sumterville, about 1000 acres
are prime oak and hickory, the ... ...
good pine land, 800 acres are ... ...
and under fence—on the premises are a
good two story dwelling with three
rooms, and every requisite out building
for a large plantation.

A tract of 240 acres adjoining the
above, 100 acres cleared and in cultivation, with a well finished house of three
rooms, and all necessary out building ...

A tract on Long Branch, two miles
from the above of 213 acres, 70 cleared and in cultivation.

Two adjoining tracts on Green
Swamp, four miles north of Sumterville of 640 acres, 250 are cleared and
cultivated, with suitable buildings for a
small farm—this will be divided to ... ts
purchasers.

To an approved purchaser the terms
will be liberal. Apply to
HENRY VAUGHAN.
October 3. ...

OCT 13, 1832

SUMTER GAZET
AND
CONSTITUTION,
ADVOCATE.

2 500
240
213
640
—————
3 593

CHERRY VALE, near Shaw Base, acquired in 1794 by Henry Vaughan II; sold in 1836 by Henry Vaughan III to his brother-in-law, John James Frierson. Now an apart- ment house for families of men at Shaw Air Force Base. (Sumter Daily Item staff photo).

BELOW IS ANOTHER VIEW OF CHERRY VALE

CHERRY VALE

It is difficult to determine the exact circumstances of Henry's move to Mississippi. Although engaged in the professions mentioned at the head of this vignette, he seems to have earned most of his money as a planter in South Carolina. Court records show he obtained much land at court sales enforcing judgements, no doubt at bargain prices brought about by market saturation; that is, everyone was growing the same thing. New Creek Indian lands opened up in Yazoo and Henry may have made an early and wise move. The true motivation was probably a combination of factors. Mississippi censuses show Henry was a planter there. Legends and Legacies says land was to be had for 50 cents an acre at the time. The first home of the Vaughan Family in Benton was the Burruss Place, built of logs. A daughter later married a Burruss. Soon Henry replaced the original homestead with a plantation, which he named Madley. Henry was a major in the Mississippi Militia and on 12 May 1837 was appointed Commissioner of the Benton-Manchester Railroad Company by Act of Legislature.

Henry prospered. In 1850 he had 222 slaves and was second only to Benjamin Roach in the county in that respect. By 1860, according to the Journal of Mississippi History (1953), Henry was the largest slaveholder in Mississippi with 293 slaves. Much of Henry's land, which was in Range 3 East of Township 11, was purchased in 1856 from the United States government through the Swamp and Overflow Act (1853-56). Although the war wiped out Henry's fortune, he regained it soon thereafter, so that he was able to give each of his children a fine home and plantation upon marriage. Legends and Legacies' contention that the family had returned to South Carolina during the Civil War has not found substantiation by this writer. Census records list Henry as the head of a household evaluated at $350,000 before the war. The 1860 census lists two non-family members in the household: Elizabeth Reilly, a 23-year-old teacher [see item on Alice W. Vaughan] and W. N. Langford, a 25-year-old overseer. Prior to the Civil War Henry had served as a delegate to

the convention whose members had voted for Mississippi's secession.

Henry and Emma's children were Mary S. (1121a), Margaret A. (1121b), Betsey (1121c), Henry IV (11211), John A. (11212), Charles B. (11213), Hugh Rees (11214), James B. (11215), Alice W. (1121d), Emma (1121e), Francis (Frank) (11216) and William (11217).

An interesting article comes from The Herald of Grenada, Mississippi of 5 May 1843: We learn from a gentleman, direct from Benton, Yazoo County, some of the particulars of a most melancholy occurance [sic]. It seems Mr. Trice had been hunting, and on his return he heard a noise in his gin house. He called out, and asked the cause--no answer was returned. He got off his horse and opened the door. A runaway negro man and his wife, the property of Mr. Vaughn, were inside of the door. The negro man raised a rifle loaded with slugs and fired at Mr. Trice, the slugs entering his body and head. He asked the negro what he shot him for--no answer was returned, where upon he raised his gun and shot the man down, at the same time severely wounding the woman. Mr. T. walked a few steps and in a few moments died.

The town of Vaughan, Mississippi was named for Henry Vaughan. According to a Mississippi gazetteer Vaughan is twelve miles east of Benton and was established in 1830, having a post office established some time in the 1830's. [This seems too early to this compiler.] According to Legends and Legacies Vaughan developed into a community when the railroad came through Yazoo County in 1857, a road being built from Vaughan to Benton in 1858. The same source says this was the only track in Yazoo County before the 1880's. There were two roads in the Benton area in 1858. One ran by the "Christian Church" and into Benton. It intersected to the west a road from Dr. Fugate's and William Pickett's that also went into Benton.

It was on 30 April 1900 that a train driven by Casey Jones crashed into a caboose of a freight train just north of the station at Vaughan. Jones assured his immortality by staying with the train to the last. He braked as hard as he could and slowed the train enough that he was the only person killed. Only by a quirk of fate was "Casey"--John Luther Jones by birth--piloting the Canton-Memphis leg of the New Orleans to Chicago Cannon Ball Express. He had piloted Engine Number 382, the Cannon Ball, north into Memphis and was due for a rest, but agreed to make the return trip south, because the return driver was ill. At 12:50 A. M., after the engine had been serviced, Casey pulled out of Memphis' Poplar Street Station with Simeon T. Webb as his fireman and J. C.. Turner as conductor. Leaving an hour and thirty-five minutes late, he wanted to make up the time before he reached Canton. No doubt Jones tugged many times on the whistle that distinguished the Cannon Ball, a six-tone calliope that always startled those on or near the tracks, because by the time it reached Goodman, ten miles north or Vaughan, the train was on schedule. Down the tracks, however, two long freights, one northbound and the other southbound, were being switched to a sidetrack east of the main track. This was not at all unusual in that day when freights were slow and easily outpaced by the much faster passenger trains. The caboose and three cars of the southbound train still protruded onto the main track when the Cannon Ball arrived. Sim Webb first spotted the caboose, gave a yell and jumped clear of the train. Jones hit the emergency brakes and stayed with the train, which derailed to the left and ended up pointing in the direction from whence it had come. Jones' valiant act resulted in only minor injuries occurring to passengers and crew other than himself. Jones' throat was pierced by a bolt or splinter of lumber. He died shortly afterwards on a baggage wagon at the depot a

half-mile away, where he had been taken on a
stretcher.

Besides the roads and the railway, Vaughan was
on a stage line and for many years was the
trading center for the county, as well as much
of Madison County to the east, across the Black
River.

MARY S. VAUGHAN (1121a)

Mary was born in 1827 or 1828, before her parents left South Carolina. Various censuses, which are the sources for her place of birth, have some discrepancies in her age. The Yazoo Democrat and the Yazoo City Whig & Political Register of 11/20/1850 carries this notice: Married on Thursday the 14th, at Madely, Yazoo Co., by the Rev. David Kerr, Mr. John O[sborn] Gnion [Guion] of North Carolina to Miss Mary S., eldest daughter of Maj. Henry Vaughan. This marriage is also recorded in Book "A", page 23 of Yazoo County Marriage Records (1845-1852).

Mary was head of household in the 1880 Mississippi Census, so her husband was likely deceased by that date. Children of the Guions were Henry (1121a1); Martha (1121aa), born about 1854; John (1121a2), born about 1857; James (1121a3), born about 1862; Hugh (1121a4), born about 1863; William (1121a5), born about 1866; and Julius (1121a6), born about 1868. The dates come from various censuses.

The 1860 census also lists in the household a Sallie Guion, general housekeeper and sister-in-law to Mary. This census says Sallie was born in North Carolina, her father in New York and her mother in South Carolina. Goodspeed (bibliography) states that Mary was alive in 1891. The information on Henry Guion comes from Henry Vaughan's will, in which he gives a bequeath to "his grandson Henry Guion." For this reason I take him to be the oldest, although he could be the youngest if born in 1869 (but he should then be in the 1880 census).

MARGARET A. VAUGHAN (1121b)

Margaret was born about 1830 in South Carolina,
daughter of Major Henry and Emma Vaughan.
According to the Yazoo City Weekly Whig of
04/28/1854: Married at Madely, on Tuesday the
18th, by the Rev. Parker Scott, Col. Henry
Allen, Jr. of Grenada, Ms. to Miss Margaret A.,
daughter of Maj. Henry Vaughan of Yazoo Co.

Mary married on 22 May 1860 in Yazoo County
Major James S. Moore. This writer is
unacquainted with what happened to Col. Allen,
but notes that the Vaughan Family was
acquainted with a James Sinkler Moore back in
South Carolina. Goodspeed states Mrs. Moore
died sometime prior to 1891.

MY IDENTICAL TWIN

Once people called each other cousin.
They knew all men were related one way or
another;
Not necessarily father, son or brother,
But other kinships were a dime a dozen.

Imagine my great, great, great shame,
When, while shaking the family tree,
I discovered two great-great-great grandfathers
the same.
And, as for my cousin, I wuz one,
And I'm closely (and distantly) related to me.

BETSEY VAUGHAN (1121c)

Betsey, daughter and third child of Henry and
Emma Vaughan, died in infancy.

PIP'S PRIZE

When my grandfather's will was proved,
Pip, as I'm called, found I had cousins of
                    every strain;
Some once removed, some twice removed,
And most should have been forever removed
                    again.

While everyone spoke of the old fellow with
                    pride,
And explained the rightness of his claim,
I found I was related on more than one side;
The fellow and I had several kin one and the
                    same.

I was taken aback to see
So many lines of relation come together,
And how many ways I'm related to me;
Each line became more a question of how than
                    whether.

They opened the will in all the confusion
And these are the words they did see;
"I leave my all to Pip, as I've come to the
                    conclusion
He's even more closely related than I am to
                    me."

HENRY VAUGHAN IV (11211)

Henry was born about 1834, before his parents left South Carolina. The 1850 census lists Henry as a student. Henry married Fanny C. Johnson of Baltimore, Maryland. The 1870 and 1880 censuses list his occupation as physician. In many other sources he is referred to as Dr. Vaughan. The 1870 census lists Henry's real estate as worth $9,500 and his wife was then thirty-three. Yazoo: Its Legends and Legacies states that Dr. Henry Y. Vaughan died on 13 December 1884 and is buried in the family cemetery. Since none of the other Henrys known to live in the area were of an age to have been a medical doctor at the time, the reference must be to the subject of this paragraph. Other Henrys in the area at the time were 1) Henry's own son, 2) Henry Yandell (son of Dr. Henry's brother James), and 3) the son of the last-named, also named Henry Yandell.

Children of Henry and Fanny were, per 1870 Mississippi census, Emma M. (11211a), born in 1856; Henry V (112111), born in 1859; and Wesley (112112), born in 1864 and known in some records as West.

Emma married on 21 October 1873 Beverly R. Grayson, member of an affluent Yazoo County family. The 1880 census indicates that two grandchildren were in Henry's household at that time: Tom (11211a1) and Mary (11211aa) Grayson, born in 1877 and 1878, respectively. Emma was not in the household, which indicates that perhaps she and Mr. Grayson were deceased by this date. The same census indicated Fanny (Franny in one source) and her parents were all from Maryland; also there was an eleven-year-old black female servant in the household named Lucy Vaughan.

A Henry Vaughan that married Molly Hendricks in Yazoo County on 14 September 1881 could have been Henry V.

JOHN A. VAUGHAN (11212)

John A., second son of Henry and Emma Vaughan, died in his teens.

LIFE'S LITTLE INSTRUCTIONS (1787)

Scratch where it itches . . . Never ask a question unless you're willing to hear the answer . . . Don't bite the hand that feeds you . . . Never wrestle with a pig; you both get all dirty--and the pig likes it . . . Never count your chickens until the eggs hatch . . . Play your cards above the board . . . Never argue with a fool; others may not know the difference . . . Neither a debtor nor a lender be . . . The way to get ahead is to use the one on your shoulders . . . Never flog a dead horse.

CHARLES B. VAUGHAN (11213)

Charles B. was the first child of Henry and Emma Vaughan born in Mississippi. According to military records he was born in 1837 in Attala County, which is a few miles to the east of Yazoo County. Perhaps he was born en route to Yazoo. Nothing indicates the family stopped over during removal from South Carolina. Charles married Mary L. Clark, one of four daughters of General William Clark, who removed in 1835 from Pitt County, North Carolina, to Jackson, Mississippi. The 1860 Mississippi census indicates Mary was 21 in that year. She is also listed as Charles' survivor in his military records, filed in Appendix XIV. The general's daughter Jane married Micajah Pickett, a wealthy Yazoo County planter, which puts Legends and Legacies' statement that Mary was Pickett's niece into question. A sketch of General Clark can be found in the North Carolina Christian of January 1925. The 1860 census lists the value of Charles' estate at $75,000 and shows an overseer, N. B. Street, in the household.

Charles was mustered into Company I of the First Regiment, Mississippi Light Artillery, on 27 April 1862. He enlisted as a private for three years or the duration of the war. At that time the unit was known as Withers' Regiment, but within days was incorporated into the Mississippi unit of the Confederate Forces, whereupon Charles' enlistment date became 3 May 1862. After a short period of instruction at camp in Jackson the unit joined the regulars. The unit participated in the Battle of Vicksburg, where Charles apparently contracted a sickness. Regimental returns for August show Charles absent on sick leave. Company muster rolls show he was back with the unit in September and October, but by 12 December was in the hospital at Vicksburg with typhoid fever. He was sent home to recuperate but instead died on 2 January 1863. Our source is a letter of Mary's sister, Jane Pickett, to another sister, Louisa Boddie, of 31 January

1863, which refutes the 21 January date in Charles' military records.

Army rolls describe Charles, a farmer by profession, as five foot five and one-half inches with dark hair and gray eyes. He was enlisted by Captain R. Bowman, probably father of the woman his nephew Henry Yandell married. Charles' brother James was a member of Bowman Chapel, likely connected with these Bowmans. Charles and James may both have been present at the siege of Vicksburg, for James was serving at this time in Wirt Adams' Cavalry.

Charlie Muteth, the only child of Charles and Mary to survive childhood, was an heir in Major Henry's will of 28 September 1870. Mary's letter to Louisa of 22 February 1863 tells of an earlier child who died in infancy, William. Charlie Mutelle, as she calls her daughter, was according to her born after Charles' death.

HUGH REES VAUGHAN (11214)

Hugh Rees was the son of Henry and Emma Vaughan. He was born in 1839 in Mississippi. At the beginning of the Civil War he joined the Confederate Army and served in Company B, Eighteenth Mississippi Infantry, rising to the rank of captain. He spent much of this period in Sumter, recovering from wounds received in battle. The following is an article from the Sumter Watchman of 23 March 1864: Another of Longstreet's heroes has gone to rest. Captain Hugh R. Vaughan died on last Friday morning [18th] at the residence of James S. Moore, Esq., near Stateburg. He volunteered at the commencement of the war and was in Barksdale's Brigade at the Battle of Sharpsburg where he was shot through the lungs; as soon as he recovered sufficiently to walk, he rejoined his command and at Gettysburg was severely wounded in the leg. He afterward rejoined Longstreet, but the hemorrhage from his wounded lung finally closed his career.

The South Carolina Historical and Genealogical Magazine (Vol. 30, page 56) says he was in the 25th year of his age. James Sinkler Moore was Hugh's cousin, having married Mary Margaret Rees, daughter of Hugh's aunt, Vermelle Rees Bradford. He may also have been his brother-in-law, as we have seen Margaret A. Vaughan married in 1860 a James S. Moore after the presumed death of her first husband Col. Allen. Mary (Rees) Moore had died in 1859. Hugh died unmarried and is buried in the cemetery of the Church of the Holy Cross in Stateburg.

Hugh's military records, which can be found in the Appendix, show that he enlisted in Yazoo County, Mississippi, on 27 April 1861 into Captain Wm. H. Luse's Company, Mississippi Volunteers. This unit was later known as just Captain Luse's Company and, upon reorganization became Company B, 18th Regiment, Mississippi Infantry. Hugh had originally enlisted for a period of 12 months and, upon reorganization on 29 May 1861, he was enlisted again for 12

months from that date by Captain Walker. The muster states he had to travel 230 miles to rendezvous with the regiment. Hugh was originally enlisted as a 2nd Sergeant in the Benton Rifles, as Luse's unit was also known, but on 26 April 1862 he was promoted to captain upon election by the unit. Colonel Griffin reenlisted him at Lees Mills on 28 April 1862 for the duration of the war. Hugh was continuously present from Yazoo to Corinth to Virginia until September 1862 because of wounds received at Sharpsburg. He doesn't appear again on the rolls until 18 May 1863. A muster of 13 August shows him once again on furlough because of wounds suffered 2 July 1863 at Gettysburg. A muster of 27 February states "died since last muster," while that of 15 July 1864 states "absent sick." A muster completed 14 July 1864 (for May and June of that year) notes "died March 18, 1864." Regimental returns indicate Company B was at Winchester in September 1862, Brucetown in October 1862, and Fredericksburg in November and December of 1862. An Engagement Listing shows Hugh present at the Battles of Manassas, 21 Jul 1861, and Leesburg, 21 October 1861; absent sick from Battles of Savage Station and Malvern Hill; present at the Battle of Maryland Heights; wounded at Sharpsburg severely; absent on furlough from both Battles of Fredericksburg, 11 December 1862 and 3 May 1863; severely wounded at Gettysburg; and absent on furlough from Battles of Chickamauga, Knoxville and Bean's Station. He is not carried on the Engagement Listing for the remainder of the nine engagements the regiment participated in before the close of the war.

JAMES B. VAUGHAN (11215)

James B. was born in 1842, fifth son of Henry
and Emma Vaughan. James was well-educated and
attended Oxford University (probably the
University of Mississippi) before the outbreak
of the Civil War. Leaving the schoolroom to
take up arms for the Confederacy, he joined the
Benton Rifles in Yazoo County the same day as
his brother Hugh Rees, 27 April 1861. On 29
May he enlisted for twelve months when the
company was attached to the Confederate 18th
Mississippi Regiment. James participated in
the Battle of Manassas, 21 July 1861, was
hospitalized at Charlottesville from 6 August
to 21 August of the same year, returned to
fight in the Battle of Leesburg on 21 October,
where he was wounded in the hip, and was
discharged on 22 November 1861. James'
discharge papers state he was 5' 1" with a fair
complexion, blue eyes and brown hair, served as
a sergeant, was born in Yazoo County and was
age 19 at discharge from the service. His last
check was entrusted to Hugh's care. Later and
to the end of the conflict, James served in
Wirt Adams' Cavalry. [See reference to Adams
on page 54--sidebar on Rees'.]

On 19 November 1867 James married Mary E.
Anderson, daughter of John W. and Adaline
(Newell) Anderson. Although the 1870 census
lists her as twenty and the 1880 census as
thirty, she was probably born in 1847. The
1850 census lists her as three years of age and
indicates her father had remarried. Mr. and
Mrs. Anderson had married within the year--her
name was Elizabeth--and the ages of Mary's
siblings show that Elizabeth was not the
mother. The Andersons were neighbors in
Mississippi and from the same area of South
Carolina as the Vaughans, before the families
migrated.

Between 1870 and 1886 James and Mary had nine
children, seven of whom survived childhood:
Emma (11215a), born about 1870, married H. F.
Russell and resided in Washington County,

Mississippi; James A. (112151), born in 1872; Samuel D. (112152), born in 1875; Henry Yandell (112153), born in 1877, married Octavia Bowman, daughter of Richard S. and Lettetia (Swayze) Bowman; Mary (11215b), born in 1880; Charles (112154) and John A. (112155), birth dates unknown.

Children of Henry and Octavia B. Vaughan are Richard (1121531); Henry Yandell (1121532); Carrie (112153a), who married Mr. Heard; Nolan Stewart (1121533), born on 25 September 1909, married Effie Lenore Hall and died 17 May 1987; and Claiborne Hayes (1121534). Nolan Stewart married on 10 April 1935 Miss Hall, daughter of Robert S. and Lenore (Robinson) Hall of Hattiesburg, Mississippi. Their children were Carolyn Lenore (1121533a), born on 5 March 1936; Nolan Stewart, Jr. (11215331), born on 22 July 1941; Cynthia Yandell (1121533b), born 27 September 1942 and Lucy Ann (1121533c), born 23 July 1946.

Charles married Cora Cox and they had a son, Charles B. (1121541) of Benton.

James was a member of the Knights of Honor and a Free and Accepted Mason. He and his wife were members of Bowman's Chapel, Methodist Episcopal Church. In 1891 James lived on the family plantation, described as 1440 acres of which 1000 were under cultivation, mostly with corn and cotton. Goodspeed states Mr. Vaughan planned to put more emphasis on livestock operations on the farm in the immediate future. James died in 1908 according to a survey of Mississippi confederate graves.

The above named John W. Anderson was probably the same as the one who served as an appraiser in the settlement of the estate of Jesse S. Brown with James' father. See page 173 of Yazoo County will settlements for March 1836 term. Beverly Grayson (probably father of the previously mentioned Beverly) was one of the executors.

Most of the above dates come from <u>Gillis'</u> <u>Genealogical Notes</u> and James' sketch in <u>Goodspeed</u>, but some were conveyed by letter to the writer by Effie (Hall) Vaughan.

English names deriving from professions (with definitions where needed): Archer; Baker; Barber; Barker (either a caller to passersby or a remover of tree bark); Booker; Bowman; Brewer; Butcher; Butler; Cantor (religious officer in charge of the singing programs); Carpenter; Carter (one who drives a cart); Carver; Chamberlain, Chamberlin (manager of royal quarters, receiver of rents, treasurer or steward of nobleman); Chancellor (judge or other high official); Chandler (a seller of candles, later of groceries and provisions in general); Clark (a clerk); Collier (coal miner or seller of coal); Cook; Cooper (maker or repairer of casks or barrels); Courier, Courrier (messenger); Crocker (maker of earthen or metal, especially iron, pots); Currier (a dresser or colorer of tanned leather or a dresser of horses); Cutler (maker, repairer, seller of knives); Draper; Farmer; Fisher; Fletcher (maker of arrows); Forrester, Forster; Fowler; Fuller (person who cleanses and thickens--fulls--cloth); Glover; Granger (farmer or farm steward); Harper; Hooker (one who fishes from a boat with lines and hooks-- Dutch hoek); Hooper (same as cooper except worked mainly on the hoops); Hunter; Joiner, Joyner (carpenter who makes doors, windows and sashes); Mason; Merchant; Miller; Monk; Painter, Paynter; Palmer (pilgrim, one who returned from Crusades with sign of the palm); Parker; Parson; Planter; Pope; Porter (gatekeeper, later one who carries); Potter; Proctor (in Britain any official charged to maintain order, but especially one who watches over students during exams); Saddler; Sawyer (one who saws for a living); Sexton (church official in charge of buildings); Shearer, Sherman (shearer of sheep); Shepherd; Shoemaker; Singer; Skinner; Smith/Arrowsmith (worker in metal); Spencer (steward or butler, formerly dispenser or de Spensor--Old French);

ALICE W. VAUGHAN (1121d)

Alice W. was born in 1844 or 1845, fourth daughter of Henry and Emma Vaughan. On 30 October 1866 Alice married James H. Burrus (Book D--1850-70--of Yazoo County, Mississippi, Marriage Records). L. C. Willis served as security on the bond. Mr. Burrus (listed as Burroughs in some sources) was a first lieutenant in Company B of the 18th Mississippi Volunteer Infantry.

Children of Mr. and Mrs. Burrus were Sophie Powell (1121da), who married James Burrus; Martha (1121db), who married Mr. Durham of Brookhaven; and Frank (1121d1) of Memphis.

Children of James and Sophie Burrus were James (1121da1); Alice (1121daa), who married Mr. O'Reilly; Sophie B. (1121dab), who married Mr. Fitzgerald; Eliza (1121dac), who married Mr. Sneed; and Emily (1121dad), who married Mr. Shakelford.

Most of the above information comes from Yazoo County Story.

English professional names (Cont'd.)

Tanner; Taylor; Tinker (a mender of pots and pans); Tucker (one who beats a drum--Middle English); Turner (worker on a lathe); Walker; Weaver; Wheeler (same as Wheelwright); Wright/Cartwright, Wainwright or Wheelwright (worker, one who has wrought, an archaic English form of worked); Farrior, Farrier (a blacksmith or veterinarian); Fielder and Fincher.

EMMA VAUGHAN (1121e)

Emma, the fifth daughter of Henry and Emma
Vaughan, was born in 1847 in Yazoo County,
Mississippi.   She lived with her family near
Benton until her untimely death at the age of
fourteen.

TIME IS OF THE ESSENCE (AND RELATIVE)

Dates used in this work are from the given
sources and presumably based on the calendar of
the day.   Most places in the United States
adopted   the   Gregorian   Calendar   effective   2
September   1752.   Some   localities   may   have
learned of the change from the Julian Calendar
late and continued to use it for a while after
that.   The change had been made to correct
faulty calculation of religious holidays caused
by   inaccuracies   in   the   Old   Style   (Julian)
Calendar.

Until 1752 the year had begun on 25 March; then
the new year was changed to 1 January.   Thus,
27 January 1749 was what we would now consider
27 January 1750.   In places where it seems
siblings were born less than nine months apart,
designated   by   (?)   in   this   work,   the   actual
separation   may   have   been   one   year   plus   the
apparent number of months.

FRANCIS VAUGHAN (11216)

Francis was born in 1849, sixth son of Henry
and Emma Vaughan. His name appears as Frank in
several records. Frank married a Mrs. Burks
and, if we rely on the 1870 Yazoo County
census, her given name was Mary E. The census
gives Frank's age as 28, which would be an
error. The same census shows a two-month-old
child Emma in the household and lists the value
of Francis' real estate at $17,500 and personal
estate at $3,700.

A grandchild of Major Henry Vaughan, Frankie
Vaughan, mentioned in Yazoo County Story, was
likely Frank's daughter. Frankie married Alan
Hicks and lived on the original Vaughan
property south of Benton until her death. The
children of Mr. and Mrs. Hicks were Hervie,
Jack and Frank of Yazoo County and Earl of New
Orleans.

Frank died at twenty-six years of age. Yazoo
County marriage Records show the marriage of a
Frank M. Vaughan to Anna A. Owings on 26 July
1871 and marriage of Anna A. Vaughan to Thomas
J. Burks on 26 December 1881. Although there
may be an error in the source of information,
the conclusion this writer draws is that
Frank's wife Mary E. Burks died sometime before
26 July 1871 and Frank married Miss Owings;
then, he dying soon thereafter, his widow
married Mr. Burks, possibly a relative of Mr.
Vaughan's first wife.

WILLIAM REECE VAUGHAN (11217)

William Reece was the true seventh son and last child of Henry and Emma Vaughan. He was born in 1854 in Yazoo County. William was the second son to have the same (phonetically) middle name. Why name a second son with the same middle name (Hugh was the other) and spell it differently is not known. Hugh died when William was ten years old.

William married Ida King. William and Ida had two children, William Reece and Alice. It is likely that William, Sr. was deceased by 1879, for Yazoo County Marriage Records show the marriage of Ida Vaughan to A. F. Lambert on 30 April of that year.

Alice (11217a) married Mr. Redmond and died in childbirth. William Reece (112171) was born 8 July 1872 and is buried in Hart Town Cemetery. He married Mattie Bennett, born 10 April 1874 and also buried in Hart Town Cemetery. Mattie's mother, Henrietta Susan, nee Anderson, was a sister to Mary E. Anderson, wife of her husband's uncle, James B. Vaughan.

Children of William Reece and Mattie Vaughan were Hugh Reece (1121711), born on 20 May 1895 and died 4 September 1947; Merle (1121712), born 1 August 1897 and died 5 September 1911; Ida (112171a), who married Mr. Presley; William Anderson (1121713), born 19 August 1909, married Martha O'Reilly and died on 3 June 1994; and Aubrey (1121714). Both Hugh Reece and Merle are buried in the Hart Town Cemetery. Major Henry is known from extant records to have had extensive dealings with the Harts.

Hugh Reece married firstly Mary Fisher. Hugh was a wagoner with the 7th Field Artillery, 1st Division in World War I. By Mary Hugh had four children: Hugh Reece, Jr. (11217111), William Lee (11217112), Mary Merle (1121711a) and Lydia Nell (1121711b). Hugh remarried and moved to Los Angeles where he is believed to have had three more daughters. Ida married A. L.

Presley and they had a daughter Peggy (11217laa). William and Martha O'Reilly Vaughan had two sons, William Anderson, Jr. (11217131) and Thomas Hugh (11217132). Aubrey married Marguerite Lewis and had a daughter Susan (1121714a), who married Mr. Edge. William Lee had a son William Reece (112171121), who also has a son William Reece, Jr. (1121711211).

The O'Reilly line above traces its lineage to Charlemagne; thus all descendants of William A. and Martha O. Vaughan or of her siblings also have this pedigree. William A. Vaughan, Jr. of 206 Martha Gene Dr., Canton, MS 39046 has done much research on this line.

JOHN ANDERSON VAUGHAN (1122)

John Anderson was the second son of Henry and
Mary Margaret Vaughan. He was born on 8 March
1803.   John attended Yale University as a
member of the Junior Class. He contracted an
illness in New Haven, Connecticut, and died on
6 November 1821 at the age of eighteen. The
family Bible states he died at the University
of Virginia. So, although John died away from
home, we may be said to have returned to the
South Carolina vein of Vaughans.

John's death notice from the Sumter Gazette of
21 November 1821 may be found on page 78 of
volume 49 of South Carolina Historical and
Genealogical Magazine and a copy of the
inscription of his headstone in the cemetery of
the Church of the Holy Cross may be found on
page 56 of volume 30 of the same publication.
The inscription states he died at Yale as a
member of the Junior Class.

VERMELLE M. VAUGHAN (112c)

Vermelle was the youngest child of Henry and Mary Margaret Vaughan. She was born on 28 June 1804 (SCHGM, vol. 30, page 56) or 28 June 1809 (Family Puzzlers--See Bibliography). This writer is inclined toward the latter and the culprit is again likely to be worn grave markers. Vermelle married firstly, on 11 March 1827, Frederick Wentworth Rees. Their children were Julia Vaughan (112ca), born 13 October 1828, married to Marcus Reynolds and died 1 June 1900; Maria Ford (112cb), born 14 November 1829, baptized 6 June 1830, died in infancy; and Margaret Mary (112cc), born 15 April 1832, married on 7 June 1853 to James Sinkler Moore and died 11 March 1859.

Frederick W. Rees died sometime between 13 November 1834 and 1 January 1835, his widow marrying secondly John Singleton Bradford, her cousin and the son of Robert Bradford, on 8 January 1839. Vermelle filed annual returns on 12 January 1841 in the settlement of Mr. Rees' estate for the previous year. Her cousin (per Major Dargan) was born on 22 September 1817 and died 27 September 1854. Their children were John Robert (112cl), born 10 October 1841 and Anna Maria (112cd), born 4 October 1839 and died 31 May 1875.

Julia married Marcus Reynolds on 16 June 1848 (____ day of June 1845 per Family Puzzlers, which uses the family Bible as its source, conveyed by Mary Britton Phillips). Mr. Reynolds was born 2 April 1817 in Armagh, Ireland, son of William and Mary Reynolds. Mr. Reynolds was the third of three brothers to emigrate to the United States. He came over in 1836, while older brothers William and George arrived in 1828 and 1820, respectively. The three were all preceded by an uncle, Joshua Reynolds of Camden, who took out naturalization papers in 1815, stating he had been seven years resident in the state. For more information on the Reynoldses see Historic Camden, pages 423-427 (Bibliography). Children of Marcus and

Julia were Mark (112cal), Maria Rees (112caa), James (112ca2), possibly the same as he who died 27 November 1895 and is buried in the Holy Cross Cemetery, and Sophia (112cab), the only reference to whom I found in Names (III, page 35). For the descendants of James Reynolds see The Friersons of Stateburg. On 5 October 1887 the younger Mark married Elizabeth Waties Anderson, daughter of William Wallace Anderson, Jr. Their four children were Mark (112call), William McKenzie (112cal2), Julia Rees (112cala) and James Wentworth (112cal3), born in 1898 and died in 1899. Dr. Mark Reynolds died on 6 March 1883.

Margaret Mary married James Sinkler Moore, son of John Isham Moore, on 7 June 1853. They had two children: John Isham (112ccl) and Margaret Mary (112cca).

Vermelle died on 6 September 1887. Much of the information in this section comes from a Vaughan Family Bible owned by Virginia Hodges Reynolds, daughter of the youngest of the above-named Mark Reynoldses.

Vermelle lived for many years at the family estate of Needwood in Stateburg, whose picture is included at the end of this sketch. This photo comes from Anne King Gregorie's History of Sumter County, as did the first of the two views of her father's estate of Cherry Vale, which incidentally burned in an accident committed by army personnel stationed at Shaw Field. Needwood passed after Vermelle's death to Benjamin Hodges, husband of her granddaughter Maria Rees (Reynolds) Hodges. Mr. Hodges was an immigrant from Salem, Massachusetts, who had originally rented the plantation in 1871 during Reconstruction and when times were lean. Mr. Hodges allowed Mrs. Bradford to remain on the plantation and married Miss Reynolds in 1886. Mr. and Mrs. Hodges had three children: Benjamin Deland, Jr. (112caal); Mark Reynolds (112caa2) and a daughter who died in infancy. Mr. Hodges, son of a merchant, John Hodges, later removed to Topsfield, Massachusetts, where he died on 12

January 1897. Thereafter, Needwood passed to Clara Frierson Reynolds, a cousin.

Virginia Reynolds Hodges has been called a cousin by Sallie Anderson, and J. Nelson Frierson said that her father was Mark Reynolds. If this be so, she was probably a fifth child of Mark and Elizabeth Waties Reynolds. She is often mentioned in conjunction with Julia Rees, the other daughter of Mark and Elizabeth Reynolds. Mrs. Hodges could have married one of the two sons of Benjamin and Maria Rees Hodges, but this is unlikely as they were both out of the area before 1897, when they would have been quite young.

According to Claude H. Neuffer's <u>Names</u> Vermelle also at one time owned Wedgefield Plantation, named for its wedge-shaped field among the Santee hills. Wedgefield had once been owned by William Rees, a well-known Tory during the Revolutionary War. He lost the property as a result of his sympathies, but it was later returned to him when he pled a grievance at law. Records refer to Vermelle as his daughter, but she was actually the granddaughter-by-marriage to his grandson Wentworth Rees. After her death Wedgefield passed to her daughters Margaret J.[?] Moore (southern part) and Julia V. Reynolds (northern part). The source for this last is Neuffer's <u>Names</u> (XIII, Pages 32-33). My records indicate Margaret's initial was M.

A VIEW OF NEEDWOOD

NEEDWOOD, on lands called Whiskey Hall by Robert F. Withers. Sold in 1827 to Frederick Wentworth Rees, who built this house, originally plastered on the exterior. Now owned by J. Frank Williams, who weatherboarded it. (Sumter Daily Item staff photo).

FRANCES VAUGHAN (11a)

Frances was the eldest daughter of Henry and Elizabeth Vaughan. Her obituary, in the Sumter Watchman of June 1857, gives 1778 as the year of her birth. The obituary appeared the same day as her death. Frances married John S. Reynolds of Camden, who also had interests in Sumter. According to the Sumter Banner of 22 November 1848 John died on 5 November 1848 of paralysis at Spring Hill Plantation. John was a planter according to the article. John's will names their children: William J. (11a1), born in 1808 and died unmarried 12 June 1881; Elizabeth Vaughan (11aa), born in April 1817, married to Lawrence M. Spann and died 20 December 1901; and Ellen C. (11ab), who married Lucien M. James.

Elizabeth and Lawrence (sometimes spelled Laurence) Spann had four children: James (11aa1); Harriet (11aaa); Bettie (11aab) and Ella (11aac). Lawrence Spann was the son of James, Sr. and Anna Spann. The wills of James, Sr. (recorded 6 May 1833) and Anna (recorded 2 October 1838) name Lawrence and his brothers and sisters. Brothers were William T., Tyre I., Charles and Timothy H. Spann. The sisters were Harriet G. Watson, wife of Walker Watson and deceased by 18 August 1837 (date of Anna's will); Anna E. F. Yates, wife of Dr. Yates; and Marie Cathcart.

Ellen C. and Lucien James, son of Holloway and Roxanna James, had five children. They were Hortensia (11aba), who married C. F. Pauknin; William J. (11ab1); Sebastian (11ab2); Ellen P. (11abb) and Mattie A. (11abc). Lucien is mentioned in his father's will, recorded 4 October 1830. His brothers were William Alexander and Benjamin Albert James. He also had a sister, Martha Ann James. James G. Spann was named as a witness in Holloway James' will and a trustee in James Spann, Sr.'s will, indicating the Reynoldses, Jameses and Spanns were closely knit or lived very near one another. James G. Spann himself left a will

recorded 5 November 1827, which must have been rather hastily written, considering the will naming him trustee for others was written on 19 September 1827.

Ellen C. James became deranged later in life and died in a mental institution in Columbia about 1880.

TRAGEDY

I once met a man all starry-eyed,
Who had just taken a beauty for a bride.
Alas, she was not schooled in the culinary arts
And forthwith he was reduced to vital parts;
So that the ensuing death certificate read:
                    chop sueycide.

ELIZABETH VAUGHAN (11b)

Elizabeth was the second daughter of Henry and Elizabeth Vaughan. She married firstly Amos DuBose, a Baptist minister who served in the High Hills Baptist Church. According to some sources Reverend DuBose was a descendant of the Huguenot immigrant Isaac DuBose. Page 91 of History of the Old Cheraws (Bibliography) states Isaac was the oldest of four sons of John DuBose, "the first of that name to remove to the Pee Dee area." A memorial in Craven County, however, states that a grant of 26 Jan 1714/1715 was made to an Isaac DuBose and conveyed to his son John by the last will and testament of Isaac of 19 Jun 1714. Rev. DuBose died in 1813. Amos and Elizabeth had eight children: Henry (11b1); Hampton (11b2); Amos (11b3), who married Martha Ann Parish, born in 1800 and died in 1883; Vincent (11b4), who married Winnie Days; Frances (11ba), who married Isaac Micheau and after his death Philip Bowers; Elizabeth (11bb), who married Blake Robinson; Martha (11bc), who married Ralph Durr; and Mary (11bd), who married Philip Bowers after her sister's death.

After the death of Rev. DuBose Elizabeth married Samuel Dwyer, who died in 1822. Elizabeth had no children by Mr. Dwyer. Mr. Dwyer left a will, dated 3 March 1820 and recorded 11 December 1822, naming a daughter Margaret Carter and a son James Dwyer. Elizabeth died sometime before 1827. An estate settlement dating to 1827 and recorded 11 March 1831 in Sumter Conveyance Records lists her children.

In the family accounts of Major Dargan he refers to Mr. Dwyer as James, but this is apparently an error.

The settlement of Elizabeth Dwyer's estate was administrated by Frances Michau. Her petition was dated 19 April 1827. It was accepted on 23 April 1827 and Caleb Rembert, James Barnes, Menasseh Michau, Willis Spann and Nathan

Christmas were appointed appraisers. Appraisal (undated, but prior to the first Monday in June) was made at $2144. John M. Dargan, Frances Michau and William L. Brunson had gone bond for $2,000 on 16 April 1827, with Vincent DuBose witnessing. Purchasers at vendue of 12 June 1827 included Frances Michau, Vincent DuBose, Willis Spann, Henry DuBose and others.

Henry Y. DuBose was born in 1794 and married firstly, in 1818, Eliza McKewn (listed in some sources as Elizabeth McKeown). Eliza died on 7 March 1832 and Henry later remarried. Henry was a medical doctor and appears in many legal documents, mostly estate settlements. According to the Directory of Deceased American Physicians Henry was an allopath who graduated from the Medical College of South Carolina in Charleston. He died on 9 November 1862. Children of Dr. DuBose and his first wife were Louisa Elizabeth (11b1a) and Jane Vermelle (11b1b). By his second wife Henry had six other children: Henry, Jr. (11b11); John Snowden (11b12); Coogler (11b13); James Madison (11b14); Julia Marie (11b1c) and Virginia (11b1d).

Amos DuBose, Jr. was born about 1796, married in 1818 Martha Ann Parish, and died sometime before 1850. Martha Ann Parish was born in 1800 in North Carolina and died in 1883 in Florence, South Carolina. Amos and Martha had at least one child, Mary Elizabeth (11b3a), born in 1820, who married about 1837 Dr. William Henry Holleyman of Sumter and Manning. Reference is Vermeille Galbreath; see also page 187 of volume 59 of SCHGM . The 1850 Sumter County census shows Martha living with the Holleymans and lists their first (probably only) five children.

Hampton was probably born between the two children listed above, if the order of listing in the 1831 conveyance is an indication. The only child of Frances and Isaac Michau (also Micheau, Michaeu) was Ann (11baa). By her second husband, Reverend Bowers (Bowen in some records and Bowens known to be in Sumter

County) Frances had Julia (11bab), Mary (11bac) and Nora (11bad).

Vincent died in August of 1883 and is known to have had three children by Winifred Days. Martha, who married Mr. Durr (sometimes appears as Dierr) had eight children.

Elizabeth had two children by Mr. Robinson. Mr. Robinson was called John by Major Dargan and, in fact was John Blake Robinson. Perhaps, then, we might surmise that Samuel Dwyer was Samuel James Dwyer. Mary Matilda married Reverend Bowers/Bowen after the death of her sister and they had seven children: Oscar (11bd1), born in Marengo County, Alabama and died in Handsboro, Mississippi; Josephine (11bda); Virginia (11bdb); Ann (11bdc); Willey (11bdd); Evaline (11bde) and Philip (11bd2). The last six were born in Mississippi.

VINCENT VAUGHAN (114)

Vincent was a son of Henry and Elizabeth Vaughan. Information on Vincent is scarce and often vague. His wife was Elizabeth, but his children are not known by either name or number to this writer. Sumter County Equity Court Records of 16 March 1814 indicate he had children. He seems to have moved shortly after 1814 to Alabama, where, according to Sumter Judgements, Package 9, Roll 137, he was believed to have died sometime before 1820. Vincent had been co-executor of his father's estate in 1810, but the estate was not settled until after his mother's death in 1815 and he had resigned his position to remove to Alabama.

J. Nelson Frierson had related to earlier researchers that Vincent had left the area with some animosity toward other family members. Frierson said that the original will of Henry Vaughan, Sr. had been considered invalid because there were only two witnesses, three being required under South Carolina law. Frierson said that Vincent stood to come out quite better under the original provisions than he did in the end, his being well taken care of because he had let the old man stay with him in his old age and had pretty much been his caretaker.

The final settlement of the estate included several court proceedings involving Vincent and his nephew Richard, son of Richard, deceased. The two heirs apparently felt they were being cheated out of their inheritance by the other heirs. Those others' contention was that Vincent and Richard had received special favors during Henry's lifetime, a contention which the courts apparently sustained. See Sumter Judgements, Package 5, Roll 84 and Package 8, Roll 122 for the proceedings. This writer does not know where Frierson got his information, but perhaps he drew his conclusions from the same sources we have.

The _Camden Journal_ of 1 April 1829 lists an unclaimed letter in the Post Office for a Vincent Vaughan.

JOHN BRADFORD VAUGHAN (114)

John Bradford was the son of Henry and
Elizabeth Vaughan. John married Sarah Gayle
Singleton, daughter of Robert and Sarah (Gayle)
Singleton. Censuses indicate John was born
about 1765, Sarah about 1768. John B. appears
in many Sumter County conveyances and many
involve the collection of debts from him. He
seems perhaps to have tried to expand too fast
or beyond his means in his land dealings. One
case involving collection of a debt from him in
Sumter County Equity Court records is dated 4
December 1805.

An interesting narrative in Sumter County
Miscellaneous Records, found in Book B, page
462 and dated 27 November 1807, relates his
pardon for a previous conviction of assault.

John owned land as early as 1812 in Jackson
County, Mississippi. A list of claims shows
John B. was awarded a plot in that year,
designated as Section 40, Township 4 and Range
6 on the Pascagoula River. A map copied from
Four Centuries on the Pascagoula is included at
the end of this sketch. A passport issued by
the state of Georgia on 24 January 1811 to John
B. Vaughan perhaps best serves as confirmation
of the date of John's move. This information
comes to us from Passports Issued by Governors
of Georgia (see Bibliography). John lived near
the Alabama-Mississippi border. Jackson County
records show that John B. was there in 1816,
yet he is on a petition, dated 12 November
1817, to add Mobile County to the state of
Alabama (Deep South Genealogical Quarterly,
Vol. 9, page 507). John B. is in the Jackson
County census of 1830, but ten years later
appears in the Mobile County, Alabama census.
Post Office records show letters in the Post
Office at Claiborne on 1 March 1824 for Jno. B.
Vaughan and at Mobile on 1 April 1824 for John
B. Vaughan, on 1 July 1824 and 1 October 1824
for B. John Vaughan. The writer suspects the
letter was the same one and remained on file
for the better part of a year. The situation

on the coast at about this time was confused.
The British had only a short time before
wrested control of the area from the Spanish,
calling the territory West Florida. Neither
the government nor the inhabitants of the area
were of a consensus as to how to parcel out the
land. At times the border seemed to extend to
the Tombigbee and at others almost to the
Pascagoula. Recently Louisiana had been
admitted as a state, but neither Alabama nor
Mississippi had. Finally a point was decided
upon for a border and a line was drawn south by
a survey crew. Although some thought the line
too far west and others too far east, the line
stood and a division had been made. Thereafter
petitions were drawn up at conventions, so that
the counties of the West Florida Territory were
incorporated into the states of Alabama and
Mississippi, the former becoming a state in
1819 and the latter a couple of years earlier.

These are the particulars we can determine on
John's children. One daughter, Elizabeth
(114a), was born 7 July 1796. Other children
appear in censuses and are mentioned in a
Sumter Equity Court proceeding of 14 February
1817. This record here abstracted, having been
extracted in turn from the Camden Equity Court
session of 21 February 1810, provides this
information: "Mr. Richardson presented the
petition of Elizabeth Vaughan, John Vaughan,
Beverly Vaughan, Robert Vaughan, Vincent
Vaughan, Henry Vaughan and Matthew Vaughan by
John B. Vaughan their next friend, praying that
their Uncle William Vaughan may be appointed
guardian of the estate of the said minors
hearing whereof it is ordered that the care and
management of the estate both real and personal
of the said minors be committed to the said
William Vaughan upon his giving bond and the
usual security and thereupon letters of
guardianship issue accordingly." The reference
of John B. as their next friend was a routine
legal term of the day. These, then, would seem
to be John's children, all of whom were minors
in 1810. The census of 1800 lists two male
children older than Elizabeth and four about
the same age, but from what we know of the

children, non-family members must have been
included in the household.

Children of John B. and Sarah Vaughan were
Elizabeth (114a), born 7 July 1796 and married
Lauchlan McKay; John Singleton (1141), born 22
February 1798, married Letitia H. Miller and
died 22 February 1856; Beverly (1142), born
about 1799; Robert (1143), born about 1800;
Vincent (1144), born about 1803; Henry (1145),
born in 1805; and Mathew J. (1146), born in
1808 and married Celitta Ann Denmark. The
children seem always to have been in the
proximity of John B. Vincent and Henry appear
in the 1830 Jackson County census; Mathew is in
the 1840 Mobile County census; and a John S.
Vaughan appears in Mobile County records at the
time John B. was there (as well as a Richard S.
Vaughan--possibly a nephew?--see compile on
Richard).

Elizabeth married Lauchlan [sometimes spelled
Lauchlin] McKay on 4 November 1813. McKay was
born on 27 May 1774 in Cumberland County, North
Carolina. Elizabeth was Mckay's second wife.
McKay was the son of Alexander and Margaret
(McNiell) McKay. Lauchlan was a pioneer of
Greene County, Mississippi, where he settled in
the fork of the Leaf and Chickasawhay, and a
man of means. He represented Greene County in
the Constitutional Convention of 1817.
Children of the McKays were Campbell (114a1),
born 2 July 1815, died about 1846 and buried
near Leaf; Lauchlan, Jr. (114a2), born 26
January 1817, married 1) Isabel McInnis and 2)
Janie Goff; Singleton Vaughan (114a3), born 10
November 1819, married 1) Sarah A. McInnis and
2) Mary Jane Coward and died 26 October 1895;
Alexander Archibald (114a4), born 17 September
1821, married Elizabeth Carter, and died 17
August 1902; Margaret Elizabeth (114aa), born
25 November 1823, married Alexander McInnis and
died 16 January 1880; Robert Singleton (114a5),
born 16 December 1825, died in 1850's and is
buried near Leaf; Sarah Ann (114ab), born 3 May
1828, married Peter McNair Fairly and died 3
August 1889; and Louisa (114ac), born 7 October
1829, married 1) William J. Evans and 2) Oliver

Cornell Cowan and died 1 April 1889. Lauchlan McKay died 23 July 1832 and is buried at the home place near Leaf, Mississippi; Elizabeth died in December of 1889 and is buried at Moss Point, near Pascagoula. Prominent descendants of Lauchlan and Elizabeth are Richmond McInnis McKay, who was a member of the lower house of Mississippi Legislature from 1936 to 1940 and his brother Edwin V. McKay, who was Clerk of Court for George County for 12 years and a State Senator from 1936 to 1938. Both were sons of Singleton Vaughan McKay. Many of the McKays intermarried with the local McInnis family and the Singleton name proliferated in both families as each continued the name in deference to parents and in-laws. Much of the information in this paragraph came from Cain's Four Centuries on the Pascagoula and more particulars on the descendants of this line can be found in that work. A letter of Mabel Ward, a great-granddaughter of Elizabeth Vaughan McKay, states that Elizabeth lived to be 93. Ward was the daughter of Sarah Elizabeth Evans Ward and granddaughter of Louisa McKay Evans, captioned above. Ms. Ward says she saw Lauchlan McKay's Bible as a young girl and copied dates from it. Elizabeth's birthdate comes from a letter of Mrs. Florence M. Bratt, believed to be information from this Bible conveyed to her by Mrs. Ward. Mrs. Bratt served as one of Cain's sources of dates. Another invaluable source of information on this line and one to which I shall refer throughout the section on John B. Vaughan is Ruth McClesky's New Limbs from Old Roots. McClesky gives December 1889 as the instant of Elizabeth's death, and, although no source is given, it agrees with Miss Ward's statement.

John Singleton married on 11 August 1828 his second wife, Letitia Hayden Miller. The name of his first wife is not known. John and Letitia's children were Sarah Jane (1141a), born in 1833, married on 30 January 1851 to Thomas J. Howell and died 8 January 1906; Mary Caroline (1141b), born 15 January 1838, married on 20 March 1856 Burr J. Coate and died 9 January 1905; Caladonia (1141c), born 15

January 1838, married Alonzo L. Norwood on 14
May 1857; John Singleton, Jr. (11411), born in
1842; Livingston (11412), born about 1845;
Joseph H. (11413), born about 1850; and
Abernathy (11414), born about 1854. Clarke
County, Alabama marriage records show the
marriage of a Mary C. Vaughan on 21 December
1853 to James M. Barr "with consent of her
parents." This was possibly a marriage of Mary
Caroline prior to her marriage to Mr. Coate.
Mary Carolyn Coates (sic) is buried in the
Tallahatta Springs Cemetery next to Livingston
Coate (1867-1931), undoubtedly her son and
named for her brother. By the 1830's John S.
was living in Clarke County and seems pretty
much to have settled there to raise his family.
Letitia, born in 1811, died 6 January 1866.
Little more is known of the life of Beverly,
Robert and Vincent except a Mobile County
document of 24 March 1814 records the
apprenticing of John S. and Robert to John
French until they reach 21.

Henry was a schoolteacher. He is believed to
have married between 1826 and 1830. He was the
postmaster of the McManus, Mississippi Post
Office in 1832. The McManus mail route died
out in the 1850's and was in George County,
north of Jackson County. Its location can be
found on a plat map that indicates the land
claim granted to Archibald McManus, the first
postmaster and man for whom the route was
named. An H. Vaughan also appears as sheriff
in 1830 on a Jackson County sheriff's list.

Mathew married about 1836 Celitta Ann Denmark.
Their children were Laura (1146a), born about
1838; Andrew A. (11461), born about 1839,
married on 1 March 1875 to Mary Goff; Mathew
J., Jr. (11462), born about 1840; Mary Louisa
(1146b), born in 1843; Savena (or Lorena or
Sarah--hard to read 1850 census); and
Elizabeth, born in 1850. It is possible that
Laura was not a daughter, since, although
showing in the 1860 census, she does not appear
in the 1850 census. The 1850 census showed
Henry Vaughan, a schoolteacher, in the
household. This was Mathew's brother. Andrew

A., the oldest son, was postmaster of Three
Rivers, Mississippi in 1858. During the Civil
War he became a member of Twigg's Rifles, 27th
Regiment, Infantry, Co. L, mustered in 2
October 1861 on the east side of Pascagoula
River for one year's service. He was mustered
for three years' service on 1 May 1862. The
army surrendered at Greensboro, North Carolina
on 26 April 1865. After the surrender the
company returned to Pascagoula with Andrew, now
a sergeant, one of seven survivors [out of an
original 118] of the campaign. See Four
Centuries on the Pascagoula for a fuller
account of the unit's itinerary during the war.

Mobile County Marriage Records indicate a John
B. Vaughan married a Mrs. Daughdrill on 7 July
1839. According to New Limbs from Old Roots
she is thought to have been Winnie (Harrell)
Daughdrill, widow of John Daughdrill.

New Limbs has an excellent summary of South
Carolina Singletons, which I recommend to those
doing study in that field, and a fascinating
account of the McKay Family mentioned in this
sketch, which I recommend to all readers. As a
matter of fact, this work is written in such an
entertaining and humorous fashion I believe
anyone should read it who gets the chance.

PLOT MAP FOR GREENE, JACKSON COUNTIES

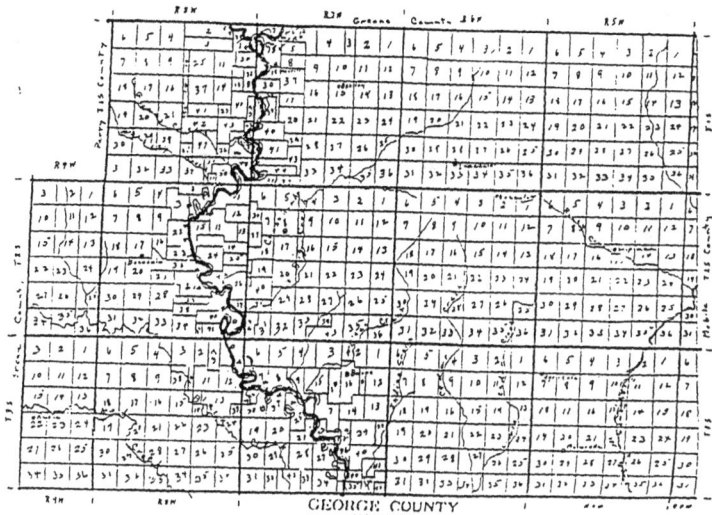

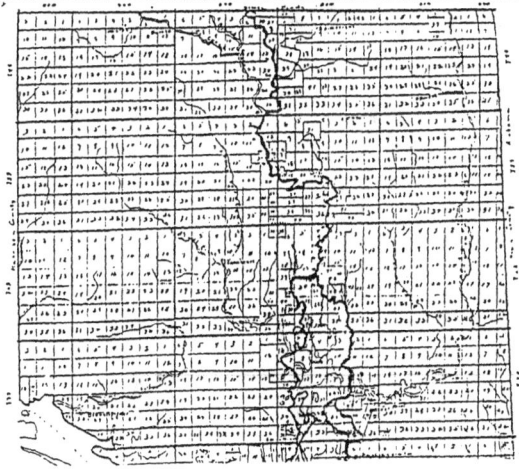

RICHARD VAUGHAN (115)

Another son of Henry and Elizabeth Vaughan was Richard. Documents pertaining to Vincent indicate Richard predeceased his father, who died in 1809, although it could also be that he died between that year and 1815, when the estate was settled. These same documents indicate that Richard's only child was also named Richard (1151). This son does not appear in any other document this writer has seen.

NOEL VAUGHAN, SR. (12)

Noel Vaughan, Sr. was the son of Frances
(Waddill) Vaughan and son or stepson of Vincent
Vaughan. He served in the South Carolina
Militia in 1782. The document at the end of
this sketch is an indent for that service.
Besides the indent, Noel received a land grant
on 15 July 1784 for Revolutionary War service.
The award of the grant may be found in the
Grant Book for South Carolina in the Archives
of that state.

Noel's wife was Winifred, also known as Winnie.
Noel and Winnie were members of the High Hills
Baptist Church, but in 1813 transferred their
membership to the First Baptist Church of
Sumter. There Noel served as a deacon until 28
January 1818, when he resigned because of
advanced age (C. C. Brown's History of the
First Baptist Church of Sumter, page 7). In
1818 Noel and Winnie were still on the Church
Roll (Brown, page 10). In a seating diagram
they are shown next to Burrell and Celia Fort.
Mr. Fort left a will in Sumter County, recorded
17 October 1832, which names, besides his wife,
a son Josiah Granderson Fort, and daughters
Sarah Pyrene and Susannah Caroline Fort. The
will also mentions Jane Elizabeth Rountree,
presumably also a daughter.

Miscellaneous Record Book XX, page 242, of
Sumter County contains an item in which Noel
and Winnie testify to have known Amy Cornet to
have been a free person of color in Northampton
County, North Carolina. This document is
copied in the Appendix and served as a source
of the origins of the Vaughans prior to their
arrival in South Carolina.

The Virginia Genealogist has an article in
Volume 6, number 2, by Cameron Allen in which
he refers to an earlier article concerning the
name of Noel Hutchins, which occurred in the
Burton Family. The original article appeared
in the Burton Chronicles of Colonial Virginia.
This article indicates Noel Hutchins was a

local hero, who had many lads named after him.
This being the case, perhaps Noel's appellation
of Hutchins does not indicate his parentage.
There were families by the name of Hutchins in
Charles City County, however, which was not too
far from New Kent County.

Noel's will was probated 17 November 1829 and
two of his sons, William, Jr. and Noel, Jr.
were administrators. Winnie is not mentioned
in the will and must therefore have predeceased
her husband.

An interesting document appears in Sumter
County Equity Court records of 28 December
1810. In it Noel is appointed trustee for the
children of his daughter, Mary Richardson, who
was separating from her husband, Abraham
Richardson.

Children of Noel and Winnie were Mary (12a),
who married Abraham Richardson and died
sometime after 1835; William, Jr. (121), born
in 1772 or 1773, married Lettetia Potter and
died about 21 September 1853; Noel, Jr. (122),
born about 1775, who married Hannah W_____ and
died 2 May 1848; and Isham (123), born 25
February 1788 and married Frances Bradford.

INDENTED CERTIFICATE FOR NOEL'S WAR SERVICE

SOUTH-CAROLINA.

PURSUANT to an ACT of the GENERAL ASSEMBLY passed the 16th of March, 1783, We, the COMMISSIONERS of the TREASURY, have this day delivered to

Mr. Noel Vaughan

this our INDENTED CERTIFICATE for [illegible]

Seven pounds eighteen Shillings and eight pence Sterling for [illegible] nineteen days Militia duty [illegible] thousand seven hundred and eighty [illegible] as [illegible]

the said Noel Vaughan his Executors, Administrators, or [illegible] will be entitled to receive from this Office the Sum of Eleven shillings [illegible] for [illegible] one Year's Interest on the Principal Sum of Seven pounds eighteen Shillings and eight pence Sterling and the like Interest Annually [illegible] Resolution of [illegible] Assembly 1783.

The said Noel Vaughan his Executors, Administrators or Assigns, will be entitled also to receive, and shall be paid, if demanded, the principal Sum of Seven pounds eighteen Shill[illegible] [illegible] pence Sterling on the Twenty Second day of June 1786.

And the said Noel Vaughan his Executors, Administrators, or Assigns, may make any Purchases at any Public Sales of Confiscated Property, (except such as shall be ordered by the Legislature for special Purposes;) and this INDENT shall be received in Payment.

For the true performance of the several payments in manner abovementioned, the PUBLIC TREASURY is made liable, and the FAITH of the STATE pledged by the aforesaid ACT.

GIVEN under our Hands at the TREASURY-OFFICE, in CHARLESTON, the Twenty Second Day of June one thousand seven hundred and eighty four.

Edward Blake
Peter Bocquet

Commissioners of the Treasury.

£ 7-18-8 Principal.

£ 11-1 Annual Interest,

No. 308

118

MARY VAUGHAN (12a)

Mary, only daughter of Noel and Winnie Vaughan, was probably born prior to 1770. This indication comes from Mary's serving as a witness to a conveyance of 16 July 1790, which may be found in Book B, pages 83-84, of Sumter County Deed Records. Law required witnesses to be twenty-one years of age. She had married Abraham Richardson sometime prior to the date of that deed. By 1810 Mr. and Mrs. Richardson had six children. In an Equity Court case of that year her father was made trustee of the three children who remained with Mary after her separation from Abraham. The conveyance was made to protect Epsey, William and Alexander should Abraham die during the separation. Mary and Abraham were later reconciled and had a seventh child. Mary died sometime after 1840.

Children of Abraham and Mary were (order indeterminate) Epsey (12aa), who married Manning D. Brunson; William Vaughan (112a?); Henry (112a?); Alexander (112a?); Milton (112a?); Seaborn (112a?) and James (112a?).

WILLIAM VAUGHAN, JR. (121)

William was born about 1772. This is
established from his age in censuses and his
statement for same that he was born in
Virginia. That means he was born before the
1772 migration from the Roanoke Rapids area.
William was designated as Junior to distinguish
him from his cousin, who was about eight years
older.

William married Lettetia Potter, daughter of
Miles and Sarah Potter, on 7 February 1797.
Lettetia is sometimes called Lettice, a common
nickname, used for instance by Laetetia
(Corbin) Lee, great-great-grandmother of Robert
E. Lee and wife of Richard Lee. The Potters
had four other children: Mary, born 2 November
1779 and died 2 February 1783; Robert and
Miles, twins born on 29 September 1785 (one
source says Robert was born 26 July 1782, but
this seems incorrect); and Levi, born 31
October 1789. Lettetia was born on 1 November
1777 and died on 16 January 1846. Some sources
give Lettetia's birthplace as Scotland, but
this is doubtful. A Miles Potter is carried on
tax lists for Brunswick County, North Carolina
for 1769 and 1772.

Many of the above dates come from a Bible that
belonged to Annie Lee Gann and said once to
have belonged to Noel A. Vaughan, a son of
William. The Bible is dated 1865, but entries
were made in varying years. Naturally the
authenticity of dates prior to 1865 are taken
on faith since they could not have been entered
at the time of occurrence. Pages from this
Bible are copied in the Appendix, but, whenever
possible, verification of dates was made from
other sources.

Children of William and Lettetia were Mary
Caroline (121a), born 19 January 1800, married
to Richard P. Cummings and died 28 September
1836; Harriett Sarah (121b), born 25 August

1804, married to Isaac H. Norton and died 14 March 1884; Winifred Elvira (121c), born 15 August 1806 and married to Henry Gilmore; William Christopher (1211), born 22 April 1809, married to Irena E. Bernard and died in 1896; Noel Anguish (1212), born 4 September 1811, married firstly to Sarah Goldsmith and secondly to Sarah C. Calhoun and died 5 August 1894; Miles Edwin (1213), born 10 April 1814, married to Mary Robeson and died 28 August 1896; and Henry Jackson (1214), born 25 June 1819, married firstly to Mary Harrison and secondly to Georgia Trawick and died 22 January 1897.

William bonded with Robert Potter in the execution of the estate of his father-in-law, Miles Potter. The will was probated on 15 November 1804. William also administrated the estate of his aunt, Naomi Hampton, in 1819. William was a witness for Richard P. Cummings in the administration of the estate of Joseph Cummings in Sumter in 1828. A deed of 11 March 1831 concerns William's conveyance of a tract of land to John Witherspoon and another deed of 28 March 1831, shortly before the family's removal to Franklin, Alabama, concerns the children's release of their dower rights.

While living in Sumter District, William was a Justice of the Quorum, roughly the same as a notary public of today. His signature appears as such on documents as early as 1810, but the first record of his appointment appears in the Resolutions of the South Carolina Legislature of 1812. He was reappointed in the Resolutions of 1819. William was a one term State Representative from Claremont County according to the Southern Chronicle. In a seating diagram for the First Baptist Church of Sumter a Vaughan is listed as seated with Isaac Norton and Captain Burrell Fort and wife Celia (C. C. Brown, History of the First Baptist Church of Sumter, page 19). This most likely was William, Jr., since his daughter was married to Norton.

William died about 21 September 1853 in Macon County, Alabama. His estate was appraised at

$14,959.12, according to estate settlement documents, Miles Edwin administrating the estate. An appraisal of 1854 valued the estate at $13, 609.87 after administration expenses, with each child's share being $1,944.27 and subshares for the Cummingses of $388.85. See Macon County Deed Records for reference.

William Vaughan, his children and the husband and families of his two oldest daughters left South Carolina in 1833 for Alabama. They went through Troup County, Georgia, where on 26 December 1833 William bought a lot from Sinik Gilder. He sold this lot on 29 December 1834 to Lazarus Atkins. We do not know exactly when the party arrived in Alabama, but the first legal reference this writer has been able to find is marriage papers for Elvira Winifred's marriage of 14 February 1836 to Henry Gilmore. Between about May and August of the same year all four of William's sons served in the Creek War. Thus it seems the family arrived in 1835 or early 1836. Papers relating to the administration of the estate of King Harrison, father-in-law of the youngest son, Henry Jackson, indicate the party first settled in Alabama in the Franklin area.

MARY CAROLINE VAUGHAN (121a)

Mary Caroline, daughter of William and Lettetia
Vaughan, was born 19 January 1800. On 1 March
1821 she married Richard P. Cummings, son of
Dr. Samuel and Susan Cummings. According to
Sumter Equity Court Records, Package 36, Roll
602, Dr. Cummings died in Sumter in 1820.
Richard's brothers were Samuel M., John, Joseph
and William. His sisters were Mary P., who
married John J. Brown, Susan, Ann, Elizabeth
and Joanna. Richard also served as executor of
the estate of Joseph, settled in 1828 in
Sumter. Mary died on 28 September 1836 and
articles in the Macon Republican establish that
Richard was also deceased by 1853. In that
year guardianship of two of the Cummings
children, Alfred and Joseph, was assigned to
Henry J. Vaughan (Macon County Minutes, 1850-
1852). When William Vaughan's estate was
administrated in 1853, the names of all the
Cummings children were given: Samuel Maxville
(121a1), who married Louisa Owenson 21 December
1849 (or '47); John Wallace (121a2); William
Richard (121a3), born in 1828 and a dentist
(1860 Tallapoosa County, Alabama, census);
Alfred Maximus (121a4); Joseph W. (121a5); and
Harriet Vermelle (121aa). In one census John's
middle name is given as Wentworth; several
censuses carry the middle name of the Cummings
children.

Richard died in or shortly before 1849. Macon
County Probate Court records show that on 12
May 1849 John Henderson entered into a bond to
administrate Richard's estate.

HARRIETT SARAH VAUGHAN (121b)

Harriett Sarah was born on 25 August 1804, second daughter of William and Lettetia Vaughan. She married Isaac H. Norton before the families left South Carolina. The Vaughan Bible gives Harriett's date of marriage as 5 May 1825. Papers in South Carolina show a marriage between Isaac Norton and Miss Jane Gordon on 22 September 1820. These two had a child, also named Jane. I have lost my source, but estate settlements concerning Jane Norton (dating to 1826 or later I believe), could cast some doubt on the 1825 date; still some estates were settled several years after the decedent's death.

Isaac Norton was early in life a wheelwright, but in Alabama established himself as a farmer and planter. He also became active in the establishment of the educational system of the new area. He took on the position of trustee of the East Alabama Female Institute.

Isaac and Harriett's children were William (121b1), born in 1826; Harriett (121ba), born in 1831; Joseph (121b2), born in 1832 and married Susan B. _____; Robert (121b3), born in 1834; Elvira (121bb), born in 1836; and Martha (121bc), born in 1840.

Deed records (and birthplaces for the children in censuses) indicate the family made a stopover in Troup County, Georgia in 1832-34, before continuing to Alabama.

According to Taproots, Vol 31, no. 2, page 84, Joseph H. Norton served as minister of the First Baptist Church of Notasulga from 1867-70 and was later pastor from January of 1878 until January 1881.

Harriett Norton died on 14 March 1884. The will of Miles Edwin Vaughan indicates most of the Nortons had migrated to the area of Eclectic, Alabama by the time of Miles' death.

WINIFRED ELVIRA VAUGHAN (121c)

Winifred Elvira was born on 15 August 1806, third daughter of William and Lettetia Vaughan. In some documents Winifred is referred to as Elvira Winifred. Marriage documents (Volume 4, A. S. D. A. R., Alabama 929.3, DAR, page 285) show she married Henry Gilmore on 14 February 1836, J. R. Sarter performing. Henry and Winifred were living in Macon County at the time of her father's death.

Little is known of Winifred, but she seems to have married soon after arriving in Alabama and she could well have met her husband en route. An item in Bobby L. Lindsey's Reason for the Tears (page 272) lists a Charles H. Gilmore deceased in Chambers County, Alabama prior to 1847 and having a brother named Henry Gilmore to survive him. Chambers County was next to Troup County, Georgia on the Alabama/Georgia border. Lindsey's work is about the forced removal of the Creeks from the eastern United States. Many Cherokees were among the deported peoples as well.

None of the descendants of Henry and Winifred are known to this writer, but Confederate Muster Rolls show a Francis M. Gilmore, who enlisted 10 March 1862 at Macon, Georgia and was on a muster roll at Loachapoka on 4 April 1862 and a W. W. Gillmore, captured 31 August 1864 near Jonesboro, Georgia and paroled 15 May 1865 in Montgomery.

Gilmore, F. M. [Pvt.] Muster roll, Loachapoka, April 4, 1862; enlisted March 10, 1862, Macon Ga, April 20 or 21 1865. Furlough Jan. 7, 1863. Francis M. Gilmore. Ocmulgee Hospital, Macon. VS hand flesh, July 22, 1864 Left batt; admitted April 16, 1865. Returned duty April 28, 1864. Residence given as Macon County.

Gillmore, W. W. [Willliam M.] [Pvt.] PW. Captured near Jonesboro, GA, Aug. 31, 1864. Paroled at Montgomery, May 15, 1865. Oath: May 15, 1865; 5'8"; dark hair; dark eyes; dark complexion.

WILLIAM CHRISTOPHER VAUGHAN (1211)

William C. was born on 22 April 1809 in South
Carolina, first son of William and Lettetia
Vaughan. Shortly after arriving in Alabama he
fought in the Creek Indian War. There is a
tale in the family that this writer has been
unable to substantiate that says William got
into a fight in a barroom brawl and killed a
fellow, so that William had to leave the area
and could only return when the incident was
forgotten. Whatever the truth of the matter,
William did remove to Lowndes County,
Mississippi and later return. On 3 August 1837
in Lowndes County he married Irena E. Bernard,
who was born about 1817 in Virginia, according
to census records. William's family appears in
the 1840 Lowndes County census, but before the
next census he had returned to Alabama.

After his return to Alabama William settled
near Notasulga and farmed and planted.
Children of William C. and Irena Vaughan were
Mary C. (1211a), born in Mississippi about 1840
and married on 7 March 1858 to Isaac Linsey
[Lindsay?]; William Alexander (12111), born
about 1842 in Mississippi and married on 17
September 1871 to E. C. Pullin; Charles C.
(12112), born about 1843 in Mississippi and
died 5 September 1861 at Fairfax Station,
Virginia, from typhoid fever; Virginia (1211b),
born about 1847; California (1211c), born about
1849 in Alabama and married Robert Lindsey; and
Joseph Benjamin (12113), born in 1854 in
Alabama, married firstly to Mary Elizabeth
Spear, secondly to Mollie McRitchie and died on
20 January 1939.

The Macon Republican of 28 February (????)
carries a notice in which William C. requests
help in locating a horse he had lost in the
area of his home at Chehaw. Chehaw was to the
south of Notasulga, about halfway between that
town and Tuskegee. This small village is today
just off the interstate highway that cuts
between the area's hills. A transaction on
page 790 of Deed Book J of Tallapoosa County

shows William had business in that area. William C. died in 1896. This writer has been unable to determine where he is buried or what he died from, but estate settlement proceedings establish the year of death.

The following pages contain papers relating to William's claim for bounty land for his service in the Creek War.

The following appeared on a printed form that
bore the mark "HERALD" PRESS, NOTASULGA:

STATE OF ALABAMA,)
  MACON COUNTY.)

On this, the (23rd) day of (August) A. D.,
one thousand eight hundred and Fifty(two),
personally appeared before me, (Samuel Reid) a
Justice of the Peace, within and for the county
and State aforesaid (William C. Vaughan) aged
(42) [sic] years, a resident of (Macon County)
in the State of (Alabama) who being duly sworn
according to law, declares that he is the
identical (Vaughn) who was a (Private) in the
company commanded by Captain (James Cobb) in
the () regiment of () commanded by () in the
war (with the Creek Indians Declared by the
united States) on the (12th) day of (May), A.
D., (1836) that he (volunteering) at
(Tuckabatcha) on the ((inserted--or about) 1st)
day of (August) A. D., (1836 had no written
discharge as will appear) by the muster rolls
of said company.
He makes this declaration for the purpose
of obtaining the bounty land to which he may be
entitled under the "Act granting bounty land to
certain officers and soldiers who have been
engaged in the military service of the United
States," passed September 28, 1850. (W. C.
Vaughan)

Sworn to and subscribed before me the day
and year above written. And I hereby certify
that I believe the said (William C. Vaughan) to
be the identical man who served as aforesaid,
and that he is of the age above stated.

(Samuel Reid) J. P.

STATE OF ALABAMA,)
  MACON COUNTY.)

(Lewis Alexander) Judge of the Probate Court of
said county, do hereby certify that (Samuel
Reid) whose name appears to the affidavit, is,
and was at the time of signing the same, an
acting Justice of the Peace in and for the said

county aforesaid, duly qualified and
commissioned as the law requires, and that
faith and credit are due his official acts.
Given under my hand and seal, this (18th) day
of (October) A. D., 185(2)

                    (Lewis Alexander)
                    (Judge of Probate)

The foregoing claim was suspended as not being
in the proper form by means of a document
bearing the heading (CIRCULAR A.) and the
marginal note "N. B.--Endorse the words
'Additional evidence' upon the envelope of all
papers addressed to this office upon business
already before it."

                    PENSION OFFICE
                    (Sept. 20,) 1855.

SIR:
    The application of (William C. Vaughan)

for Bounty Land under the act of 3d March,
1855, No (51600) has been examined and the
claim suspended.

        Service is alleged to have been rendered
in (Capt. J. Cobb's Co. Ala. Vols.)

        As the Auditor reports ("No Rolls.")

and as the third section of said act requires
service to be established by record evidence,
parole testimony is inadmissible. The claim
will, therefore, remain suspended until the
service is established by record evidence, as
contemplated by said act.

                    Very respectfully,
Crossed out--E. W. Bayzer, Esq.   J. MINOT
                    Notasulga   Commissioner
                         Ala

As a result of the suspension record evidence
was constructed:

The State of Alabama)   On this the 28th day
   County of Macon   )   of July A. D. 1856
before me William K. Harris an acting Justice
of the Peace within and for the County and
State   aforesaid,   personally   appeared
Littleberry   Strange   and   Lewis   Alexander
residence of the said County and State
aforesaid, who being duly sworn according to
law, declare, that William C. Vaughan who made
application for Bounty Land under the act of
"3rd of March 1855" No 51,600, and whose
application has been suspended for further
proof. That the said William C. Vaughan Served
in the Creek War of 1836, for more than
Fourteen days (14). The affiant's were in the
same service under Captain Cobb, and know that
said company and the said William C. Vaughan
did actual service more than Fourteen (14)
days.
                    Littleberry Strange
               Lewis Alexander

Sworn to and subscribed before me on the day
and year above written, and I certify that
Littleberry Strange & Lewis Alexander are
certifiable witnesses. Wm. K. Harris J. P.

The State of Alabama) I Lewis Alexander Judge
County of Macon   )   of the Probate Court in
& for said County and State, do hereby certify
that William K. Harris whose genuine signature
is affixed to the above affidavit is & was at
the time of signing of the same an acting
Justice of the Peace in & for the county and
state aforesaid, duly qualified and
commissioned as the law directs and that full
faith & credit is due his official acts as
such. Given under my hand & seal of office
this the 30th July A. D. 1856. Lewis Alexander
                    Judge of Probate

State of Alabama)   Know all men by these
Macon County   )   that I, William C.
Vaughan, of the County and State aforesaid,
have constituted and appointed and by these
presents do constitute and appoint A. F. Posey
of Greenville, Ala, my true and lawful attorney
to attend to my claim No. 51,600 for services

130

in Capt. Cobb's Co Ala Volunteers Creek War
1836.

And I hereby revoke any and
all authority heretofore given to anyone else
to attend to said claim: and I authorize the
said A. F. Posey to do all things necessary and
proper in relation to said claim, and to
receive my warrant when issued In testimony
whereof, I hereunto set my hand and seal this
18th day of Sept. 1858.
Attest
Alexander Vaughan   William C. Vaughan (LS)
Irena E. Vaughan

MARY C. VAUGHAN (1211a)

Mary C. was the first child of William C. and
Irena Vaughan. She was born about 1840 in
Lowndes County, Mississippi. On 7 March 1858
she married Isaac Linsey [Lindsey?] according
to Chambers County, Alabama Marriage Records,
Book 5, page 447b. The marriage was held at
the home of her uncle, Noel Anguish Vaughan,
with John Britton officiating.

It is likely that Isaac and Mary had at least
two children. In the 1870 census Ida and
Robert Linsey are listed "at home" in the
household of William C. Vaughan. The 1880
census lists them in the same household and
names Robert as a grandson. Considering the
ages of the family members [California, the
other daughter who married a Lindsey, was not
born until 1849], it would seem these were
Mary's children, so the parents were probably
deceased by 1870.

Many Lindseys lived in Chambers County. School
records for Ward's Mill School Class of 1845
[Township 23, Range 27] list an Isaac Lindsey,
son of Robert, attending. The lineage of this
particular Lindsey is uncertain, but two
brothers, Thomas and John Lindsey, who settled
near Berryville, Virginia in 1740 and later
moved to Newberry District, South Carolina, had
many descendants in Chambers County. No
connection has been established from Robert to
either of the brothers, but several lines of
descent are incomplete for about five
intervening generations. See Bobby Lindsey's
Reason for the Tears, pages 213 and 279-281 for
more information on the Lindseys.

WILLIAM ALEXANDER VAUGHAN (12111)

William Alexander was born about 1842 in Lowndes County, Mississippi. On 17 September he married E. C. Pullin. Alexander is believed to have been a tailor by profession. Early Auburn, Alabama records list a tailor of that name as having a shop in the town. In 1896 Alexander was living in Lafayette County, Arkansas. Macon County records document his granting power of attorney to his brother Joseph B. Vaughan of Notasulga (Miscellaneous Records, Book 1, page 83). This document was dated 12 October 1896 and filed 4 February 1897 and related to the settlement of the estate of William C. and Irena Vaughan, deceased.

CHARLES C. VAUGHAN (12112)

Charles C. was the second son of William C. and Irena Vaughan. He was born in Lowndes County, Mississippi. Census records indicate he was born in the latter half of 1843, although military records say he was nineteen when he died on 5 September 1861. Young men often lied about their age in order to join the service, but this would not have been necessary for Charles, as he was over sixteen upon joining. The same records (in the Appendix and abstracts following immediately) describe Charles as five foot eight, of light complexion, hazel eyes, light hair and, by profession, a farmer.

Charles enlisted in Company B, 6th Regiment of the Alabama Infantry on 7 May 1861 at Loachapoka. He was enlisted by John M. Kennedy. On 15 May he was mustered in for 12 months in Montgomery by Major McLean.

Charles died on 5 September 1861 from typhoid fever at Fairfax Station, Virginia. He was unmarried. Narrative material from Charles' military service follows.

DOCUMENTS RELATING TO CHARLES' MILITARY SERVICE

I Certify that the within named Charles C. Vaughan, a private in Captain Kennedy's Co (B) of the Sixth Regiment of Alabama Volunteers, born in Lowndes County, State of Mississippi, aged nineteen years five feet & eight inches high, light complexion, hazzle (sic) eyes, light hair; and by profession a farmer, was enlisted by me at Loachapoka Alabama on the 7th of May, eighteen hundred and sixty one to serve for one year, and died on the fifth day of September eighteen hundred and sixty one.

The said Charles C. Vaughan was last paid by paymaster E. H. Harris to include the 30th day of June eighteen hundred and sixty one, and has pay due him from that date to the time of his death, the fifth day of September eighteen hundred and sixty one.

There is due him two 93/100 Dollars retainer(?) pay for eight days.

He is indebted to the Confederate States nothing.

Given in duplicate at Yorktown, Va. this the 26th day of April 1862.

> Jno. M. Kennedy Capt
> Co B, 6th Regt Ala Vols

Declaration for Pay of
Fathers Claim

The State of Alabama)   On this 22nd day of
Montgomery County   )   July 1862 Before me
Thomas Durden an Acting Justice of the Peace within and for said County Personally came William Vaughan aged fifty two years a resident of the County of Macon and State of Alabama who being duly sworn declares that he is the reputed father of Charles C. Vaughan who was a private in Co (B) commanded by Captain Kennedy in the 6th Regiment of Ala Volunteers during the War with the United States in 1861, that his son the said Charles C. Vaughan enlisted at

Loachapoka Ala on the 7th day of May 1861 for
the term of twelve months and continued in
actual service in said War until he died, that
he died on the 5th day of September 1861 at
Fairfax Station Va from sickness contracted
while in the service of the Confederate States
and while in the line of his duty as a soldier
& that he left no widow or child surviving him
and that the declarant is the only legal heir &
claimant.

He makes this declaration for the purpose of
obtaining from the government of the
Confederate States the arrearages of pay
cummalative (sic) retained pay & all other
allowances that may be found due the said
Charles C. Vaughan up to the time of his death
as well as the proceeds of all or any effects
he may have left And he desires that in case
the claim is allowed that the amount be sent to
Thomas Durden
Montgomery Ala

Sworn to and subscribed before me this day and
year first above written
William C. Vaughan
Th. Durden JP

We the undersigned residents of the County of
Macon & Montgomery and State of Alabama do upon
our oaths declare that we knew Charles C.
Vaughan in his lifetime and always understood
from him that he was the son of Wm. C. Vaughan
whose signature we have witnessed to the
foregoing declaration And we know that the said
Charles C. Vaughan died leaving no widow nor
child surviving him, and that the declarant is
the only legal heir of the deceased and that we
are disinterested.

Sworn to and subscribed before me this 22nd
July 1862.
Henry J. Vaughan
M. E. Vaughan
Th. Durden JP

The State of Alabama)   It is hereby
Montgomery County   )   certified that
satisfied proof has been exhibited before me by
affidavits of H. J. Vaughan and M. E. Vaughan
two creditable witnesses that Wm. C. Vaughan is
the reputed father of Charles C. Vaughan dec'd
and that I am disinterested
Sworn under my hand at office   T. H. Durden JP
this 22nd July 1822

The State of Alabama)   I David Campbell
Montgomery County   )   Judge of Probate
for and within said County do hereby certify
that Thomas Durden Esq before whom the
foregoing declaration and affidavits were
signed was at the time an Acting Justice of the
Peace within and for said County duly
commissioned and sworn

In testimony whereof I hereunto set my hand and
offer my Seal of Office this 24 day of July
1862

                        David Campbell
                        Judge of Probate

A certificate followed written upon a form
letter:

THE CONFEDERATE STATES
        To (Charles C Vaughan) ,deceased
        late of Capt. (Kennedy's) Co. (B),
        (6th) Reg't. (Alabama Volunteers) Dr.

        For pay from (30th June 1861 when
last paid to 5th September 1861 when he died
Two months & five days at $11 per mo. $23.83
Retained pay for eight days $ 2.93
                                   $26.76
As per report of Capt J M Kennedy herewith

VIRGINIA VAUGHAN (1211b)

The second daughter of William C. and Irena Vaughan was Virginia. Census records indicate she was born about 1845 and the last child in the family born in Mississippi. She appears to have married a Mr. Trot and removed to Columbia County, Arkansas. Mr. Trot granted power of attorney to Joseph B. Vaughan for his wife's interest in the settlement of her father's estate (Macon County Probate Court Records, dated 12 October 1896 and filed 4 February 1897). Both of the other daughters in the family are known to have married Lindseys (Linsey, Lindsay).

The 1870 Macon County census lists a Minnie Vaughan in the household of William C. and Irena (as well as a second child, Mary Vaughan, about the same age). The 1880 census for Macon County lists a Minnie Trot in the same household, but Mary does not appear in the latter.

Conclusions this writer would draw is that Minnie (and possibly Mary) were children of Virginia, who probably died quite young and Mr. Trot was left to look out for his daughters' share of the estate. Since he was then in Arkansas, he assigned power of attorney to J. B. Vaughan. Perhaps this writer will find more records pertaining to this estate in the future.

CALIFORNIA VAUGHAN (1211c)

California was born about 1849, the first child of William C. and Irena Vaughan born in Alabama. She married Robert Lindsey. Robert was probably a relative of Isaac Linsey, husband of California's sister Mary. As it appears Mary and Isaac died young and their children stayed in the Vaughan household, a close association with the Lindseys would be expected. The 1880 Lee County census indicates that California had at least one child: a son, Marvin (1211c1), born in 1878.

ALAGOLD PUMPKIN VEGETABLE SCALLOP
(FROM AUBURN COOKBOOK)

1/2 Pumpkin   1 Small Onion   1 Green Pepper
2 T. Butter   Salt, Pepper, Paprika
1/2 C. Buttered Bread Crumbs

Peel, steam and mash pumpkin. Cut the onion and green pepper fine and brown in butter. Add to the pumpkin and season with salt, pepper and paprika. Turn the mixture into a greased baking dish and cover the top with buttered crumbs. Bake at 400 degrees for 20 minutes or until golden brown.   Serves 6 to 8.

JOSEPH BENJAMIN VAUGHAN (12113)

Joseph Benjamin was born on 16 September 1854 in Macon County, Alabama. He was the last child of William C. and Irena Vaughan. According to Lee County Marriage Records, Book A, page 511, Joseph married on 22 April 1886 Mary Elizabeth Spear, A. J. Cousins performing. Mary, born in 1855, was the daughter of Mary A. Spear of Russell County, Alabama. The 1900 Lee County census and an item from Lee County Deed Book 213, page 419, indicate that Joe and his first wife had no children. A notice of 1887 in the **Universalist Herald** (a short-lived Notasulga newspaper published by John C. Burruss) states, however, that Mr. and Mrs. Joe Vaughn (sic) had recently lost an infant child.

The 1900 Lee County census lists Joseph as a farmer living in Precinct 5. The census shows Joseph and his second wife, Mollie McRitchie, had been married 5 years and that the Vaughans had three children, all living. Mollie, who was born 8 November 1873, was the daughter of Thomas and Mary A. McRitchie. The 1900 Lee County census shows they lived next door to their daughter. The year Joseph's first wife died, he and his second wife were members of Notasulga Baptist Church, a membership they later resigned. Mollie seems to have resigned in 1896 and Joseph in 1897. Shortly thereafter they joined the Loachapoka Baptist Church, which may indicate a move about that time.

Thomas McRitchie was born in Scotland and Mary A. was born in Georgia. Mary was probably a Hill before marriage, the 1910 Lee County census showing Rosline Hill, a sister-in law to Thomas, in the household. According to grave markers in the Loachapoka Cemetery, Thomas was born on 13 July 1829 and died on 12 November 1912. Mary was born on 17 July 1846 and died on 7 June 1916. Mary's parents were Georgia natives. Thomas and Mary had eight children according to the 1900 Lee County census, all of whom were living, four still in their household.

One son was John B. McRitchie, who was age 16
in 1900. He is involved in later deed
transactions with Joseph and his wife. One
of these is a sale of 175 acres by the
Vaughans to J. B. McRitchie for $200 (Lee
County Deed Book 164, page 203). This
property was part of Mollie's inheritance and
was located in Sections 22 and 24 of Township
19 and Range 24. A later sale of a parcel of
Section 24, Township 18 and Range 24 is also
on file.

Censuses and Joseph's obituary at the end of
this sketch reveal that Joe and Mollie had
seven children: William, Cecil and Jessie H.
(1900 census); Mary E., Nettie M. and Lois A.
(1910 census); and B. H. (obituary). There are
inconsistencies in ages when the two censuses
are compared, but definite dates are available
for two of the children, who have grave markers
in the Loachapoka Cemetery. The grave markers
also put to the question the accuracy of the
1910 census, which lists Jessie as age 9 (but
known to be alive at the time of the 1900
census) and Mary Ellen as age 7 (but known to
have been born in early 1901). Thus we
summarize: William Thomas (121131), born 15
July 1895, died 22 May 1923 and buried in
Loachapoka Cemetery; Cecil (121132), born about
1897 and died before 1910; Jessie (H?)
(12113a), born in April 1899; Mary Ellen
(12113b), born 3 February 1901, died 3 January
1923 and buried in Loachapoka Cemetery; Nettie
M. (12113c), born about 1905; Lois A. (12113d),
born about 1907; and B. H. (121133), born after
1910. Joseph's obituary states the two
youngest girls married C. J. Manley and Frank
Densham, while not indicating which married
which.

Joe B. died on 20 January 1939, his wife
surviving him until 5 September 1950. Joe's
obituary was carried in the 21 January 1939
edition of the Opelika Daily News: J. B.
Vaughan, 84, dies Loachapoka, be buried today:
Funeral services for J. B. Vaughan, 84,
lifelong resident of East Alabama, were to be

held this afternoon at 4 o'clock at the
Loachapoka Baptist Church. Mr. Vaughan passed
away at his home in Loachapoka Friday night at
11:15 after several years of illness.
His body will be laid to rest in Loachapoka
Cemetery. The Rev. Mr. Bentley and Rev. Mr.
Culpepper will officiate at services. C. R.
Summers is in charge of arrangements.
Mr. Vaughan was born in Macon County but he had
lived in Lee County nearly all his life. He
was married to Miss Mollie McRitchie of
Loachapoka. Mr. Vaughan was a member of the
Baptist Church.
Surviving are his widow, Mrs. J. B. Vaughan;
one son B. H. Vaughan, both of Loachapoka;
three daughters, Miss Jessie Vaughan of Union
Springs, Mrs. C. J. Manley of Zebulon, Ga. and
Mrs. Frank Densham of Dothan and three
grandchildren.

The aforementioned John B. McRitchie is buried
in the Loachapoka Cemetery (and listed as John
R. on his headstone). John was born on 1 May
1884 and died on 13 May 1953. His wife, Carrie
Lou McRitchie, born 5 December 1896 and died 12
July 1920, is buried next to him.

Other items on Joe B. may be found in Taproots,
Vol. 31, no. 2, pages 84 and 85. First a
mention is made that new hymnbooks for the
First Baptist Church of Notasulga were
purchased by contributions made by several
members, one being a $.75 contribution from Joe
B. Vaughan. The books were received 2 May
1886. On page 85 it is mentioned that Joe B.
was on 6 April 1889 a member of a committee to
look into the construction of the belfry and on
4 April 1896 was appointed one of three members
to build a baptismal pool for the church.

NOEL ANGUISH VAUGHAN (1212)

Noel Anguish, second son of William and Lettetia Vaughan, was born on 4 September 1811 in Sumter, South Carolina. As the family was leaving Troup County, Georgia, Noel served as a witness when his father sold his land tract there in 1834 (Troup County Deed Book E, page 55).

On 29 January 1850, as recorded in Chambers County marriage Records, Book 4, page 314, Noel married his first wife, Sarah Ann Martha Goldsmith, nee Leary (also Lary, O'Leary). The ceremony was performed by Hugh and E. C. Carmichael, MG's, with John W. Spears signing as witness. Sarah was the daughter of George W. and Amy (Johnson) Lary and had previously been married on 4 November 1838 to John T. Goldsmith by whom she had four children. After Mr. Goldsmith had died and his widow remarried, the children became a part of the Vaughan household. The children are named in Goldsmith's will of 1843 and in court proceedings of 1858 relating to that will: George Madison, Amanda Permelia, Frances Logenia and Caroline S. Goldsmith. Amanda married on 28 May 1857 at the home of Noel Vaughan, Frank Lovejoy, John Britton performing and Noel signing as guardian for the bride. [Chambers County Marriage Records in the Taproots publication name the husband Jeremiah Freeman Lovejoy.]

Sarah died on 26 July 1883 of a fever and was buried near Camp Hill, but was later disintered at night and secretly reburied in a grave with her sister Eliza Catten in Forsythe, Georgia. Her dying wish had been to be buried with her sister. Children of Noel and Sarah were Noel Alexander Campbell (12121), born 28 December 1850 and died 3 November 1851; Harriett Ann Elvira (Hattie) (1212a), born 5 April 1852, married Nathaniel Barber on 18 October 1870; Joanna Virginia (1212b), born 3 March 1855, married Dr. Joseph J. Camp on 10 December 1876 and died 17 June 1883; Noel Henry Alexander

Campbell (Buddy) (12122), born 20 March 1858, who married Katie Crow and moved to Texas; and Mary Anna Lee (1212c), born 14 July 1862, married George W. Gann and lived in Greenville, Texas and died 3 March 1950.

Noel married secondly, on 12 November 1885, Sarah Catherine Calhoun, in rites performed by J. F. Bledsoe. Sarah was born on 23 May 1827 in Monroe County, Georgia, daughter of Thomas Milton and Ann (Hudson) McKee. Sarah married firstly on 5 December 1848 in Harris County, Georgia, James Malcolm Calhoun, son of Duncan and Sarah (McNeal) Calhoun, themselves natives of Georgia. James Calhoun died in December of 1864 from wounds received on 30 November 1864 at the battle of Franklin, Tennessee. Information from Thomas Dorrough, a descendant through Sarah's eldest daughter, Sarah A., and her husband John C. Dorrough, is that Sarah had 8 children by Mr. Calhoun. The 1910 Lee County census shows Sarah living in her daughter's household and says she had nine children, of whom seven were yet living. Sarah died on 9 June 1913 in Waverly and was buried in the Roxana Cemetery across from a daughter and two grandchildren.

Noel was a Methodist and at one time served as a delegate to the Methodist Convention. Later he became a Campbellite, the name of the early Christian Church. Noel's son-in-law, George Gann, was a Campbellite and it is probably not coincidence that two of Noel's children were named Alexander and Campbell.

Noel was a doctor by profession and lived most of his life in Chambers County. Mrs. Weber of California has an account book which belonged to Dr. Vaughan. In it he marked patients who could not pay "Paid, Dec. 25."

Noel was the second of four brothers to fight in the Creek War of 1836. Like his brothers he obtained 160 acres bounty land for his services. Noel was involved in many land transactions, many of which are abstracted in the Appendix. Besides his land purchases, he

was an heir in the settlement of his father's estate. The 1860 slave census credits him with seven slaves. The 1870 census for Chambers County lists a Wallace William Vaughan in Noel's household; he seems to have been a nephew.

Noel died on 5 August 1894 and is buried in the Camp Hill Methodist Cemetery. His obituary is in the Alabama Archives vertical file. It states he was of humanitarian nature and had extensive holdings around Camp Hill: a large grist mill, plantation home (Pinelli), fish pond, saddle and leather goods shop and slaves [earlier, of course]. At age 82 he had quit practising, but was asked to come see a sick baby, was caught in a rainstorm, caught pneumonia and died. He had a small cancer on his upper lip. As a boy Judge Vaughan Trammell, father of Francis Trammell, lived with Dr. Vaughan.

Noel's will, recorded in Chambers County, left his property to his wife Sarah, who was to be bond-free executrix. The will was dated 30 November 1893 and filed 8 August 1894 (Book 3, page 645). At the foot of this article are pictures of Noel and his first wife, copies and extracts of papers relating to Noel's military service, and a picture thought to be that of Noel's second wife and some of her relatives. Also in the Appendix are copies of pages from a Bible that belonged to Noel.

PHOTOS OF NOEL AND SARAH ANN VAUGHAN

A DORROUGH FAMILY PHOTOGRAPH

The old Dorrough place located in hill country across Sougahatchee Creek, about 10 miles north of Notasulga, Alabama. Standing in front of fence, L to R: John Clark Dorrough, Edward L. Dorrough (youngest child), Sarah Ann (Sally) Calhoun Dorrough. Seated, probably Sarah Catherine McKee Calhoun Vaughan. Standing behind fence, perhaps William Franklyn & James Marvin Dorrough. Time: early 1900's.

FILE HEADING FOR NOEL'S BOUNTY LAND APPLICATION

PROCEEDINGS IN NOEL'S BOUNTY LAND APPLICATION

The State of Alabama)   L. S.
Chambers County   )   On this 7th day of
May A. D. One Thousand Eight Hundred and fifty
five personally appeared before me Nathan Y.
Hunter a Justice of the Peace within and for
the County and State aforesaid, Noel A. Vaughan
aged forty three years a resident of Chambers
County in the State of Alabama who being duly
sworn according to law declares that he is the
identical Noel A. Vaughan who was a private in
the Company commanded by Captain James Cobb,
but cannot state to what Regiment said Company
was attached in the War with the Creek Indians
in the year A. D. 1836 that he volunteered at
Tuckabatchie Town in Macon County Alabama about
the month of April or May of 1836 at the
commencement of hostilities and continued in
actual service in said War for more than
fourteen days and was honorably discharged at
Tuckabatchie Town in Macon County at or about
the close of said War, but did not receive any
written discharge none being given to any of
said Company so far as he knows or believes.

He makes this declaration for the purpose of
obtaining the bounty land to which he may be
entitled under the act approved March 3rd 1855
He also declares that he has not received a
Warrant for bounty land under this or any other
act of Congress nor made any other application
therefor

                    N. A. Vaughan

We Henry Williamson and Strother Gaines
residents of Chambers County in the State of
Alabama upon our oaths declare that the
foregoing declaration was signed and
acknowledged by Noel A. Vaughan in our presence
and that we believe from the appearances and
statements of the applicant that he is the
identical person he represents himself to be
                Henry Williamson
                Strother Gaines

The foregoing declaration and affidavit were
sworn to and subscribed before me on the day
and year above written and I certify that I
know the affiants to be credible persons that
the claimant is the person he represents
himself to be and that I have no interest in
this claim Nathan Y. Hunter J. P.

The State of Alabama) I, Samuel Pearson, Judge
Chambers County   )of Probate for the County
and State aforesaid and by these laws of said
State, Ex-Officio Clerk of the Court of
Probate, and Keeper of the records of said
County, hereby certify, that Nathan Y. Hunter,
whose name appears to the foregoing declaration
and affidavit, signed J. P., is an acting
Justice of the Peace, in and for the County and
State aforesaid; duly commissioned and
qualified according to law; and that his
signature, as written thereto, is genuine.
                Given under my hand and seal
                of office, at La Fayette,
                Alabama, this 7th day of May
                1855.
                        Saml. Pearson
                        Judge of Probate

NOEL ALEXANDER CAMPBELL VAUGHAN (12121)

Noel Alexander Campbell, first child of Noel
and Sarah Vaughan, was born on 28 December
1850. He died in infancy on 3 November 1851.

HORSELESS CARRIAGE
(WITH APOLOGIES TO THE HORSE)

There was once an old fellow named Clive,
Who was ever so lucky to arrive alive.
Said his friends, "Why in the heck
Are those who have the most wrecks
The first to tell you how to drive?"

HARRIETT ANN ELVIRA VAUGHAN (1212a)

Harriett Ann Elvira, also known as Hattie, was born on 5 April 1852. On 18 October 1870 she married Nathaniel James Barber, J. A. Curry performing at her father's house (Chambers County Marriage Records). Nathaniel was born on 4 July 1845, the son of Nathaniel C. and Elizabeth (Hardin) Barber. Elizabeth was the elder Barber's second wife. His first wife, Comfort Ann Barber, died on 4 June 1829 according to the Columbia [S. C.] Telescope. Nathaniel J. was the grandson of John and Margaret Barber of Ireland. The Texas Archives has a file on Nathaniel Barber, which this writer has not yet had the opportunity to see. Hattie's tombstone gives 24 February 1889 as the date of her death.

Children of Nathaniel and Harriett were Sara(h) Elizabeth (1212aa), born 23 September 1872, who married Spain Payton Barber and died in 1953; Nathaniel Marvin (1212a1), born 29 September 1875, married to Ira Oliver and died in 1942; Vaughan McTyeire (1212a2), born 8 July 1877 and died in 1895; and Celestia Anna (1212ab), born 12 June 1880, who married Rufus Allen Patrick and died on 7 July 1944.

JOANNA VIRGINIA VAUGHAN (1212b)

Joanna Virginia was born on 3 March 1855. She was known as Joe. On 10 December 1876 she married Dr. Joseph J. Camp, Rev. John F. Bledsoe performing at the home of Noel A. Vaughan (Chambers County Marriage Records, Vol. ___, page 275a). Joanna died on 17 July 1883. Dr. and Mrs. Camp had two children: Johnny (1212b1), born 12 December 1877 and Herman Dawson (1212b2).

SHEPHERD'S PIE (FROM THE AUBURN COOKBOOK)

1 T. Fat   1 Onion, sliced   2 C. Cooked Meat
2 C. Tomatoes   2 C. Mashed Potatoes
Salt and Pepper

Melt fat, add sliced onion, and brown lightly. Add meat, tomatoes, salt and pepper. Simmer 10 minutes. Line a greased 1-quart baking dish with 1 cup mashed potatoes. Add meat-tomato mixture and cover with remaining cup of mashed potatoes. Bake in a moderate oven (350 degrees) for 30 minutes or until brown. Serves 6.

NOEL HENRY ALEXANDER CAMPBELL VAUGHAN (12122)

Noel H. A. C., also known as Buddy, was born on 20 March 1858. This writer has little information on Buddy. He married Katie Crow and removed to northern Texas. He later removed to the northwest, rumored to have been Colorado or Utah. Pat Weber says that his marriage to Katie Crow was his fourth and that he moved to Seattle, Washington. Known children of Buddy and Katie were Charlie (121221), Bessie (12122a), Arthur (121222) and Claude (121223).

PET PEEVE

My boss is the most vicious you have ever met:
Arrogance, contumely, chutzpah, hubris--you
bet.
One day he went into shock 'cause I was a
minute late by clock;
But, instead of calling for the doc,
We up and sent him to the vet.

154

MARY ANNA LEE VAUGHAN (12122c)

Mary Anna Lee was born on 14 July 1862. On ___
December 1893 in Hunt County, Texas she married
George W. Gann, a Campbellite preacher. A
record may be found in Book H, page 203 of
Chambers County Marriage Records. Mary died on
3 March 1950.

WHAT'S IN A NAME

There were once two boys from Jersey,
Totally indecisive, absolutely without poise;
So that for a name they considered Yesno,
But it sounded like they were from Fresno;
So they settled on Noyes.

MILES EDWIN VAUGHAN (1213)

Miles Edwin was born on 10 April 1814 in Sumter, South Carolina. He migrated with the family to Alabama and, shortly after his arrival, fought in the Creek War. Like his brothers, he received bounty lands for his service. On 6 February 1840 Miles married Mary Lucretia Robeson, also known as Molly. Molly was born on 9 September 1822 in South Carolina. Mary's uncle, Allen Vines Robison, was a dance instructor in Macon County, Alabama. Advertisements in the <u>Macon Republican</u> (10 June 1858) announced Robison's classes at G. W. Brewer's hotel.

Mr. Robison moved to Screven County, Georgia in 1827 and to Montgomery, Alabama in 1832. He was widely travelled in his profession and also played the violin. He married his wife, Caroline Amanda, on 9 May 1837 in Wetumpka, Alabama. Their son, Horatio H., lived with Miles Edwin for many years and helped him with his farm. Horatio married Mary Francis Adams. Horatio had a son, Elbert Vaughan Robison (born 18 October 1881 and married Laura Hill), one of whose sons, Vaughan Hill Robison (born about 1917), was for years an Alabama State Senator. Allen Vines died near Loachapoka on 25 June 1880 and Horatio died at Wetumpka on 9 January 1914. Horatio had served in Company I of the 3rd Alabama Regiment during the Civil War. He received most of Miles' estate after the latter's death on 28 August 1896. Miles' death is recorded in the Bible of A. V. Robison, which has been passed down in his family. An old story in the Vaughan Family relates that Miles had asked his brother Henry J. to come live with him so that the latter could help him with his farm and Henry's wife could cook for the old bachelor and, that, if they would do so, he would give them all his property when he died. This story seems to be one of those rumors that crop up in families: Miles was no bachelor (as the purveyor of the tale didn't seem to know) and, being only a few years older than his brother, there was no certainty he

would predecease his brother. The story went on to relate how Henry's wife was afraid of the Indians who remained in the area and refused, whereupon the estate went to Robison, who had served in Henry's stead.

Miles E. had considerable property in the vicinities of Loachapoka and Notasulga. He had a grist mill, sawmill and cotton gin run by waterpower and with an undershot wheel, a rarity in that day. The mill was on Broome's Creek below the dam. Nearby areas were Armstrong Church and the Beehive Community. Miles' mill was known as the Lower Mill, while that of his brother Henry was known as the Upper Mill. Three of the brothers were known to have had mills.

Miles Edwin was well-versed. He is listed on page 82 of Macon County's ledger of doctors. In 1883 he bought some land from Mary W. Allen of Texas and built the Miles Vaughan House Place. This house, pictured in this article, was architected by Miles and featured low ceilings, novel for that period. He sold this tract in 1894 to J. L. Wise and, as of the early 1970's, the house was still standing, but almost completely in ruins (in recent years it was being raided for firewood). Miles often served as conductor of elections for Macon County. In 1850 he served as manager for the Loachapoka Beat for judicial and bailiff elections (Macon Republican, 18 April 1850), Henry J. serving as the Returning Officer. Same notice appears in the 11 July 1850 edition. Miles served as conductor of general elections for Loachapoka in 1851 (Republican, 3 July 1851) and in 1854 as manager for Loachapoka Beat School Commission election (Republican, 13 April 1854). This issue also lists Col John G. Robison as a manager as well as other Robisons--R. C., Henry and John L. It is uncertain if any of these Robisons were related to Miles. Miles was listed as a subscriber to the Macon Republican on the Franklin Route (Taproots, Volume 7, Number 2).

The locale of Franklin seems to be the area in which the Vaughans first settled after their arrival in Alabama. Besides the subscription list of the _Republican_, the writer notes that Miles' brother Henry J. had a father-in-law, King Harrison, who owned property in the Franklin area, which place Henry probably met his future wife. The Vaughans' movement seems to have been eastward through Chehaw, Notasulga, Loachapoka, Waverly/Roxana/Camp Hill and Opelika.

Court documents show that Miles was involved in court sessions in Russell County in the 1840's, possibly as a witness and perhaps in the assessment or partition of estates. In many estate settlements around Chambers County he is listed as a creditor/debtor to the estate. Miles was also a merchant and had a store in Loachapoka. One court docket listing, which can be found in the _Taproots_ publication, shows Miles was involved in a gaming house suit. The listing does not, however, indicate in what manner he was involved. Only two names are listed, so one would suspect he was either the plaintiff or the operator.

The 1871 Macon County Tax List (page 56) carries Miles as having paid or been assessed $25 for 320 acres of land. The January 1874 Macon County Minutes carries a tax assessment for Miles on page 60, while on page 61 is an assessment for his brother, Henry Jackson. Miles administrated the estate of his father William after the latter's death. Extracts of deeds relating to the administration are filed in the Appendix. On following pages are copies of four notices that relate to this administration.

On the mill site atop a hill is a cemetery, called the Ferrell Cemetery. The annotations on the stones there are copied on the following pages. This was apparently the family from which Miles obtained the land in 1869 and 1870. These transactions are also extracted in the Deeds Appendix.

The <u>Macon</u> <u>Republican</u> of 12 January 1854 lists an unclaimed letter for Mrs. M. L. Vaughan, Miles' wife. Mary died on 2 March 1879 and is buried next to her husband in the Loachapoka Cemetery.

Horatio Robison's petition for probate of Miles' will appears in Macon County Wills and Appraisements (1892-1904, page 271). Witnesses for Robison were T. L. Samford of Notasulga and A. W. Fincher of Vaughan's Mill. The will, on page 272, gave to Lettie V. Thomas half-interest in mill and gin and half-interest in ten acres of land on which mill and gin were situated (S14, T19, R24, Lee County), to Henry J. Vaughan $5, and to Horatio Herrin Robison the remainder of real and personal property. The will was dated 24 August 1896, four days before Miles' death. This land later passed to the hands of Lewis A. (Bing) Harmon, after which the mill burnt. John Harmon bought the Upper Mill, which also burnt. Later the Lower Mill property passed to a group which established the Vaughan's Mill Fishing Club. When interest flagged, the property was sold to Peter Preer, passed to his daughter, Myrtle S. Preer, and later was sold to a doctor couple of Columbus, Georgia.

An interesting account concerns the visit of a Tom Clower to his native Alabama, where he made a call on his old friend, Miles Vaughan. Alexander Nunn's article, which recounts this account and appeared in the <u>Opelika</u> <u>Daily</u> <u>News</u>, is copied at the foot of this vignette.

Mrs. Hosea Vaughan, who died at ninety-nine in 1989, related to the writer a few years before her death remembering, as a young girl, seeing Miles ride by the house where she lived on the way to Loachapoka. The house was on the route between the mill place and "town." She said she remembered he always rode a white horse and "sat straight as an arrow in the saddle."

A source the writer once saw stated Miles commanded Company A of the State Militia during the Civil War. The writer now enters this

information, because recently the 1907 Lee County Confederate Census has become available to him. A listing for Isham Edwards informs that he re-enlisted at Loachapoka in September 1864 in the county reserves under Captain Miles Vaughan of Company A until April 1865, when the company was disbanded at Tuskegee, having originally enlisted at Camp Watts in the reserve.

Miles Edwin and Molly had no children.

NOTICES FROM MACON REPUBLICAN ON ESTATE OF WILLIAM VAUGHAN

Macon Republican
10 November 1853
17 November 1853
24 November 1853
1 December 1853
8 December 1853
15 December 1853

Macon Republican
3 November 1853
10 November 1853
17 November 1853
1 December 1853

ADMINISTRATOR'S SALE.

ON the 1st Monday in January next, on the Court House square in Tuskegee, within the usual hours of sale, I will sell to the highest bidder for cash, all the negroes belonging to the estate of William Vaughan, dec'd, to wit: Jim, Amy, George, Jack, Eliza, John, Steve, Willis, Charles, Reuben, John, Mariah Daniel, Dave, Sam, and Violet; sold by order of Probate Court for division amongst the heirs of William Vaughan, deceased.

MILES E. VAUGHAN,
nov. 3—tds   Adm'r.

ADMINISTRATOR'S SALE.

BY virtue of an order of the Probate Court of Macon county, I will, on the 1st Monday in December next, at the late residence of William Vaughan, dec'd, sell to the highest bidder for cash, the perishable property of said deceased, consisting of horses, cattle, hogs, &c. Also, all articles of household furniture and farming utensils. In short, all the personal estate, except the negroes, and enough provisions to feed the family till 1st January, 1854.
Sold for division amongst the heirs of said deceased.

MILES E. VAUGHAN,
Nov. 3—tds   Adm'r.

Macon Republican
5 January 1854
12 January 1854
17 January 1854

Macon Republican
10 November 1853
17 November 1853
24 November 1853
8 December 1853

ADMINISTRATOR'S SALE.

BY virtue of an order of the Probate Court of Macon county I will on the 3rd Monday in January 1854, it being the 23d day of said month, at the Court-house square in the town of Tuskegee, sell to the highest bidder, the following lands to wit: a tract as follows, commencing on the east line of the section at the half-mile stake, east line of the original north-east corner of section 33, township 19, and range 21, and thence a west course with the section line to Risley's line then a south course to a pine post near Risley's fence, east to the corner of Shells fence, thence due south to Fears line, and being a part of west half of the above described section. Also a parcel of land containing five acres in the northeast corner of section 33, township 19, range 21, sold as the real estate of Wm. Vaughan deceased. Sale within the usual hours.
Terms, credit till 1st Jan. 1855.

jan 5—tds   M. E. VAUGHAN, Adm'r.

ALABAMA—MACON COUNTY.

Probate Court—Special Term—31st day of October, 1853.

THIS day came Miles E. Vaughan, Administrator of the estate of William Vaughan, dec'd, and presented his petition praying for an order to sell the real estate of said dec'd, to wit: One hundred acres on N. 1-2 of Section 33, T. 19, and Range 21, and five acres on the North East corner of the South 1-2 of said section, for the purpose of division among the heirs of said dec'd, which petition was ordered to be filed, and set for hearing on the 2d Monday in December next. And it appearing that John W. Cummings, Wm. R. Cummings, Alfred M. Cummings, are heirs of said dec'd, are non-residents of the State of Alabama, it is ordered that publication be given in the Macon Republican for four successive weeks, notifying the said Henry J., Wm., and Noel A. Vaughan, and the heirs of Mary Cummings, dec'd, John W., Wm. R., and Alfred M. Cummings to be and appear at a regular term of the Probate Court of said county, to be held on the 2d Monday in December next, and show cause why said order should not be granted.

LEWIS ALEXANDER,
nov. 3—4w   Judge of Probate.

VIEW OF LOACHAPOKA HOME OF MILES E. VAUGHAN
(ca 1970) WITH LOW CEILINGS AND OTHER FEATURES

DESCRIPTION OF FERRELL CEMETERY
AT VAUGHAN'S MILL

VAUGHAN'S MILL CEMETERY

Contributor: Mr. James L. Braswell, Jr.
Copied by: Mr. James L. Braswell, Jr. and his son, William Chambless Braswell, March 15, 1964.

Location: Situated near Vaughan's Mill in Macon County, Alabama, on North side of county road (about 50 yards West of private road leading to old mill site) which runs from Armstrong Church to a point on U. S. Highway # 29 which is about 1½ miles Northeast of "Y" (U.S. #80 & U. S. #29); it is also about ¼ mile Southeast of point where this county road passes over I-85, in S¼Quarter of Southeast Quarter of Section 30, Township 18 N. and Range 25 E.

The following described markers are quite singular in that they are apparently placed in memory of the same person. They are placed side by side and bear the same name and dates. The only difference is that one of these "slab Type" markers is square on all four corners while the other is rounded on the two upper corners. Long years have passed since these markers were laid side by side, and yet one cannot but wish to know the sotry behind them.

(1)   In Memory of   Sacred
       William Ferrell   To the Memory of
     Born Jan 18th, 1791   William Ferrell
     Died Oct. 6th, 1855   Born Jan 18th, 1791
                                            And departed this life
                                                 Oct. 6th, 1855

Two or three adult graves and one or more infant graves marked only with native rocks.

In Memory of William Alexander , Son of L. S. and Martha Scott, who was born April 19, 1857, and died May 4, 1858, Aged 1 year and 15 days.

Julia C. Harrell, Born Oct. 2, 1860, Died March 8, 1902.
     "She was too good, too gentle and fair
     To dwell in this cold world of care."

From East Alabama's Past

More On Tom Clower

By Alexander Nunn 7-11-71

. Last Sunday we left Thomas Holliday Clower visiting cousins in Opelika. After having left East Alabama in 1857, he had returned 17 years later for a long visit. This diary was a record of his kin and friends whom he saw and of conditions he found. Today's installment begins on Friday, Oct. 9, 1874.

* * * * *

"I left (Opelika) about half after 10 o'clock for Auburn. After a dirty ride I reached Auburn about 11 o'clock. I dined at Aunt Agnes' house near the depot and stayed until about 3 o'clock. At this time, about 5 o'clock, I am writing this sitting in front of Aunt Jane's residence.

Saturday, 10 o'clock. I stayed all night at Aunt Lou's and after breakfast went over to the college and looked at that. The Halls were perfectly splendid and there was libraries connected with the Halls, 1 to each. I left Auburn at 11 o'clock, arrived back at Loachapoka about half after eleven. I say around town until late in the eve, then took up a line of march for Uncle Mos Hayley's place. I found them all well and not looking for me.

Sunday, 11th October. This morn I walked up to Loachapoka and church. There was Sunday School going on at the Methodist Church. Stopping there I listened to some charming music by the choir. After Sunday School was over I proceeded to the Baptist Church where I heard a good sermon and more good music.

Next morn, 12th day of Oct. I was off again for town from my uncle's and from town went out to Dr. Mahonie's where I remained all night.

Tuesday, 13 of October. Cool enough for frost but I did not see any. I left Dr. Mahonie's about 7 o'clock in a buggy, passed through my father's old plantation that I worked on 17 years ago. It looks very old and worn. I could hardly believe it was the same place everything (was) so much changed. I crossed Loachapoka Creek at Coss, now Reid's Mill. Walking about 300 yards I came up to John F. Yarbrough's place. Dr. Yarbrough and his wife were my old teachers in fact the la 2 teachers I ever went to in Ala or anywhere else. I had not seen any of the family for 17 years but recognized them in a moment. I spent the day and night at Dr. Yarbrough's and a more pleasant time I never had anywhere.

WEDNESDAY, 11th. A killing frost. After dinner today I went in to call on more of my old friends, B. Jones' family. I remained all night and next morning, the 15th, bid them all farewell and left for Loachapoka. And then back again to headquarters, Uncle Mos Hayley's, where I am now writing these lines. Uncle Mos and his two sons have gone to Opelika. They left last night about midnight. They are expecting to get back tonight.

Friday, 16th. They all arrived from Opelika about midnight. There was rain and a heavy hail storm in places this evening.

Sat. 17 Oct. I have been all day doing nothing as usual.

Sunday, 18th. A beautiful day. After breakfast I started to the association at Farmville. The road was rough, hilly, and rocky but I got there all safe about 10 o'clock. There were about 1,000 people assembled on the ground; a better dressed and better looking crowd would be hard to find in any country. There were two sermons and after them a little collection made. By this time it was 2 o'clock. The crowd had plenty on the ground to eat and that of the very best. After eating and walking around a few minutes, I started back. I never had the pleasure of visiting Farmville but once and that was 20 years ago, so I recognized but few persons present.

Monday, 19th Oct. I pretended to help the some potatoes today. My uncle is making a very poor crop this season.

20th, Tuesday. As yesterday, I worked.

21st, Oct., Wednesday. I idled around all morning and in the eve made a visit to see one of my old friends, Miles Vaughn who is living on Loachapoka Creek about 3 miles from where I have been staying.

Wednesday a.m., 22 Oct. I spent the night at Mr. Miles Vaughn. I had a very bad cold and did not rest well, in fact, could not sleep any during the night. Thurs. I left Mr. Vaughn a soon after breakfast and traveled to around Loachapoka.

Thursday, 23rd. I passed this evening at Mr. Tom Peddy's, also stayed there until morning. I returned to headquarters.

I find that the majority of the people in this county, Lee, in debt and no chance of ever paying out. There has been two failures in crops, last year and this, which has almost ruined this county. I have heard many say they are completely bankrupt and unless things change for the better many people will actually suffer for the necessities of life during the coming year. In many places that I have visited, the crop will not bring near as much as the cost of cultivating it. I am confident that many crops of cotton will not make more than 250 lbs. seed cotton per acre, and corn is not much better.

Sat. 24th of Oct. A heavy rain last night. I have sat about all day doing nothing at all except eating and drinking.

Sunday, 25th I arose early this morning, dressed up in my best clothes, and was off to see some of my old friends again, Mr. Jesse Page and Mr. Fletcher Yarbrough's family. I stayed all day—took dinner at Mr. Page's, and it was a splendid one. I

left Mr. Page's about 3 o'clock and stayed awhile at Mr. Yarbrough's, leaving there about 1 hour before night.

Monday, 26th. I am preparing to go back to Mississippi on tomorrow. Uncle Addison Hayley is expecting to go with me. The next train is at 5 o'clock tomorrow morning. It is about 4 (p.m.) as I write this.

27th day of October. Tuesday. I roused up early this morning, took some coffee and a little lunch, after which Cousin Walter Hayley, Uncle Addison Hayley (and I) left for Loachapoka where we got about 1 hour before day. At 5 o'clock the train arrived and Uncle and me jumped aboard for Montgomery. About 8 o'clock the train rolled into the city. We stood around watching the loading and unloading of baggage (and) the changing of cars, until a few minutes after 9 when we took another train bound for China.

ABOUT THE VISITOR. His Hosts, and Hostesses, T. H. Clower and Mrs. A. W. Bennett were married Nov. 4; 1888 in Lee County, Ala. by Rev J. Bancroft at the residence of J. R. McTee. We have not learned whether "T. H." was "Thomas, Holiday" Clower.

Aunt Lou—nee Louise J. Warren, widow of the Clower brother Thomas M. who had died in 1871.

Dr. Mahonie'r—Dr. T. F. Malone, dentist (1834-1895), who practiced in Loachapoka for many years and is buried there.

Coss, now Reid's Mill—what was later to become Langley's mill, on the southside of the Saugahatchee on the way to Roxana. Today, mill gone, bridge gone, road gone. Use of the word "Coss" intrigues us. It usually refers to an old Indian town on the Coosa River, not far from Childersburg.

John F. Yarbrough—came to Loachapoka in the early 1850's as a young graduate right out of Emory College to become principal of the Academy. Married his music teacher, Miss America Leftwich. Was one of the first superintendents of education in Lee County, later held other important county offices. Many descendants in East Alabama.

B. Jones—must have been the V. B. Jones family of the 1860 Census.

Miles Vaughn—Miles E. Vaughn of Loachapoka. The Opelika Democrat of April 11, 1889 said of him and his brother: "M. E. and H. J. Vaughan are active gentlemen of the old school, who were brought from South Carolina, before the Indians left here in 1836. They are farming, milling, ginning, and trading, and H. J. Vaughan individually owns other mills and lands." From this family came the names Upper Vaughan's mill (Reid's, Langley's) and Lower Vaughan's, near Armstrong, on the Chetafalua.

Mr. Jesse Page—Jesse Boring Page, grandfather of Principal J. D. Page of Smith Station Schools. Lived most of his life north of the Saugahatchee, and about 4 miles from Loachapoka. Was badly injured facially in the battle of Vicksburg Story is that Mr. Page was firing from behind a barrel when a Yankee bullet actually entered the bore of his gun and caused it to explode.

Uncle Addison Hayley—A 45 year old farmer in 1860. Living with him were Jonathan and Martha David and their three children, Charles A. Hester, overseer, and John A. Glenn, student. Cousin Walter Hayley has not been identified. All the early Census records spelled the name, "Haley."

IN THE PREPARATION of these notes I have had the benefit of the counsel and records of Peavy Wright and Earle Vaughan of Auburn, the latter being a great great grandson of H. J. Vaughan; descendant of Miles E; the records of Banker George W. Clower, Jr. of Atlanta and Maybelle Clower Byrd of Winston-Salem, N.C., the latter a granddaughter of the owner of the diary. The knowledge of a number of others about families and locations has been most helpful. The marriage record is from "Marriage Records of Lee County, Ala., 1867-1893," published by East Ala Genealogical Society.

Next Sunday: A Confederate soldier in the fortifications near Richmond, Va. hears the Yankees cheering over Abraham Lincoln's reelection. Nov. 9, 1964.

From the Opelika Democrat of 11 April 1889:

LOACHAPOKA

A GRAPHIC DESCRIPTION OF SOME
OF ITS OLD LANDMARKS

Not Dead, Nor Sleeping--Its Water
Power, Churches, Mills, Granite,
Railroads, Schools, etc.

(From Our Special Reporter.)

At one time, Loachapoka was one of the busiest little villages in the State--then came the somnolent period--and now comes resuscitation.

With the growth of Opelika, and smaller towns surrounding, the effect was produced, but now the village has come to the conclusion that, in her immediate vicinity, there are such advantages to be availed of, that permanent prosperity can be secured. The land surrounding is good. Splendid water powers are within one and a half or two miles, and the best of granite taps the village in inexhaustible supply.

Loachapoka now has five stores, a good cotton gin and excellent flour and grist mills not far away. The population is 380. The churches are Methodist and Baptist, and an excellent school taught by Miss R. S. Fowler, a graduate of the Nashville Normal, has generally fifty pupils. Two Sunday Schools are well attended, and no one can poke fun at Loachapoka's lack of morality. The region is a rich cotton producer, and vegetation of every description is indigenous to the soil.

The Saugahatchee Creek with excellent volume and rock bottom, is a gift of nature, ready at hand, for manufacturing.

The Vaughan Mills, located thereon, were built fifteen years ago. They grind from 300 to 400 bushels a month for the Western Railroad of Alabama, and have a capacity of 200 bushels per day.

At this point there are fifteen feet fall--enough for any factory. M. E. and H. J. Vaughan are active gentlemen of the old school, who were brought from South Carolina, before the Indians left here, in 1836.

They are farming, milling, ginning and trading, and M. E. Vaughan individually owns other mills and lands.

The Saugahatchee Mills are also on this creek--are about a mile below Vaughan's, and have fifteen feet fall at least. It is a splendid location for a cotton factory and the chief expense would be in the building, as the fall is a natural and the bottom solid rock. It is the property of J. H. Williamson, who is a born miller and chose the location in preference to all others. He has a modest gin thereon, and is now exercising his inventive genius on a water power lath mill. The granite abounding near Loachapoka has been quarried, and is a blue gray, susceptible of taking a beautiful polish. That on the Haynie estate, I hear will have a railroad from the main line this fall and quarrying be done on a scale worthy of the first-class quality of the granite.

Loachapoka has been receiving a regular brushing up. The Methodist parsonage has received an addition. The church has been repaired and the Baptists are following suit.

F. Haynie has built a model barn, which for convenience and ingenuity should be patterned after, and the improvements upon his cottage, and grounds, will make it an ideal home. John Daley, Jr., the able railway, telegraph and express operator has a growing business . . .

DOCUMENTS CONCERNING
MILES' BOUNTY LAND APPLICATION

The State of Alabama)   On this the 1st day of
Macon County   )   January in the year 1858
personally appeared before me James Clopton an
acting Justice of the Peace in & for said
County and State, William F. Pullen who being
duly sworn deposes & says that Miles E. Vaughan
(who have made application for Bounty Land
Warrant No 177.940 said application having been
rejected by the Department) did service in the
Creek War of 1836 in the company commanded by
Captain _____ Cobb.   That Miles E. Vaughan
volunteered in said company at Tuskegee Ala on
or about 1st May----1836 and continued in
actual service for more than fourteen (14)
days, and was honourably discharged on or about
the 1st day of Aug 1836 He further states that
affiant was a private in said company and knows
the facts to which he testifies of his own
knowledge.   Further states that he received a
Land Warrant for his service in said company,
No 65-175, for 160 acres.   He further swears
that he is a disinterested witness & resides in
said county & state
                    W. F. Pullen

Sworn to & subscribed before me day & year
aforewritten & I certify the W. F. Pullen is a
credible witness. James Clopton
                    Justice of Peace

The State of Alabama) Personally appeared
       Macon County   ) before me Robt. A.
Johnston an acting Justice of the Peace in
aforesaid County, Lewis Alexander who on oath
states that Miles E. Vaughn, who has applied
for Land Warrant No 177.940 did serve in the
company commanded by Captain Cobb, the War with
the Creek Indians of 1836.   That said Vaughn
volunteered in said War at Tuskegee Ala. &
served in said War in the company commanded by
Captain James Cobb for more than 14 days & was
honorably discharged at Tuskegee Macon County
Ala on or about the 1st day of August 1836.
Affiant served in said Company with the said
Miles Vaughn and therefore knowing of the said

166

service of his own knowledge. He further says
he recd 2 Land Warrant for his service under
Capt Skenery McGeorge for 80 acres each but
sold the same & cannot now recollect the
numbers. He further says he is a disinterested
witness. Lewis Alexander

Sworn to & subscribed before me August 4th 1858
& I hereby certify that Lewis Alexander is a
creditable person.
                    Robt. Johnston
                    Justice of Peace

The State of Alabama) I Lewis Alexander
    Macon County   ) Judge of the Probate
Court in afore said County & State do herby
certify that James Clopton & Robt. A. Johnston
whose names appear to the foregoing affidavits
are & were at the time of signing the same
acting Justices of the Peace in & for said
County duly elected, qualified & commissioned
as required by Law & that full faith and credit
are due to all their official acts as such.
Given under my hand & official seal on this the
9th Sept 1858
                    Lewis Alexander
                    Judge of Probate

The State of Alabama) On this the 18th day
    Macon County   ) of June A D 1855
personally appeared before me Milton S. Kelton
an acting Justice of the Peace in & for the
county aforesaid Miles E. Vaughn aged 41 years
old a resident of Macon Co State of Alabama,
who being duly sworn according to law declares
that he is the identical Miles E Vaughn who was
a private in the Company commanded by Captain
James Cobb not in any Regiment but a detached
company of Alabama Militia in the War with the
Creek Indians declared by the United States on
or about the 7th May 1836, that he volunteered
in Macon Co Ala on or about the 12th May 1836
for the term of three months & continued in
actual service for 14 (fourteen) days & was
honorably discharged on or about the 12th of
July A. D. 1836. He makes this declaration for
the purpose of obtaining the Bounty Land to
which he may be entitled under the act granting

bounty Land approved 3rd March 1855. He also declares that He has not received a Warrant for bounty Land under this or any other act of Congress or made application therefor, and desires when issued to be sent to Paine & Mayes Tuskegee Ala.

Miles E. Vaughan

We John Robison & John G. Pond residents of Macon County in the State of Alabama upon our oaths declare that the foregoing declaration was signed and acknowledged by Miles E. Vaughn in our presence, and that we believe from the appearance and statement of the applicant that he is the identical person he represents himself to be.John L. Robison

John G. Pond

The foregoing declaration & affidavit were sworn to and subscribed before me on the day & year above written and I certify that I know the affiants to be creditable persons that the claimant is the person he represents himself to be and that I have no interest in this claim.

Milton S. Kelton
J. P.

The State of Alabama) I Lewis Alexander
Macon County   ) Judge of Probate
for said county do hereby certify that Milton S. Kelton whose name is signed to the above affidavit is and was at the time of signing the same an acting Justice of the Peace in and for the County aforesaid and qualified and commissioned as the Law requires and that faith and credit is due his official acts

Given under my hand and
Seal of office this 22nd day of
June A. D. 1855
Lewis Alexander
Judge of Probate

FILE HEADING FOR MILES' BOUNTY LAND APPLICATION

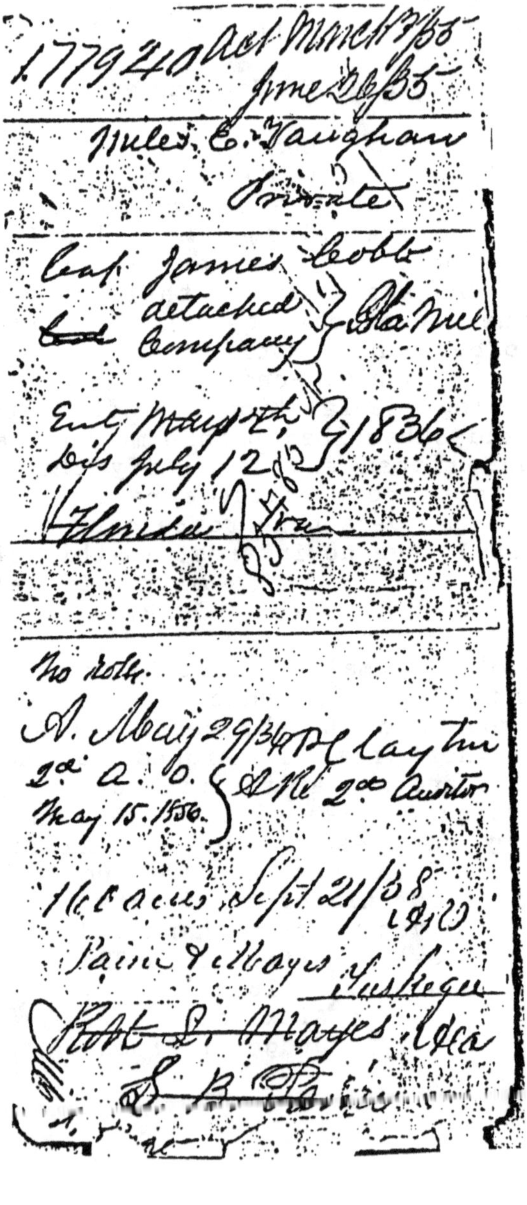

177940 Act March 3/55
June 26/55

Miles E. Vaughan
Private

Capt James Cobb
detached Company } Ala Mil

Ent May 4th } 1836
Dis July 12th

Florida War

No rolls.

A. Abay 29/34 B Clayton
2d A. O. } 2d Auditor
May 15. 1856.

160 acres Sept 21/58

Paine & Mayes Tuskegee

~~Robt S. Mayes~~ Ala

S. B.

HENRY JACKSON VAUGHAN (1214)

Henry Jackson was born on 25 June 1819 in Sumter, South Carolina. On 9 December 1841 he married Mary Anne Harrison, known as Mollie, daughter of King and Rebecca Mary (Parmer) Harrison, with C. J. Atkins, J. P., performing the ceremony. Mary Anne was born on 27 January 1826 and died 21 (26?) July 1864, while Henry was off fighting in the Civil War. (Rebecca Antoinette's Bible gives 21 June as the date.) King Harrison died in 1837 and his estate was administered by his widow and later by son-in-law Henry Jackson. It is not clear whether they co-administered or Henry took over after Rebecca's death. In the estate settlement the commissioners (C. I. Atkins, et al.) sold a parcel of land (West half, Section 12, Township 17, Range 22) which Henry received in a monetary transfer with the commissioners.

Henry's second wife, whom he married 5 February 1867, was Georgia Ann Trawick, daughter of Isom and Sarah Trawick of Georgia. Georgia had previously married, on 18 November 1858, George W. Phillips, C. A. Stanton officiating. Mr. Phillips was also a casualty of the Civil War. The 1900 Lee County census shows Georgia was born in 1843 and that her father was born in Georgia, her mother in South Carolina; the 1910 census shows both her parents having been born in Georgia. Henry had served in his youth in the Creek Indian War, the fourth of four brothers to have done so. His second wife still received a pension for his service at the time of her death on 25 June 1930. Records concerning Henry's service are included at the end of this article.

Rumor has it that Henry and his son Henry King enlisted at the same time in Company F of the 46th Alabama Infantry Regiment; however, Henry's obituary states he enlisted in 1863, while records show that his son enlisted in 1862.

Henry was a miller by trade and owned the Upper
Vaughan's Mill on the Saugahatchee Creek.
After his father's death in 1853 he became
guardian for the minor children of his sister,
Mary Cummings, for their part in the settlement
of the estate.

Henry died on 22 January 1897 and is buried in
Loachapoka Cemetery. His gravestone,
manufactured by Rosebrough of St. Louis, reads
"Our Husband and Father."

Children of Henry and his first wife were
William Miles (12141), born on 31 October 1842,
married to Mary E. Walton and died 26 September
1918; Henry King Noel (12142), born 4 July
1844, married to Louisa C. Ross (nee Rowe) and
died 24 June 1917; Rebecca Antoinette (1214a),
born 26 January 1846, married to Benjamin H.
Reynolds and died 17 October 1913; George Louis
(12143), born 29 December 1847, married thrice,
lastly to Ida (Betty) Taylor; Wallace Walton
(12144), also known by several other names,
born 24 November 1849, married to Ida
Rutherford and died 8 January 1874; and
Lettetia Vermelle (1214e), born 5 June 1861,
married to Josephus N. Thomas and died on 6
August 1909. A list of six other children who
died young comes from a Bible of Fanny Vaughan
conveyed through Pat Weber. They were Mary
Saphronia (1214b), born 3 June 1852 and died 24
February 1854; Martha Elmira (1214c), born 8
October 1853 and died 22 November 1856; James
Marlin (12145), born 17 May 1855 and died 22
November 1856; Exenia Lavonia (1214d), born 22
February 1857 and died 30 September 1861;
Jackson Harrison (12146), born 2 May 1859
(apparently died the same day); and Ora
Anguilla (12147), born 9 April 1864 and died 3
June 1865. Support for the verity of the
information comes from the Harrison Bible with
birth and death dates for Ora Anguilla, the
death date struck over changing 1865 to 1866.
Henry and Georgia had no children.

The following obituary for Henry Jackson
Vaughan appeared in The Alabama Christian
Advocate of 15 April 1897:

VAUGHAN--Henry Jackson Vaughan, the subject of this notice, was born at Sumter, Sumterville District, South Carolina, June 25, 1819, and died at Loachapoka, Ala., January 22, 1897.

In early life he came to Troupe County, Georgia, and from thence in a few years to Alabama. When only eighteen years old he volunteered and served in the Indian war, for which he was drawing a pension when he died.

In 1841 he was married to Miss Mary A. Harrison; to them were born six children, five of whom are living, and a granddaughter, the representative of a son who preceded him to the grave.

In 1863 he went to the Confederate army and served until the close of the war. During this absence from home his wife died. After the war he was married to Mrs. Georgia A. Phillips, nee Trawick, who still lives. While young he joined the Baptist church.

Brother Vaughan was the sole survivor of a family of four sons and three daughters. All the brothers, except himself, lived over four score years, he lacking only two years of reaching that age; and of the sisters, one lived beyond it.

In many respects Brother Vaughan was an exemplary man. In the conduct and management of his business he displayed superior judgement, and as an evidence of the investment of skill and forethought his entire estate was settled by the heirs without arbiters or legal counsel.

He was a man of sterling integrity, and, perhaps, lacked patience with those whose conduct was not based upon principle. He made no compromise with doubt of uncertainty, nor formed any partnership with policy. His purpose was to know the right and perform it. Industry, energy and frugality were his prominent characteristics. He was punctual to every promise he made to others, and a violation of those made to him made him skeptical as to the sincerity of the obligator.

Estimating friendship as sacred, his was indeed valuable to all who secured it, and enjoyed his confidence.

Outside of the material things bequeathed to his children and his griefstricken wife, he left them a goodly heritage in that "A good name is rather to be chosen than great riches."
GEORGE FONTAINE
Loachapoka, Ala.

HENRY J. VAUGHAN'S
NOTICE OF SETTLEMENT OF ESTATE ACCOUNT

Macon Republican
27 October 1853
3 November 1853

ALABAMA—MACON COUNTY.
Probate Court—Special Term—14th day of
October, 1853.

THIS day came Henry J. Vaughan, guardian of Joseph W. Cummings, a minor, and presented his account current and vouchers for a final settlement of the estate of said minor, which was ordered to be filed, and set for hearing on the 2nd Monday in November next.

And ordered that publication be made in the Macon Republican for three weeks successively, notifying all persons interested to be and appear at a regular term of the Probate court of said county, to be held on the 2nd Monday of November next, and show cause why said account and vouchers should not be allowed.

LEWIS ALEXANDER,
Oct. 20—3w   Judge of Probate.

9 TO 5

Why the sages so fervently express
The virtue of labor I cannot guess,
But it makes my blood boil
When the fruits of my toil
Are confiscated by the I R S.

FILE HEADING FOR HENRY'S BOUNTY LAND APPLICATION

274,616 Act Mar 3 | 55

Oct 5 | 58

Henry J. Vaughan

Private.

Served as Henry Vaughan

Capt James P. Cobb

Cole

Ala. Vols

Florida War 1836

160 acres Oct 16

A. F. Posey Esq.

Greenville

Ala.

FOLLOWING ARE PAPERS RELATING TO HENRY'S
PENSION AND BOUNTY LAND AWARDS

State of Alabama   ) On this 17th day of
County of Macon   ) September A. D. 1858,
before me a Justice of the Peace in and for the
County and State aforesaid, personally came
Henry J. Vaughan, aged 40 years a resident of
the County and State aforesaid, who being duly
sworn according to law, declares that he is the
identical Henry J. Vaughan who was a private in
the company known as the "Tuckabatchie Guards"
commanded by Capt James P. Cobb of Alabama
Volunteers in the War with the Creek Indians in
Ala: That he volunteered at Tuckabatchee Ala,
about 1st May 1836 and continued in actual
service until July 1836 and was honorably
discharged with the said company at
Tuckabatchee, Ala
He makes this declaration for the purpose of
obtaining the bounty land to which he may be
entitled under the act of March 2nd 1855. He
further declares that he has never received any
bounty land under this or any other act of
Congress, nor made any other application
therefor.
He hereby constitutes and appoints A. F.
Posey of Greenville, Butler County. Ala, his
attorney to attend to this claim and to receive
his warrant when issued
                Henry "J" Vaughan

We Allison Scroggins and Joel H. Godwin
residents of Macon Co. Ala, upon our oaths
declare that the foregoing declaration was
signed and acknowledged by Henry J. Vaughan in
our presence and that we know him to be the
person he represents himself to be
                Allison Scroggins
                Joel H. Godwin

The foregoing declaration and affidavit were
sworn to and subscribed before me on this day
and year first-above written; and I certify
that I know the affiants to be credible
persons, that the claimant is the identical
person he represents himself to be and that I
have no interest in his claim.

William E. Winn J. P.

The State of Alabama)   I Lewis Alexander
Macon County   )   Judge of Probate
in and for Said County do hereby Certify that
William E. Winn whose given signature appears
to the above Certificate as justice of the
Peace is and was at the time of signing the
same an acting Justice of the Peace in and for
said County duly qualified and commissioned
according to law and that full faith and credit
is due to all his official acts as such.
    Given under my hand and seal of office this
    21st day of September A. D. 1858
    Lewis Alexander Judge of Probate

FORM LETTER FOR PENSION CLAIM IN NATIONAL
ARCHIVES

INDIAN WARS

Claim of Soldier for Service Pension Under Act
of July 27, 1892.

To be executed before some officer authorized
to administer oaths for general purposes. The
official charter or signature of any such
officer not required by law to use a seal must
be certified by the clerk of the proper court
giving dates of beginning and end of official
term. A full and explicit reply is required to
all questions indicated by this blank.

STATE OF (Alabama))
    County of (Lee))
    On this ( ) day of ( ), A. D. one thousand
eight hundred Ninety-(two), personally appeared
before me, a ( ), for the County and State
aforesaid, (Henry Jackson Vaughan), aged (73)
years, a resident of (Loachapoka, Macon Co) in
the State of (Alabama), who being duly sworn
according to law, states that he is the
identical person who served under the name of
(Henry Jackson Vaughan), as a (private) in the
Company commanded by Capt. (James P. Cobb), in
the (Vols) Regiment of (US Infantry), commanded
by (Capt James P. Cobb), in the (Creek) War;
that he enlisted at (Tuccabatchee, Macon Co) on

or about the (30th) day of (April), A. D.,
18(36), for the term of (two months), and was
honorably discharged at (Tuccabatchee, Macon
Co), on the (last) day of (June), A. D. 18(36);
that he also served in ( ) Co., ( ) Regt., ( )
Vols., from ( ), 18( ); and in ( ) Co., ( )
Regt., ( ) Vols., from ( ), 18( ); to ( ), 18(
); that he has not been employed in the
military or naval service of the United States
otherwise than as stated above.

That at the time of entering the service
claimed for he was (22) years of age, (5) feet
(6) inches in height, with (blue) eyes, (black)
hair, (fair) complexion, by occupation a
(farmer), and that he was born at
(Sumpterville), county of (Sumpter), State of
(South Carolina).

That since leaving the service he has resided
at (Loachapoka Macon Co Ala) years, at ( ), ( )
years, at ( ), ( ) years, at ( ), years, at ().

That he was married to (Mary Ann Harrison) on
the (25th) day of (November), A. D. 18(41), at
(Tuskegee Macon Co Ala); that his said wife is
now (dead), having died on (21st) day of
(July), A. D., 18(64), that he has ( ) since
remarried, and that the number of his claim
being ( ); that he has ( ) heretofore made
application for bounty land, the number of his
land warrant being (forgotten)

That he is a citizen of the United States,
and makes this application for the purpose of
obtaining a pension under the provisions of the
act approved July 27, 1892, and hereby appoints
(Edgar B. McBath), of (Washington District of
Columbia) his true and lawful attorney.

That his post office address is No. ( )
street, (city or town of) (Loachapoka), County
of (Lee), State of (Alabama)
                    (Henry Jackson Vaughan)
                  Signature of claimant in full.

Attest:
(N. A. Vaughan))
(M. E. Vaughan))
    Also personally appeared (James Wooten), aged
(72) years, residing at No. ( ) street, in
(Loachapoka Lee County, Ala), and (William H.
Johnson), aged ( ) years, residing at No. ( )

178

street, in (Loachapoka Lee County Ala), persons
whom I certify to be respectable and entitled
to credit, and who, being by me duly sworn, say
that they have known the said (Henry Jackson
Vaughan) for (30) years and ( ) years,
respectively; that they were present and saw
him sign his name (or make his mark) to the
foregoing declaration; that they have every
reason to believe, and do believe, from the
appearance of said claimant and from their
personal acquaintance with him, that he is the
identical person he represents himself to be;
and they further say that they are fully
satisfied that he is the identical person who
rendered the service alleged in the above
application (in the company of Capt. (James P.
Cobb), in the regiment of ( ), in the (Creek)
War), by the following facts and circumstances,
viz.: (By being personally acquainted with
applicant for quite a number of years and he
has rendered himself a perfect gentleman) and
that they have no interest in this claim. ( )

                                    (James Wooten)
If witnesses sign by   (W. H. Johnson MD)
mark, their signatures   Signatures of
must be attested by   Witnesses
persons who write.

    Sworn to and subscribed before me this (7)
day of (Sept), A. D., 18(92); and I hereby
certify that the contents of the above
declaration, etc., were **fully** **read** **and**
explained to the applicant and witnesses before
swearing, including the words ( ), added, and
the words ( ), erased; and that I have no
interest, direct or indirect, in the
prosecution of this claim.

                          (J. B. Fielder)
(L. S.)   (N. P. & ex off J. P.)
                       Official character.
8811b-5m

The State of Alabama) Office of PROBATE COURT
    Lee County.   )

I, (W. C. Robinson), judge of the Probate Court
in and for said County, and Ex-Officio Clerk
and Keeper of the files of Papers, Records and

Seal thereof, the same being a Court of Record, hereby certify that (J. B. Fielder, N. P. & Ex off. J. P.) whose name is signed to the foregoing (Instrument of writing) as a (Notary P & Ex officio Justice of the Peace) is and was a (bonded officer, as above named) in and for said county, at the date thereof, duly elected, commissioned and qualified as prescribed by law, and fully authorized and empowered, under the Constitution and Laws of the State of Alabama, to administer oaths, take affidavits, and take proofs of deeds and acknowledgements of conveyances; that his signature is genuine, and his acts as such are entitled to full faith and credit. And I further certify that this, my certificate, is in due form of law, and the proper officer.

> Given under my hand and seal of office at Opelika, Lee County, Alabama, this (9th) day of (September), A. D., 18(92).
> (W. C. Robinson)
> Judge of Probate

The State of Alabama)
County of Jefferson) Before me this day personally Mrs. Mary C. Reynolds, aged 54 years and P. O. address Woodlawn, Ala, who being duly sworn says:

I am a sister of Mrs. Georgia Ann Vaughan, of Loachapoka, Ala, and formerly in that section, said sisters maiden name was Trawick when she married in Macon Co. Ala to George W. Phillips and they so live and were living at his death in the confederate Army, which occurred at Corinth, Miss. May 22, 1862, as reported by his brother (now dead) a comrade who returned

said sister remained a widow until Feb. 5, 1867 when again married Henry J. Vaughan, whose widow she now is not having again married.

The said Henry J. Vaughan had a former wife whose maiden name was Mary Ann Harrison, who died 26 July 1864 and his next and last marriage was with Mrs. Georgia Ann Phillips, as above stated.

The facts above stated all occurred in the vicinity where Mrs. G. A. Vaughan now and has

180

lived for many years (except the <u>place</u> of death
of her former husband Phillips,) and is what is
known and accepted in the families and
community without doubt of question; and that
there was no legal bar to the marriage of the
said Henry J. Vaughan & Georgia Ann Phillips.
        I have no interest direct or indirect in
this statement.

                Mary C. Reynolds

Next on file are papers, the identical form as
that completed by Henry J. Vaughan on 7
September 1892, but completed this instance by
his wife shortly after his death in order to
receive a pension in his stead. It varies with
the previous deposition in that she is the
deponent and her description of her husband is
age 19 at entry, five foot three inches tall,
and of light hair. She further stated that he
had lived "at or near Notasulga" about 28 years
after his service and at Loachapoka for 30
years after that. She states that she married
Mr. Vaughan on February 5, 1867 at her home,
Lee Co. and that Rev. Louis Dowdel, a Minister,
presided. She states that her husband had
previously married Mary Ann Harrison on the 1st
day of December A. D. 1841. She states that
her husband died at his home in Loachapoka on
22nd day of January, A. D. 1897. She lists the
claim number of pension as 2337. S. C. and
Gussie Mahone were witnesses.

Also personally appeared (W. Johnson), aged 64
years, residing at No. (Loachapoka) street, in
(Lee Co Ala), and (J. O. Warren), aged (38)
years, residing at No. (Loachapoka) street, in
(Lee Co. Ala), persons whom I certify to be
respectable and entitled to credit, and who,
being by me duly sworn, say that they have
known the said (Georgia A. Vaughan) for (30)
and (25) years, respectively; that they were
present and saw her sign her name (or make her
mark) to the foregoing declaration; that they
have every reason to believe, and do believe
from the appearance of said claimant, and from
their personal acquaintance with her, that she
is the person who was the wife of the identical
(Henry J. Vaughan) who rendered the service

alleged in the above application (in the
company of Capt. (James P. Cobb, in the
regiment of (Volunteers) in the (Creek war), by
the following-named facts and circumstances:
(She has lived near us for 20 or 25 years and
she and Mr Henry Jackson Vaughan lived together
as man & wife for the last 20 or 30 years) and
that they have no interest in the prosecution
of this claim.

(W. H. Johnson)
(J. O. Warren)
Signatures of Witnesses.

Sworn and subscribed to before me this (15) day
of (February), A. D. 18(97); and I hereby
certify that the contents of the above
declaration, etc., were read and explained to
the applicant and witnesses before swearing,
including the words ( ), added, and the words (
), erased; and that I have no interest, direct
or indirect, in the prosecution of this claim.

(J. B. Fielder)
(L.S.)   (N. P. & Ex off J. P.)
                Official character.
8812 b--5 m

The above document is filed in the appendix.
There is also what appears to be a ledger of
claims, notarized by an R. DuPont Thompson that
has the notation "Indian War, No. 7025, Georgia
A. Vaughan, wid. Henry J. Vaughan Capt Cobbs Co
Ala Vols., Creek War 1836" on it; also "Filed
by A. F. Posey, atty, Greenville, Ala"

A Drop Report states that Georgia Ann Vaughan
was dropped July 17, 1930 due to death June
24/30. Finally there is a receipt roll for
clothing issued by Co F, Ala Regt of Apr 30
1864 and a register of St. Mary's Hospital, La
Grange, Ga. stating Henry was transferred to
Notasulga on June 26, 1864.
From Mrs. Fitzpatrick, I received a document
concerning a transfer of membership of Henry J.
and his wife from the Baptist Church. A
transcription of its contents are as follows:

State of Alabama) The Baptist Church of Christ
Macon County   ) at Pine Level do hereby

182

certify that our beloved Brother Henry J.
Vaughan and his wife Sister Mary Vaughan are
members with us in full fellowship and are
hereby dismissed from us when joined to an
other Church of the same faith and order Done
by order of the Church in conference
December 13th 1857   Pat Cadenhead
                               Prod pro tem:
Charles A. Stanton--Clerk

THE HARRISON-PARMER HERITAGE

Mary Anne Harrison was the daughter of King
William and Rebecca (Parmer) Harrison.
Parmer seems to have evolved from Palmer of
earlier generations.   Rebecca married Mr.
Harrison in 1825.   Brothers of Mary, the
oldest child, were James A., born 10 December
1827 and died 17 September 1844; Jonathan,
born on 25 August 1829, married Eliza ____
and died 11 December 1854; Josiah, born 9
June 1832, married 9 September 1858 to Julia
A. Parmer, F. M. T. Tankersley performing
(Julia seems to have been from the old
Virginia line of Parmers); Jackson, born 6
October 1834, married 22 March 1855, Mr.
Welch performing, Susan H. Murrell (born 6
January 1839 and died 24 August 1907) and
died 15 August 1908; and King W., born on 17
April 1837 and died 12 May 1870.

King William, Sr. was the son of George
Harrison, born about 1762.   George was
probably born in North Carolina, lived in
South Carolina between 1790 and 1804, Georgia
from 1805 to 1818 and came to Alabama by
oxcart in that year.   His wife appears in
some places as Rachel, some places as Katie
Hammond.   From Rachel's age in a family
Bible, she would have been too young to have
had a child in 1789, the year George's oldest
child was born. He may have been married to
one, then the other.   King William was born
on 17 September 1807 and died on 27 January
1837, before his last child was born.
Rebecca Parmer was the daughter of Josiah and

Mary Parmer and born on 9 January 1807.
After the death of King William she married
secondly Reuben Segrest. Rebecca died on 29
December 1844.

Josiah Parmer was the third child of Thomas
and Phoebe Palmer, there being thirteen
children in all. He was born on 27 September
1787, married firstly Mary Moseley and
secondly, on 20 April 1846, Eliza Tankersley,
and died 1 August 1869. Mary was born on 11
September 1788 and is thought to have died on
13 October 1845; Eliza was born on 5 February
1809 (or 1805--Bible unclear) and thought to
have died 23 March 1864. Eliza Tankersley's
parents were Robert D. and Margaret (Peggy)
(Vann) Moseley. Margaret died on 10 October
1849. She and Robert had married about 1782.

Thomas Palmer was the son of Reuben Palmer by
the latter's first wife. His birth date is
unknown, but he died on 18 November 1826 in
Montgomery, Alabama. He married Phoebe
Westbrook, daughter of Amos Westbrook, the
latter born about 1737 in Ireland.

Little is known of Reuben Palmer. He was one
of three sons born to Robert and Prudence
(Jeffrey) Palmer between 1705 and 1711.
Reuben was married twice but the name of
neither wife is known. By his first wife he
had two sons and possibly a daughter; by his
second wife he had five children and possibly
the daughter above whose mother is uncertain.
This daughter married Amos Westbrook, who may
have been the father-in-law of her brother
Thomas (and another brother William) or a son
of that father-in-law.

Robert Palmer married Prudence Jeffrey, who
died between 1714 and 1718. Robert died on
12 March 1732 and 2 July 1733 (probably the
same will with dates of writing and
recording). After Prudence died he married
secondly Martha _____.

Prudence Jeffrey was the daughter of Edward Jeffrey of N. Farnham Parish, Richmond County, Virginia. His will is recorded in 1709-1717 Book, pages 190-1, probated on 7 July 1714.

A more comprehensive treatment of these lines is not possible in this work, but much more information is available on both parallel and downlines of each generation of this lineage. My source has been for the most part Verna Fitzpatrick. Anyone interested on more information may, however, contact this writer.

WILLIAM MILES VAUGHAN (12141)

William Miles, first child of Henry Jackson and
Mary Anne Vaughan, was born on 31 October 1842
in Macon County, Alabama. According to
Chambers County Marriage Records (Volume 6), he
married Mary Elizabeth Walton on 16 October
1866, J. F. Bledsoe officiating. Mary, usually
called Molly, was born in Meriwether County,
Georgia on 23 August 1845, daughter of James
Foy and Margaret A. Walton. According to their
headstones in the New Harmony Cemetery James
was born on 13 February 1824 and died 12 March
1892; Margaret, born 25 March 1826, died on 22
September 1887.

William Miles enlisted in the Confederate Army
on 22 January 1863 for a three year period. He
served as a private in Company K, 1st Regiment
Alabama Volunteers. Extracts of his service
records follow this narrative. A sketch of his
tour shows him present at a unit muster for
November 1863, having been captured on 9 July
1863 at Port Hudson, Louisiana, but paroled
within three or four days. After 1 December he
was detailed to the Selma Arsenal, subsequent
to his request of 24 November for release from
assignments requiring rigorous activity. In
his request he stated he suffered vertigo when
overheated due to a blow to the head when
kicked by a horse during his youth. Through 16
April he remained at the Selma Arsenal while
the regiment was dispatched to Fort Gaines. On
12 February 1865 he was admitted to Way
Hospital in Meridian and on 23 February was
detailed to the Surgical Center.

In an account of Company K, entitled My Three
Years in the Confederate Service, Lt. Daniel P.
Smith states (pages 46 and 47): "On December
26th [1862] Lieutenant Tuttle and Corporal John
Hearn left for Alabama to secure recruits for
Company K. They returned in February having
secured 45, as follows . . . Wm. Vaughan,
Lowndes Co. . . ." From page 86 of 12 October
1863: "Of Co. K, according to such imperfect

information as the writer has at his command, the following men reported at Capersville, or soon thereafter at Meridian, Miss. . . . Wm. Vaughan . . . " There may be an error in the residency of William Miles in this account, but the dates seem accurate and Miles may have been residing with relatives of his mother, known to have lived in Lowndes County.

In the 1907 Lee County Confederate Soldier Census William Miles states he enlisted as a private in July of 1861 at Notasulga in Co. G of 1st Alabama Cavalry, remaining with them until June 1862, when discharged at Tupelo, Mississippi due to sickness. He states he reenlisted at Montgomery in February 1863 in Co. K. This fits very well with Smith's account and it appears Miles was recuperating in Lowndes County, which he considered to be Montgomery because of its proximity. William Miles adds he was captured at Selma by Wilson's Raiders and kept in prison until the end of the war and that his birthplace was Chehaw.

After the war Miles lived in Waverly, Alabama until about 1910. The 1900 Lee County census lists William Miles in the Gold Hill precinct. In 1910 he moved to Opelika, where he lived at 19 Clanton Street in a house he later bought from his son. The 1910 Lee County census lists William Miles in household #14 of the Roxana Beat, near his daughter Annie C. Mayberry. Apparently the census was taken before they moved to Opelika. Also in Miles' household were his wife, his son Hosea, Hosea's wife, Eva M., their one-year-old son, Hosea, Jr. and a boarding merchant, Wilson A. Dent, age 45. William Miles died on 26 September 1918 and his wife on 11 July 1928; they are buried in Rosemere Cemetery in Opelika. Miles' death certificate is copied on the following page.

William Miles and Molly Vaughan had six children: Mary Lillian (12141a), born on 20 August 1867, married to James M. Gardner and died on 5 August 1885; Ida Lavonia (12141b), born on 10 March 1869, married Phil H. Greene and died 18 September 1899; Annie Cora

(12141c), born on 15 July 1871, married W. H. (Bud) Mayberry and died in 1923; Walton Henry (121411), born on 12 January 1874, married firstly Lena Mae Jones, secondly Fannie V. Price and died on 27 October 1955; Willie Miles (12141d), born on 27 September 1880, married Phil H. Greene and died 16 April 1968; and Hosea Frederick (121412), born on 18 September 1887, married Eva Mae Wright and died 13 June 1953.

The following obituary appeared in the Opelika Daily News of 26 September 1918:

VETERAN DEAD

William M. Vaughan Died at Age of 75 Years Early Today at Home in This City

William Miles Vaughan, aged 75 years, well known Confederate veteran, died this morning at 3:20 o'clock at his home, No. 19 Clanton Street, after an illness of two years, with paralysis.

The deceased was born in Macon County on October 31, 1842, and had lived in this city the past eight years, moving from Waverly.

Mr. Vaughan was formerly engaged in farming until late years.

On October 16, 1866, he married Miss Mary E. Walton, of near Waverly.

He is survived by his wife and two sons and two daughters. The children are W. H. Vaughan and H. F. Vaughan of this city, Mrs. W. H. Mayberry of Waverly and Mrs. M. V. Green of Birmingham. Two brothers survive, who are H. K. Vaughan of Hurtsboro and G. L. Vaughan of Betty, Texas. Seventeen grandchildren, three great-grandchildren and a number of other relatives survive this well known veteran.

Funeral service will be held from the home on Clanton street at 10:00 o'clock Friday morning, Dr. Rush officiating, the deceased being a member of Trinity church. Interment will be at Rosemere cemetery. Pallbearers will be L. F. Dickson, J. M. Holloway, W. J. Ware,

W. F. Harrison, R. C. Spratling and R. Z. Tatum.

The death certificate of H. K. Vaughan proves he died on 24 June 1917 and the statement of this brother surviving William M. is incorrect. See article on H. K. Vaughan.

SOME COMMON NICKNAMES

MARY ANN(E)	MOLLY OR MOLLIE
MARY ELIZABETH	POLLY, MOLLY OR MOLLIE
MARGARET	PEGGY OR MEG
LETTETIA	LETTIE OR LETTICE
ANTOINETTE	NETTIE
HENRY	HAL OR HARRY
HAROLD	HAL OR HARRY
JAMES	JIM OR JIMMY
JOHN	JOHNNY OR JACK
WILLIAM	WILL, WILLIE, BILL OR BILLY

WILLIAM MILES' DEATH CERTIFICATE

I, Dorothy S. Harshbarger, State Registrar of Health Statistics, certify this is a true and exact copy of the original certificate filed in the Center for Health Statistics, State of Alabama, Department of Public Health, Montgomery, Alabama, and have caused the official seal of the Center for Health Statistics to be affixed.

Dorothy S. Harshbarger

Dorothy S. Harshbarger, State Registrar

JUNE 19, 1992   Claude Earl Fox, M.D., M.P.H., State Health Officer

---

CERTIFICATE OF DEATH
STATE OF ALABAMA—BUREAU OF VITAL STATISTICS
STATE BOARD OF HEALTH

File No. for State Registrar Only.

203

1 PLACE OF DEATH
County _____
Town or City of _Opelika_   No. ____   St. _____   Ward ____

(If death occurred in a hospital or institution, give its NAME instead of street and number)

2 FULL NAME _W. M. Vaughn_

(a) Residence. No. _____   St., ____   Ward ____

(Usual place of abode)   (If nonresident, give city or town and State)

Length of residence in city or town where death occurred   yrs.   mos.   ds.   How long in U. S., if of foreign birth?   yrs.   mos.   ds.

PERSONAL AND STATISTICAL PARTICULARS	MEDICAL CERTIFICATE OF DEATH
3 SEX M **4 COLOR OR RACE** W **5 SINGLE, MARRIED, WIDOWED, OR DIVORCED** (Write the word)	**16 DATE OF DEATH** (month, day, and year) _Sept 26_ 19 _8_
5a If married, widowed, or divorced HUSBAND of (or) WIFE of	**17** I HEREBY CERTIFY, That I attended deceased from ____ 19 ____ to ____ 19 ____ that I last saw h____ alive on ____ 19 ____ and that death occurred, on the date stated above, at ____ The CAUSE OF DEATH was as follows: _Paralysis_
6 DATE OF BIRTH (month, day, and year)	
7 AGE Years Months Days If LESS than ____ hrs. or ____ min.	(duration) yrs. mos. ds.
8 OCCUPATION OF DECEASED (a) Trade, profession, or particular kind of work (b) General nature of industry, business, or establishment in which employed (or employer) (c) Name of employer	CONTRIBUTORY (Secondary) (duration) yrs. mos. ds.
9 BIRTHPLACE (city or town) (State or country)	**18** Where was disease contracted if not at place of death? Did an operation precede death? Date of ____ Was there an autopsy? What test confirmed diagnosis? (Signed) ____ M. D. ____ 19 ____ (Address)
10 NAME OF FATHER	
11 BIRTHPLACE OF FATHER (city or town) (State or country)	
12 MAIDEN NAME OF MOTHER	**19** State the DISEASE CAUSING DEATH, or in death from VIOLENT CAUSES, state (1) MEANS AND NATURE OF INJURY, and (2) whether ACCIDENTAL, SUICIDAL, or HOMICIDAL. (See reverse side for additional information.)
13 BIRTHPLACE OF MOTHER (city or town) (State or country)	
14 ____ Informant (Address)	**19 PLACE OF BURIAL, CREMATION, or REMOVAL DATE OF BURIAL** ____ 19 ____
15 Filed _Oct 1_ 19 _8_ Registrar	**20 UNDERTAKER** _Jas. T. Frederick_ **ADDRESS** _Opelika_

PHOTOGRAPH OF WILLIAM MILES VAUGHAN

OFFICIAL PAPERS CONCERNING WILLIAM MILES'
REQUEST FOR REASSIGNMENT TO NON-FIELD SERVICE
(TRANSCRIBED)

                 Camp 1st Ala Regt near Meridian Miss
                        Nov 24th 1863
Col--
       I have the honor respectfully to request a
discharge from active field service for the
following reason--Eight years ago I received a
blow on my head which carried away a portion of
my skull--and every time I heated by over-
exercise I am greatly troubled by vertigo or
dizziness in my head, so much so as to
incapacitate me from active duty.
During the siege of Port Hudson La I was very
much affected by the heat & constant exposure
to the sun, so that I was seldom fit for duty.
I do not desire a full discharge from the army,
but merely one from active service.
                 I am Col very respectfully
To   Your Obt. Servt
   Col Benj S. Ewell   W. M. Vaughan
   N. A. Genl. Private Co. "K" 1st Ala Regt.

Private Wm. M. Vaughan having applied for a
certificate on which to ground an application
on which to ground an application (sic) for
relief from field duty, I certify that I have
carefully examined this private and find him
incapable of doing active field duty because of
an injury received in his head, causing a
considerable loss of bone thereby producing
vertigo and great suffering when exposed to the
sun or taking active exercise--I therefore
respectfully recommend that he be assigned to
duty that does not require exposure or
excitement.
                        J. H. Hamilton
                        Surgeon 1st Ala

MARY LILLIAN VAUGHAN (12141a)

Mary Lillian, known as Lillie, was born on 20 August 1867. On 11 December 1884 she married James M. Gardner, J. F. Bledsoe officiating (Chambers County Marriage Records, Book 8, page 304b). Mary and her husband, son of W. V. and M. E. Gardner, were married at the residence of her father. The Gardners were originally from Georgia, but removed to the Dadeville, Alabama area. Mary died in childbirth on 5 August 1885. She is buried at Midway Methodist Church, 8 miles northwest of Oak Bowery, Alabama.

193

IDA LAVONIA VAUGHAN (12141b)

Ida Lavonia was born on 10 March 1869. She married Phil H. Greene. Ida died on 18 September 1899 and is buried at New Harmony Presbyterian Church next to her son Vivian Daniel. Phil and Ida had five children: Lynn Edwin (12141b1), born 21 June 1891 and died 3 March 1962; Vivian Daniel (12141b2), born on 6 August 1893 and died 22 October 1896; Philip I. (12141b3), Mary (12141ba); and Milie Alice (12141bb), known also as Baby, who married Phillip Mitchell, and had one son, Phillip, Jr. (12141bb1).

Besides Ida and Vivian, the oldest child, Lynn E. Greene, is buried at New Harmony. The writer had the occasion to meet Mr. Greene a few times when both visited Eva Mae Vaughan, his aunt and the writer's grandmother. Phil Greene is buried in Rosemere Cemetery in Opelika near his wife's parents' graves, rather than the New Harmony Cemetery. Mr. Greene's parents and what would appear to be a brother and sister are buried at New Harmony. Phillip H. Greene was born on 22 February 1865 and died on 17 October 1913. He was the son of William Alston and Elizabeth C. (Daniel) Greene of Georgia. William A. Greene was born on 29 June 1821 and died on 29 October 1905; his wife Elizabeth was born 15 March 1827 and died on 29 March 1890.

After Ida's death Phillip Greene married her younger sister Willie Miles.

Some Greenes and relatives buried in the New Harmony Presbyterian Church Cemetery (5 miles NE of Waverly):
--Ida L. Greene, 03/10/1869-09/18/1899, wife of P. H. Greene
--Vivian Daniel, 08/06/1893-10/22/1896, son of P. H. and Ida
--Leon [Lynn] Edwin Greene, 06/21/1891-03/03/1962
--Thomas W. Greene, 1860-1890

194

--Mary Elizabeth Greene Campbell, 05/10/1844-
01/14/1914
--John B. Campbell, born 11/18/1823 in
Chesterfield Co., S. C. and died in Auburn
06/29/1879 (husband of above?)

ANNIE CORA VAUGHAN (12141c)

Annie Cora was born on 15 July 1871. She married William Harris (Bud) Mayberry, one-time mayor of Waverly. J. H. Lockhart presided on 9 February 1890 at the ceremony. Mr. Mayberry was born in 1868 (in Illinois according to the 1900 Lee County census which may be in error), son of Charles W. and Lucy J. (Cooper) Mayberry. The 1910 census shows Annie and Bud living between her parents and his.

Annie Cora had six children by Mr. Mayberry: a daughter of unknown name (12141ca); Exo Myrtle (12141cb), born about 1893, who married a Mr. Ward; Mary Willie (12141cc), born on 5 November 1894 and died 28 April 1896; Homer Sanford (12141c1), born on 27 December 1896 and died 23 January 1897; Washington Myles (12141c2), born on 21 February 1898 and died 13 October 1956; and Annie L. (12141cd), born about 1905. The unknown daughter is assumed to have been the oldest, because, according to the 1910 census, she is known to have been still alive, but not at home, so that it is likely she was married.

Annie Cora died in 1923 and Bud in 1940. They are both buried in the Waverly Cemetery.

MAYBERRYS GROW IN WAVERLY

Charles Washington and Lucy J. (Cooper) Mayberry came to Waverly in the latter half of the 1800's. Although the 1910 Lee County census says Charles' parents were from North Carolina and Tennessee, this is incorrect. The 1900 census correctly lists Illinois as Charles' birthplace. The 1910 census says Lucy and her parents were from Georgia. In the 1907 Lee County Confederate Soldier Census Charles says he was born in Illinois and enlisted in February 1864 as a private in McDonald's Company of the Home Guards, serving until the close of the war at Notasulga. Charles and Lucy had thirteen children, of whom eight still lived at the

time of the 1910 census.

Charles' father was James Washington Mayberry, born in 1790 in Birmingham, England, who came to America about 1805. Charles' mother's name is unknown to the writer, but she was born in France. James W. Mayberry died on 18 March 1872 and is buried among the Mayberrys in the Waverly Cemetery.

A list of Mayberrys buried in the Waverly Cemetery follows:
--James Washington Mayberry, 1790-1872
--Annie A. Green, born in 1862 at Menefee Home in Gold Hill and died on second Sunday in May, 1888, wife of James Washington Mayberry [This writer does not know the meaning of the statement, perhaps there was another James Washington Mayberry, brother to Bud or Charles W.]
--Charles W. Mayberry, 06/08/1827-12/05/1910
--Lucy J. Mayberry, 03/04/1832-04/10/1912
--James (Tuck) Mayberry 07/04/1854-10/25/1940 [See Annie A. above.]
--Jack Mayberry, 12/22/1858, at Oak Bowery-06/01/1860 at Waverly
--Jack's twin sister, 12/22/1858, stone at Waverly, buried at Oak Bowery
--Charles Mayberry, 02/28/1862-06\23/1950
--Carrie P. Mayberry, 10/19/1858-02/18/1932
--Charles B. Mayberry, 08/23/1892-05/14/1957 Alabama, S2 USNRF, WWI
--Alva H. Mayberry, 02/15/1934-??
--Guy W. Mayberry, 06/14/1902-09/11/1938
--Susan Mayberry, 02/26/1864-06/05/1865
--Frances Isabella Mayberry Hoffman, 05/30/1866 in Waverly 01/25/1928 in Columbus, Georgia, wife of Walter Henry Hoffman
--Infant son, 07/04/1886-07/04/1886, and infant daughter, 08/05/1890-11/01/1890 of above
--William H. Mayberry, 1868-1940
--Annie Cora Vaughan Mayberry, 1871-1923
--Mary Willie Mayberry, 11/05/1884 [1894]-04/28/1896
--Homer Sanford Mayberry, 12/27/1896-08/02/1897
--Washington Myles Mayberry, 02/21/1898-

```
                              10/13/1956
--Vermelle    Hill    Mayberry,   10/03/1900-
                              05/29/1973
```
--Ruby Hall Mayberry, 08/12/1909-10/30/1968
--Henry Upton Mayberry, 09/03/1872-01/01/0917
--Lucy Ruth Mayberry, daughter of Henry U.
Mayberry and Susan H. Shoffeitt, 01/22/1909-
                              11/30/1926
--   Lucy Mayberry Allen, 1876-1951
--   Omer P. Mayberry, 1887-1961
--   Maggie W. Mayberry, 1890-1981

Also buried in the New Harmony Presbyterian
Cemetery, 5 miles NE of Waverly (of which as
  of 05/01/1980 Maxie Mayberry was a deacon):
--John Millard Mayberry (Father), 08/19/1887-
                              08/14/1959
--Mrs. Mary Mayberry [Mother?], 02/27/1885- -
--Walter Mayberry (Son),   04/19/1905-
                              06/08/1957

Buried in the Brown Cemetery at Auburn:
--Nancy Henrietta Mayberry,   11/10/1868-
         12/20/1939, wife of J. T. Martin
--   J. T. Martin, no dates
--Susan   Murphy   Mayberry,   07/28/1829-
         11/30/1902, wife of James Mayberry

Notes: Other records show that Charles
Mayberry and Carrie T. (Patrick) Mayberry
were married on 23 December 1882 in
Tallapoosa County, Alabama, Jon S. Holt
performing (Tallapoosa County Marriage
Records, Book 9, page 226a).   The Susan
Murphy Mayberry buried in Brown Cemetery was
the wife of James Washington Mayberry
(probably a second wife). Two of their known
children were James Monroe Mayberry, born on
25 November 1864 in Opelika, and Nancy
Henrietta Mayberry, born on 10 November 1868,
also in Opelika. James Monroe married Willie
Oscar Brown. Two of their children, born in
Opelika, were Carrie Mayberry, born on 18 May
1913 and Thomas Heflin Mayberry, born on 21
January 1921. Nancy Henrietta married J. T.
Martin, as above indicated.

WALTON HENRY VAUGHAN (121411)

Walton Henry was born on 12 January 1874, the first son of William Miles and Molly Vaughan. On 30 April 1899 he married Lena Mae Jones at the home of C. P. D. Taylor, a business associate. Lena was born on 19 June 1876. She was the daughter of John A. Jones of Chambers County and a niece of Mr. Taylor. The John Allen Jones listed on Beat 2, Opelika, in the 1910 Lee County census was probably Lena's brother, there being several generations of John Allen Joneses.

Walton was a businessman and grocer in the Opelika area from the turn of the century until his death on 27 October 1955. He also dealt extensively in stocks and conducted many land transactions. His business associate, Charles P. D. Taylor, appears in the 1907 Lee County Confederate Soldier Census. He states he was born 15 June 1840 in Early Co., Ga., enlisted as a private in Co. B, 23rd Alabama Infantry on 13 September 1861 at Montgomery and served until captured at Union Springs on 7 June 1865, where he was paroled. The 1910 Lee County census lists Walton as a policeman.

Walton and Lena had four sons: Edgar D. (1214111), born about 1900; Herbert Walton (1214112), born about 1902, married Susie Love Jones and died 15 December 1970; Bernard Wilton (1214113), born 7 February 1906, married to Frances Whatley and died 11 May 1962; and Otis H. (1214114), born about 1909 and married Katharine M. _____.

Lena died on 28 August 1945 and Walton married on 7 January 1952 Fannie Vaughan Price, his first cousin and daughter of Henry K. Vaughan.

Walton and his first wife are buried in Rosemere Cemetery in Opelika, near the graves of William Miles and Molly Vaughan, Walton's son Bernard, and brother-in-law, Phil H. Greene.

The 1910 Lee County census is the source of the approximate birth dates for all the sons except Bernard.

EDGAR D. VAUGHAN (1214111)

Edgar was the first of four sons of Walton H. and Lena Vaughan. He was born about 1900. He lived for many years in Birmingham, Alabama. Although this writer does not know the name of Edgar's wife, marriage records show that an Edgar D. Vaughan married on 26 October 1932 Bessie Howard.

HERBERT WALTON VAUGHAN (1214112)

Herbert Walton married Susie Love Jones. Herbert lived in Opelika and was a grocer. At times he was also a farmer and owner of a flower shop and a clothing store. Herbert was a member of the Kiwanis Club. He died on 15 December 1970.

Herbert and Susie had three children: Marylyn (1214112a), who married Mr. Moore; Herbert Walton, Jr. (12141121), born on 7 February 1933; and Susie Love (1214112b).

BERNARD WILTON VAUGHAN (1214113)

Bernard Wilton was born on 7 February 1906. He
married Frances Whatley. Bernard died on 11
May 1962 and is buried in Rosemere Cemetery in
Opelika near his father. Bernard and Frances
had six children: Mary Elizabeth (1214113a);
Frances Virginia (1214113b), born on 20 August
1936 and married to Robert James Yarbrough, son
of Marcus J. and Mary Shepard Yarbrough, on 4
June 1954; William Walton (12141131), born in
1945; Michael Christian (12141132), born in
1949; Sarah Lynn (1214113c), and Bernard
Wilton, Jr. (12141133).

OTIS H. VAUGHAN (1214114)

Otis was the last child of Walton H. and Lena Vaughan. He was born about 1909. Otis married Katharine _____. He lived for many years in Marietta, Georgia.

WILLIE MILES VAUGHAN (12141d)

Willie Miles, known as Milie, was born on 27 September 1880. On 3 January 1900 she married Phil H. Greene, formerly the husband of her sister Ida. Milie resided for many years at 3202 Norwood Blvd. in Birmingham, Alabama, before her death on 16 April 1968. She is buried in Elmwood Cemetery in that city.

By Mr. Greene Milie had one child. Her daughter Frances (12141da) was born in January of 1901. She married Walter Anderson, a Spanish-American War veteran. After her husband's death Frances lived with her mother until the latter's death.

HOSEA FREDERICK VAUGHAN (121412)

Hosea Frederick was born on 18 September 1887 on his parents' farm near Waverly. On 21 November 1907 Hosea married Eva Mae Wright, daughter of Charles Leonidas and Octavia (Christian) Wright of the Armstrong Church Community. Eva's maternal grandfather was John Humphrey Christian of Randolph County, Alabama, who served as a captain in the Confederate Army. He was a prisoner of war at Johnston Island at the close of the conflict.

By profession Hosea was a farmer, but he also served a term as Deputy Sheriff of Lee County. In the second decade of the present century he lived with his father on Clanton Street in Opelika. He purchased the home from his father in 1917. After William's death in 1918 Hosea and Eva continued to live there until the house burned. After that they sold the lot to Brady Uldric and moved to the home on Society Hill Road, where Mrs. Vaughan lived until her death on 18 February 1989.

Children of Hosea and Eva were Hosea Frederick, Jr. (1214121), born on 30 August 1908 and died on 7 February 1911; Miles Leonidas (1214122), born 5 December 1911 and married on 1 November 1941 to Edith Lorene Baker; Edna Earle (121412a), born on 10 March 1914, married on 28 July 1939 to James Joseph Cagle and died in 1976; Mary Elizabeth (121412b), born on 20 January 1916, married firstly to Raymond C. Millican and later to Ed Untreiner and died in July of 1982; Eva Wright (121412c), born on 31 May 1918, married to William Herman Woods on 7 June 1936 and later to Nolan Garner, Olin G. Hinkle and Frank Vinson; Homer Frederick (1214123), born on 30 August 1922; James Douglas (1214124), born on 5 January 1925 and married on 25 January 1948 to Bette Ann Moore; and Barbara Ellen (121412d), stillborn on 13 July 1934.

PHOTOGRAPH OF HOSEA FREDERICK VAUGHAN

HOSEA FREDERICK VAUGHAN, JR. (1214121)

Hosea Frederick, Jr. was born on 30 August 1908 in Waverly. He is listed in the 1910 Lee County census in the household with his father and grandfather. On 7 February 1911 Hosea Frederick, Jr. died from an illness. He was buried originally in Waverly, but was later removed to Rosemere Cemetery in Opelika to rest in the plot with his father.

MILES LEONIDAS VAUGHAN (1214122)

Miles Leonidas was the second son of Hosea and
Eva Vaughan. He was born on 5 December 1911 at
Gold Hill. During the depression and while
quite young, he quit school to help the family
survive those difficult years. In a few years
he returned to school and on 18 May 1934 took
his diploma from Beauregard School. After
graduation Miles went into the employ of the
Alabama State Highway Department. He moved to
Montgomery in 1941. He and Edith Lorene Baker,
both lived at the boardinghouse at 524
Washington Avenue, when he received his draft
notice in March of 1941. On 1 November of that
year he married Miss Baker, his high school
sweetheart and daughter of Albert B. and
Freddie Baker.

In the army Miles served as a private in the
9th Armored Replacement Battalion, Company A,
from 23 May 1941 to 29 September 1941. He was
trained for Filler Replacement for Armored
Force. On 13 September 1941 at Ft. Knox,
Kentucky, he was promoted to Lance Corporal.
On 29 September 1941 he was transferred to
Enlisted Reserve Corps. Miles returned to his
civilian address of 99 Auburn Avenue in
Opelika. He resumed employ with the State
Highway Department, but on 30 January 1942 was
recalled to active duty with Company B of the
748th Tank Battalion as a Technician 5th Grade.
On 26 August 1942 he was promoted to Technician
4th Grade at Camp Rucker, Alabama.
Subsequently Miles was promoted to Sergeant and
in the European Theater served in Company D of
the 47th Tank Battalion. In this capacity he
became a tank commander, section leader and
acting platoon leader. As such Miles
supervised and was responsible for 5 tanks and
25 men. Miles served in the Battles of the
Rhineland and Northern France, designated as GO
40 WD 45 and GO 46 WD 45, respectively. He
departed for the European Theater on 31 March
1944, arriving 6 April 1944, and made the
return departure on 7 September 1945, arriving
at Ft. McPherson, Georgia on 16 September 1945.

Miles was separated there on 22 September and arrived in Opelika on 24 September. Miles' service number was 34104164. After separation Miles was in the Enlisted Reserves until 21 September 1948, when he received his honorable discharge.

After Miles' return from the service Mr. and Mrs. Vaughan lived for a time at Opelika, R. F. D. 2, but in 1946 moved to Montgomery, living at 1150 Norman Bridge Road (changed to 3928 Norman Bridge at last note) until 1950. The rest of his life Miles lived at 4602 Cleveland Avenue.

When first employed by the state, Miles worked in a machine shop, operating a lathe and doing general machine shop work. He also repaired highway testing equipment and for a few months drove a diesel tractor. Soon he went to work in the asphalt testing laboratory. For years he travelled the state collecting asphalt samples from road construction sites. He tested these and turned reports in to the office in Montgomery. Eventually Miles became head of the bituminous department located in Montgomery. In his professional capacity Miles was a member of the American Association of Asphalt Paving Technologists and the American Association of State Highway & Transportation Officials. One of his projects that Miles was most proud of was his part in designing the asphalt specifications for the Talladega International Speedway. In 1978, after 39 years in its employ, Miles retired from the State.

Miles was a member and past commander of Arthur W. Ansley VFW Post #4176. He was a member of Woodmen of the World. Miles was a member of St. James Methodist Church in Montgomery. He was an avid hunter and fisherman. Miles died on 9 November 1985 from pulmonary failure. He was a victim of emphysema. As a child Miles suffered a severe case of pneumonia and was subject to asthma and bronchitis most of his life. His lung problems seemed to stay with

him as he worked with the asphalt and its harsh chemicals.

Miles and Edith had three children: Miles Leonidas, Jr. (12141221), born 22 July 1942 and married to June Rawlinson; William Terry (12141222), born 5 July 1944 and married to Marion Hendley, nee Hazelwood; and Robert Earl (12141223), born on 28 May 1949, married firstly to Linda Harrod and secondly to Sherry Lambert.

OF BAKERS AND WRIGHTS,
BUT NOT BUTCHERS OR CANDLESTICK MAKERS

Miles and Edith had a common ancestor in the fourth generation of their ancestry on the Wright line. A common ancestry was just that in the days before the nation's population became so mobile.

Miles' mother was Eva (Wright) Vaughan, daughter of Charles Leonidas and Octavia (Christian) Wright. Eva was born on 6 July 1889 and died on 18 February 1989, thus lacking a few months of reaching the century mark in age. She was a remarkable woman, who could still recount many episodes of her childhood well into her nineties. The Wrights lived on the Wire Road (so called because in the olden days the telegraph line ran along this route) near Armstrong Church. A road from Vaughan's (Lower) Mill intersects the Wire Road there and it is this road that Miles Edwin Vaughan used when he rode into Loachapoka and of which Eva said he sat like an arrow upon his white steed. Eva had a brother and three sisters.

Charles Leonidas Wright was born on 27 May 1858, the son of Charles and Amanda (Culbreath) Wright. Some sources say the elder Charles had an initial of C., but Eva said he had no middle initial. Charles Leonidas married about 1886 Octavia Grimes Christian, daughter of John Humphrey Christian, previously mentioned in this

volume, and his wife Sarah (Grimes) Christian. Charles died on 7 February 1931 and is buried in the Armstrong Church Cemetery. Octavia was born on 30 July 1866 and died on 29 April 1917. Charles Wright was born in 1821, married Amanda Eunice Culbreath and died on 17 June 1864 as a casualty of the Civil War and is buried in Virginia. Amanda was born on 17 December 1829 and died on 23 November 1872. John Humphrey Christian was born on 31 January 1830. His wife Sarah Stokes Grimes was born in 1847. She had two sisters and four brothers. One of these brothers, John (1843-1862) was brought home after he took ill in Virginia during the War between the States by his captain, Mr. Christian. Sarah met her future husband at this time. John Grimes did not survive his sickness and was the first person buried in the Armstrong Cemetery. John Christian died on 25 November 1914 and Sarah in 1927. Charles Wright was the son of Samuel B. and Elizabeth (Wilmot) Wright. Samuel Wright and Elizabeth Wilmot were both born in 1797. Elizabeth died in 1866 and Samuel in 1887. Amanda Culbreath was the daughter of Thomas Culbreath and his wife Eunice _____, who died in 1851. Sarah Grimes was the daughter of Henry H. Grimes, born on 31 March 1802 and died on 10 January 1872, and Sarah Stokes or Crawley, born in 1818 and died in 1871. Since I have found Sophia with both last names, she may have been married twice. Samuel B. Wright's father was named Charles and the latter had a sister named Dorcas, who married William Matthews. This generation of Wrights was from Georgia, but, other than what I have here said, to the writer the Wrights fade into the clouds of the past.

Albert Brewer Baker was born on 25 December 1882, son of Julius Richmond and Frances (Zuber) Baker. In 1907 he married Freddie Wright and he died on 5 June 1971. Freddie Wright was born on 9 October 1886 and died on 29 March 1971. Both are buried in the Loachapoka Cemetery. Julius Richmond Baker

was born on 4 May 1857, son of John J. and
Julia (Gilmore) Baker. Julius married
Frances Virginia Brunnie Zuber. He died on
12 November 1911. His wife was born in 1860,
daughter of Lovick Pierce and Elizabeth
(Westwood) Zuber. Her death date is not
known to the writer. Freddie's parents were
Lewis Alonzo Wright and the former Wylante
Josephine Yarbrough/Kellum. Lewis was born
on 31 December 1848 and married his wife on
17 December 1878. He died on 3 June 1919.
Wylante was born on 8 September 1858 and died
on 10 July 1945. Her parents were killed by
invading Union forces during the Civil War
and the children were taken up by the
Kellums, whose name they assumed. The names
of her birth parents are unknown to the
writer. John J. Baker was born on 30 March
1830 and married Miss Gilmore on 21 December
1852. An item in the Taproots publication,
taken from a Notasulga paper (Herald?),
states that in 1907 Mr. Baker was one of
Macon County's few surviving Civil War
veterans. Mr. Baker died on 9 November 1910.
His wife Julia Ann Gilmore was born in 1833
and her death date is not known to the
writer. Lovick Pierce Zuber was born in 1816
and his wife Elizabeth Westwood was born in
1824. Lewis A. Wright's father, William
Wilmot Wright was born in 1825, married on 30
March 1848 Barbara Ann Thompson, and died in
1905. Mrs. Wright married Dink Smith after
her first husband's death. Other than that
all the writer knows about her is that she
was the daughter of Thomas and Nancy
(Robertson) Thompson. Lovick Pierce Zuber
was the son of Charles Zuber. John J. Baker
was the son of Benajah and Tabitha
(Voss/Vance) Baker. According to the
Tuskegee Republican of 1 March 1858, Benajah
died about that same date. His wife, who was
born in 1807, appears as Vance in some
records, Voss in others. The records naming
her as Voss list a brother Charles G. Voss
and her father William Voss. Thomas Thompson
died on 1 July 1859; Nancy (Robertson)
Thompson was born in 1807 and died in 1888.
William Wilmot Wright was the son of the

aforementioned Samuel B. and Elizabeth (Wilmot) Wright and thus a brother to Charles Wright. There is much information available on the families in this digression, but room does not allow further treatment in this volume. Much of the information here came from Lee County and Her Forebears, Yesterdays in and around Loachapoka, and Glimpses of the Past from My Grandfather's Trunk. I recommend those works to anyone interested in study of the brothers and sisters of those here mentioned or a fuller treatment of those subject to the above paragraphs. See the bibliography for more information.

Edith Lorene Baker was born on 15 November 1918, seventh child of Albert and Freddie Baker. As the only daughter she had seven brothers, of which six survived to adulthood. Her brothers were in order of birth J. A., R. H., Seth L., Willie B., who died at age 10, Carlton, James Noel and Albert Love. Of these only Albert Love was born after Edith. Edith also attended the Beauregard School, where both she and Miles played on their respective basketball teams. After graduation Edith worked in the bakery in Opelika. After moving to Montgomery Edith worked at Loveman's Department Store, Guaranty Savings Life Insurance Company, McConnell's Plymouth dealership, and the Baptist Hospital.

MILES LEONIDAS VAUGHAN, JR. (12141221)

Miles Leonidas, Jr. was born on 22 July 1942 in Opelika, Alabama. When his father returned from the war, the family moved to Montgomery. Miles spent his childhood there and attended Sidney Lanier High School. He left before graduation to serve in the U. S. Army. Miles was assigned to the 82nd Airborne Division, where he served as a paratrooper. While in the service he got his certificate, later attended Troy State University, and graduated from Auburn University with a degree in aerospace administration. After getting his degree Miles served a second term with the service in Vietnam. Having gotten his commission while in the National Guard, Miles was a captain in the late conflict. Returning to the National Guard at the war's end, Miles was promoted to the rank of major.

Miles married the former June Rawlinson, daughter of Florence Rawlinson of Elmore, Alabama. Mr. and Mrs. Vaughan currently reside in Auburn, where he is an officer with the Parole and Probation Board. Miles and June have three children: Kristin Alise (12141221a), born 16 September 1972; Amy (12141221b), born 13 December 1974; and Miles Edwin (121412211), born 17 June 1976.

WILLIAM TERRY VAUGHAN (12141222)

William Terry was born on 5 July 1944 in Opelika, Alabama. Soon after his birth his parents moved to Montgomery, Alabama, where Terry, as he is known, spent his youth. Terry attended Sidney Lanier High School, graduating in 1962. Terry began his college studies at the University of Alabama, but later transferred to Auburn University, where he graduated in 1967.

After graduation Terry went to service in the U. S. Army. He was assigned to 8th Signal Battalion of the 8th Infantry Division. With a primary military military occupational specialty of radio-teletypist, he nonetheless served for the most part as a cryptoclerk. After a tour of duty in Germany Terry returned there to attend the interpreter's institute (Dolmetscheninstitut) of the University of Heidelberg (1970-1971). Later he followed with graduate study in German Language and Literature and Comparative Literature at the University of South of South Carolina.

On 5 November 1977 Terry married the former Marion Happy Hazelwood, in Longwood, Florida. Happy, as his wife is known, is the daughter of Mary Jane (Albritton) Hazelwood and the late Fred Hazelwood of Mayfield, Kentucky. Since moving to Florida in June of 1977, Terry has resided in Fern Park, St. Cloud, Winter Park and presently Orlando. For five years Terry taught at the high school and college level, and for the last eighteen years has been in the employ of the Florida Department of Health and Rehabilitative Services. His wife has worked as a hospital administrator, secretary, store manager, administrative assistant and real estate saleswoman.

ROBERT EARL VAUGHAN (12141223)

Robert Earl was born on 28 May 1949 in Montgomery, Alabama. He attended Sidney Lanier High School, from which he took his diploma. He was known as Bobby in his younger years and attended Troy State University. Robert, as he is now known, like his brothers, graduated from Auburn University, where he took a degree in Civil Engineering.

On 12 July 1969 Robert married Linda Diane Harrod, daughter of James and Louise Harrod, also of Montgomery. Robert subsequently married a second time in 1988 the former Sharon Elizabeth Lambert of Cincinnati, Ohio, but they divorced in 1992.

Robert initially began his working career with the Alabama State Highway Department in Montgomery after taking his Civil Engineering degree. He later worked and travelled rather extensively while working in engineering consulting and construction. His work experience is in engineering consulting, transportation, environmental remediation and construction management. He is a Registered Professional Engineer in several states and a Licensed Land Surveyor in his home state of Alabama. His construction project experience includes highways, bridges, airports, buildings, environmental remediation and waste disposal facilities on government, military, industrial, commercial, medical, hazardous-waste and educational sites.

Robert's work has taken him (or enabled him to travel) to the American southeast, southwest, west, New England and Midwest and of foreign countries, Saudi Arabia in the Middle East, Thailand and Hong Kong in the Far East and The Netherlands in Europe.

His work in Saudi Arabia covered about 18 months during a short stint in 1981 and a longer period in 1983 and 1984.

Robert retired from U. S. Reserve military service in 1989 after 20 years as a Lieutenant, Junior Grade, from the Civil Engineering Corps of the Naval Reserve (Seabees). The first seven years of his military career began with the 20th Special Forces Group of the Alabama National Guard where he was a paratrooper and radio operator. When he left the Alabama Guard to take a commission in the Naval Reserve, he held the rank of Sergeant First Class and was the supervisor of all the radio operators in his unit.

Robert has two children by his first wife: Jeffrey Michael (121412231), born on 2 September 1974; and Keith Christopher (121412232), born on 28 October 1979.

EDNA EARLE VAUGHAN (121412a)

Edna Earle was born on 10 March 1914. On 28 July 1939 she married James Joseph Cagle, also of Opelika. Edna and her husband, a housing contractor, soon moved to Mobile, Alabama, where they resided for many years on Dog River Road. Edna was by profession a teacher, but held several secretarial positions in her career and was a representative for World Book Encyclopedia. Edna died of cancer on 21 March 1976 and her husband yet survives her.

Children of James and Edna Cagle are Douglas Oranton (121412a1), born on 27 July 1940, married firstly to Margie Smith and secondly to Diane _____, by whom he has a son, Kevin (121412a11), most recently the family residing in Lafayette, Louisiana; and Edna Earle (121412aa), born on 6 April 1943, married firstly to Robert Goodman, by whom she has four children: Robert, Jr. (121412aa1), Melissa (121412aaa), Anita (121412aab), and Stephanie (121412aac). Mr. and Mrs. Goodman were divorced on 15 April 1975 and Edna Earle married Donnie Howell. At this writing Edna Earle lived at 711 St. Mary Street in Pascagoula, Mississippi. She is now Mrs. Ray.

MARY ELIZABETH VAUGHAN (121412b)

Mary Elizabeth, known as Polly, was born on 20 January 1916, second daughter of Hosea and Eva Vaughan. Polly married firstly Raymond C. Millican. She and her husband resided in Mobile, Alabama, where Ray was an electrician at Brookley Air Force Base. Ray was also a Free and Accepted Mason. Polly was employed as a secretary most of her career, but also was a nurse for many years. After her first husband's death Polly married Ed Untreiner, with whom she lived in Creola, Alabama. Polly died on 6 July 1982 from complications of pulmonary disease.

By Mr. Millican Polly had one child. Horace Raymond (121412b1) was born on 28 June 1947 and married on 16 June 1967 Patricia Thompson.

EVA WRIGHT VAUGHAN (121412c)

Eva Wright was born on 31 May 1918. On 7 June 1936 she married William Herman Woods. After Mr. Woods was killed in an automobile accident, Eva married Nolan Garner, a local farmer. Mr. Garner was the son of Ross and Nannie Garner. The 1910 census shows the Garners living in the Ridge Grove Precinct. Ross was a farmer, also an Alabama native. Nolan was seven years old at the time of the census and had two younger brothers, Jones and Lawson, and two younger sisters, Lilian and Lida. In 1910 Ross and Nannie were 27 and 30 years old, respectively.

On 2 June 1967, after Mr. Garner's death, Eva married Olin Hinkle, a farmer from Lafayette, son of Oscar Olin and Lillie Bell (Landrum) Hinkle. Mr. Hinkle has since died as has Eva's fourth husband, Frank Vinson.

Eva worked for many years as a clerk and secretary at East Alabama Office Supply in Opelika. Eva and her first husband had two children: William Frederick (121412c1), born 16 August 1937, married firstly Judy Kerr on 18 November 1961, by whom he had two daughters, Lisa (121412c1a) and Candy (121412c1b), and secondly Mae Strozier; and Barbara Ellen (121412ca), born on 1 September 1940 and married on 20 October   to John Strozier, brother of Mae Strozier Woods, by whom she has three children: Susan (121412caa), Sheryl (121412cab), and John, Jr. (121412ca1).

Eva lives on the Lafayette Highway, north of Opelika. Her son has been employed for many years with the Department of Agriculture in Washington, D. C. Ellen worked for many years with the Department of Parks and Recreation in Opelika.

HOMER FREDERICK VAUGHAN (1214123)

Homer Frederick was born on 30 August 1922. On 27 September 1941 he married Edna Ruth Speir, daughter of Mrs. H. K. Speir. The ceremony was performed at Trinity Methodist Church in Opelika by Reverend W. H. McNeal, after which the Vaughans lived for a period at 306 Edge Street of that city. While still young Homer enlisted in the U. S. Navy. After his discharge from the Navy, Homer moved to California, where he lived for several years in Gardenia and worked for the Cadillac Automobile Company. Homer later remarried four times. His second wife was Bonnie _____; his third wife Vlasta Cesnolidek, known as Val; his fourth wife Riva _____; and his fifth wife Jo _____. Homer lived the latter part of his life in Phoenix, Arizona. Homer died on 8 June 1990 in Phoenix.

Homer's children are Frederick Eugene, known as Ricky, (12141231), born on 26 August 1944, who married on 6 February 1970 Cindy Mitchell; Karel Douglas (12141232), born on 25 December 1948 and married on 12 June 1988 to Marni Anne Kallis; Vlasta Kathie (1214123a), born on 1 February 1952, who married John Arthur Brazinski; and Pamela Octavia (1214123b), born on 3 October 1957, married firstly to Keith Lawrence Kelley and second to Keith Andrew Lindsay.

FREDERICK EUGENE VAUGHAN (12141231)

Frederick Eugene, known as Ricky, was born on 26 August 1944. On 6 February 1970 he married Cindy Mitchell.

KAREL DOUGLAS VAUGHAN (12141232)

Karel Douglas was born on 25 December 1948 in Los Angeles, California. He attended medical school and currently specializes in sports medicine. On 12 June 1988 Douglas married Marni Anne Kallis in Beverly Hills. Marni was born in Los Angeles on 30 May 1957 and teaches school.

The first child of Mr. and Mrs. Vaughan, born on 10 August 1989, is Jesse Clayton Vaughan (121412321).

VLASTA KATHIE VAUGHAN (1214123a)

Vlasta Kathie was born on 1 February 1952 in
Culver City, California. She attended San
Diego State University, where she received her
B. S. in microbiology. Kathie is a medical
technologist by profession. Kathie married
John Arthur Brazinski, an attorney. Mr.
Brazinski, son of Adolph B. and Anne (Hamley)
Brazinski, was born on 28 May 1946 in
Elizabeth, New Jersey. Mr. Brazinski took his
degree in political science from Holy Cross and
a Doctor of Laws from Georgetown University.
Mrs. Brazinski is the daughter of Vlasta
Cesnolidek. The Brazinskis live in Jackson,
Wyoming at this writing.

Children of the Brazinskis are: Charles Cole
(1214123a1), born 10 September 1987 and Kira
Anne (1214123aa), born on 21 June 1992.

PAMELA OCTAVIA VAUGHAN (1214123b)

Pamela Octavia was born on 3 October 1957 in Gardenia, California, a suburb of Los Angeles. As of this writing Pamela lives in Philadelphia. In February of 1975 she married Keith Lawrence Kelley in West Chester, Pennsylvania. Octavia, as she is known, was later divorced from Mr. Kelley. The Kelleys had one child: Jessica Myra Kelley (1214123ba), born on 19 July 1974. Octavia married secondly Keith Andrew Lindsay, son of Don and Phyllis (Delius) Lindsay, on 12 April 1985 in Fayetteville, Tennessee. Their daughter Erin Worth Lindsay-Vaughan (1214123bb) was born on 19 May 1986. Octavia lived in Sarasota, Florida in 1990 while she attended Sarasota School of Massage Therapy. Later she studied electronics at Rosemont College in Rosemont, Pennsylvania.

At this writing Jessica attends the University of Utah and Erin has attended school in the Pennsylvania public school system for about a year.

JAMES DOUGLAS VAUGHAN (1214124)

James Douglas was born on 5 January 1925. On 25 June 1948 he married Bette Anne Moore. Douglas, as he is called, resides on lands that are adjacent to and were once a part of his parents' property. Douglas' professional career was with the U. S. postal Service. He worked at the Opelika Post Office until some years ago when he retired.

Douglas and Bette are the parents of three daughters: Elizabeth Anne (1214124a), born on 22 June 1949 and married to James K. Norman; Nancy Charlotte (1214124b), who married Kent Moore; and Joy Louise (1214124c), who on 16 June 1979 married Wayne G. Kimberly.

ELIZABETH ANNE VAUGHAN (1214124a)

Elizabeth Anne was born on 22 June 1949. She attended Auburn University and on 31 October 1968 married James K. Norman. The Normans lived for a time in Fort Walton Beach, Florida, while Mr. Norman was in the service. Later they lived in Miami, Florida. The Normans' son is David (1214124a1).

228

NANCY CHARLOTTE VAUGHAN (1214124b)

Nancy Charlotte was the second daughter of
James Douglas and Bette Anne Vaughan. Nancy
attended Duke University in Durham, North
Carolina. She studied in the field of biology
at both the undergraduate and graduate fields.
Nancy married Kent Moore.

JOY LOUISE VAUGHAN (1214124c)

Joy Louise was the third daughter of James Douglas and Bette Anne Vaughan. Joy attended high school in Opelika. On 16 June 1979 Joy married Wayne G. Kimberly.

BARBARA ELLEN VAUGHAN (121412d)

Barbara Ellen, daughter of Hosea and Eva Vaughan, was stillborn on 13 July 1934 and is buried in Rosemere Cemetery in Opelika.

SOURCE OF SOME NAMES IN THE VAUGHAN FAMILY

Noel: From Frances Waddill's brother Noel: 3 Noels, Noel Anguish, Henry King Noel, Noel Alexander Campbell, Noel Henry Alexander Campbell

Miles: From Lettetia Potter's father Miles: Miles Edwin (2), William Miles, Willie Miles (2), Miles Leonidas (2)

Leonidas: From Eva Wright's father Charles Leonidas: Miles Leonidas (2).

King: From Mary Harrison's father King: Henry King Noel, Ora King (2)

Jackson: From Andrew Jackson, hero of the War of 1812 and Seminole War of 1818: Henry Jackson

HENRY KING VAUGHAN (12142)

Henry King was born on 4 July 1844, second child of Henry J. and Mary Anne Vaughan. He enlisted in the Confederate Army on 5 May 1862 at Tallapoosa, Alabama. His enlistment by M. L. Woods was for three years or the duration of the war. Henry joined as a private in Captain Baggett's Company of the 46th Regiment of Alabama Infantry. The company was later designated as Company F.

Henry was promoted to sergeant and, when he was captured at Vicksburg on 4 July 1863, was listed as sergeant-major. Henry was paroled from his capture on 10 July 1863 and his company was furloughed on the twenty-second of that month at Enterprise, Mississippi. At the time of his capture Henry's unit, as were most of the units in the theater, was involved in the battles at Baker's Creek and Champion's Hill. Rumor has it that Henry served as a courier for General Pettus or the latter's commander, General Joseph Johnston. An extract of Henry's parole note follows and copies of muster roll information is in the Appendix.

Sergeant-major Vaughan was listed in service in the second quarter of 1864 on a clothing receipt roll, issued on 30 April 1864. At that time the unit was designated as Company F & S, 46th Ala. Regt.

In one source we find that Henry married on 23 December 1866 in Tallapoosa County Louisa Catherine Ross, nee Rowe, also known as Lula. A reference in Taproots, however, gives the marriage date as 12 December 1866 (reference Book 6, page 558 of Tallapoosa County Marriage Records), listing John Trammell as bond and H. R. McCoy performing minister. Lula was the daughter of William and Emily Rowe of Georgia, and had previously been married to Mr. Ross.

Henry, known in some records as Henry Noel or Henry King Noel, became a Justice of the Peace in Tuskegee after the war. C. Boroms, J. A.

Ellison and R. M. Hall went bond for Henry when he was J. P. in Tuskegee. Tallapoosa County Marriage Book 9, pages 109a and 118b show that H. K. was performing as J. P. in that county in 1881. Later Henry moved to Auburn (in the mid 1880's it is believed) where he served as marshall and, according to R. L. Polk's 1886-87 Business Directory, ran a boarding house. Records from the Alabama Archives indicate Henry was again serving as a J. P. in Tallapoosa County in 1888. Late in life Henry lived in the Phenix City/Hurtsboro area, where it is also believed he served as a Justice of the Peace.

A story exists that Henry ran away from home to join the Confederate service. This story coexists with the one that he and his father joined at the same time. The latter has already been dismissed, but the former may have been true. We know Henry K. exhibited a patriotic and militaristic fervor that befitted his day of birth. Early in the war families were not expected to send sons to war if they were already represented by a soldier in the family. Also many parents were not wont to see their young sons depart for the conflict, even though later, when the war deepened and seemed to reach into all aspects of everyday life, they answered the call themselves. The eager son scenario seems to fit developments in this Vaughan family.

Despite the assertion in William Miles' obituary that he was survived by Henry King, the latter's death certificate proves that rumors Henry was still alive were greatly exaggerated. Henry died on 24 June 1917 in Hurtsboro from arterio-scleritis and nephritis. Henry is buried in Hurtsboro Cemetery, a Confederate marker distinguishing his grave. Children of Henry and Louisa were Wilemma T. (12142a); Mary Lou (12142b); Sarah Allen (12142c), who married William H. Simmons; a stillborn daughter (12142d); Ora King (121421), colorfully known as O. K.; John (121422), who died a bachelor; Fannie (12142e), born 27 November 1883, married to 1) Mr. Edwards, 2) J.

S. Johnson, 3) Dr. J. M. Price and 4) on 7 January 1952 her cousin Walton H. Vaughan; and William Rowe (121423), who died a bachelor in October 1958 in Mt. Olive, Texas. Except for William and Fannie, all the children died prior to 1958.

EXTRACT OF HENRY KING'S PAROLE NOTE

VICKSBURG, MISSISSIPPI, JULY (9) 1863.
TO ALL WHOM IT MAY CONCERN, KNOW YE THAT:

I (H. K. Vaughan) a (SergtMajr) of (Co(F)46th) Regt (Ala) Vols. C. S. A., being a prisoner of War, in the hands of the United States Forces, in virtue of the capitulation of the city of Vicksburg and its Garrison, by Lieut. Gen. John C. Pemberton, C. S. A., Commanding, on the 4th day of July, 1863, do in pursuance of the terms of said capitulation, give this my solemn parole under oath--
That I will not take up arms again against the United States, nor serve in any military, police, or constabulary force in any Fort, Garrison or field work, held by the Confederate States of America, against the United States of America, nor as guard of any prisons, depots or stores nor discharge any duties usually performed by Officers or soldiers against the United States of America, until duly exchanged by the proper authorities.
H. K. Vaughan Sergt Major

Sworn to and subscribed before me at Vicksburg, Miss., this (9) day of July 1863.
(Jno C. Ivy 20th) Reg't (Ohio) Vols.
(Maj) AND PAROLING OFFICER.

DEATH CERTIFICATE OF HENRY KING VAUGHAN

I, Forest E. Ludden, Ed.D., State Registrar of Vital Statistics, certify this is a true and exact copy of the original certificate filed in the Bureau of Vital Statistics, State of Alabama, Department of Public Health, Montgomery, AL, and have caused the official seal of the Bureau of Vital Statistics to be affixed.

Forest E. Ludden, Ed.D.

Forest E. Ludden, Ed.D., State Registrar

June 15, 1987

218

fore making certificate read "Suggestions" on the reverse side of this form.

Form No. 2

CERTIFICATE OF DEATH

Full name of deceased *H. K. Vaughn*

[Do not fail to give Full Name]

Date of death: Month *June* day *24* 19— Hour *10* A.M. P.M.

Place of death (county) _____ beat *6* _____

City or town *Hurtsboro* ward _____ street and No. _____

Place of birth of deceased (state or country) *Ala*

White or colored *White* Male or female *Male* Occupation *R. R. [?]*

How long did deceased reside at place of death *2½ years*

Where was disease contracted? _____ Duration of illness *3 months*

Principal disease causing death *Entero Col[itis]*

Contributory disease causing death *Nephritis*

If homicidal, suicidal, or accidental, state definitely how accomplished _____

Did deceased undergo a surgical operation, and if so, when and of what nature? _____

Age: years *73* months _____ days _____ single, married or widowed *married*

Full name of father of deceased *H. J. Vaughn*

Birthplace of father (state or country) *Ala*

Full name of mother of deceased *Mary Ann Vaughn*

Birthplace of mother (state or country) *Ala*

Place of interment *Hurtsboro*

Remarks: _____

Reporter *R. M. Hanks*

Date of Report *July 1* 191— Post Office *Hurtsboro, Ala*

WILEMMA VAUGHAN (1214a)

Wilemma T., known as Emma, was the first child
of Henry K. and Lula Vaughan.

TO NAME A SCOTTISH CHILD

Name the oldest son for the paternal
                              grandfather.
Name the second son for the maternal
                              grandfather.
Name the third son for the father.
Name the oldest daughter for the maternal
                              grandmother.
Name the second daughter for the paternal
                              grandmother.
Name the others as you see fit.

MARY LOU VAUGHAN (12142b)

Mary Lou, known as Minnie, was a daughter and second child of Henry K. and Lula Vaughan.

SOURCES OF NAMES (CONT'D)

Walton: From William Miles' wife's maiden name: Walton Henry, Herbert Walton

Lettetia: From Lettetia Potter: Lettetia Vermelle

SARAH ALLEN VAUGHAN (12142c)

Sarah Allen, known as Sallie, was the third
child of Henry K. and Lula Vaughan.   She
married William H. Simmons.   The Simmonses had
five children (order indeterminate):   Tommy
(12142c1);   William   H.   (12142c2);   Sarah
(12142ca);   Louise   (12142cb);   and   Vaughan
(12142cc), who is buried at Shorter, Alabama.

UNNAMED DAUGHTER (12142d)

Henry K. and Lula's fourth child was a stillborn daughter, who was not named.

ORA K. VAUGHAN (121421)

Ora King was the fifth child and first son of
Henry K. and Lula Vaughan.   Ora was often
called "O. K."   Ora resided at one time in
Dennison, Texas.   He had three children, of
which only one is known to this writer: Ora
K., Jr. (1214211).

ORA KING VAUGHAN, JR. (1214211)

The only information this writer has on Ora King Vaughan, Jr. is that he was one of three children.

JOHN VAUGHAN (121.422)

John Vaughan, second son of Henry K. and Lula
Vaughan, was born in 1879. He died a bachelor
sometime before 1958.

FANNIE VAUGHAN (12142e)

Fannie was born on 27 November 1883, youngest daughter of Henry K. and Lula Vaughan. Fannie married four times. She married firstly a Mr. Edwards. Secondly she married J. S. Johnson, by whom she had a daughter, Vivian Vaughan (12142ea), who married Paul K. Grey. Thirdly Fannie married Dr. John M. Price, by whom she had two daughters: Dorothy Louise (12142eb), known as Dot, who married Walter B. Elkins; and Dellie Stanton (12142ec), who married B. A. Lanford. On 7 January 1952 Fannie married a fourth time, to her cousin Walton H. Vaughan.

After Walton's death in 1955, Fannie moved to Texas and in 1958 was living at 2406 Prairie Avenue in Fort Worth, primarily to care for her brother, William Rowe, who was ill at the time.

WILLIAM ROWE VAUGHAN (121423)

William Rowe was the last child of Henry K. and
Lula Vaughan. He never married and died at Mt.
Olive, Texas in October of 1958. He had
contracted an illness in September of that
year.

REBECCA ANTOINETTE VAUGHAN (1214a)

Rebecca Antoinette, more commonly known as
Nettie, was the first daughter of Henry J. and
Mary Vaughan. Her date of birth is believed to
have been 26 January 1846, although her Bible
lists the date as 29 January of that year. The
latter date appears to have been entered by one
of her daughters. Rebecca married Benjamin
Herbert Reynolds on 12 August 1865 (17 August
according to her Bible). Mr. Reynolds was an
ordained Methodist minister and served as a lay
minister whenever needed. He was pastor of
Roxana Methodist Church from 1878 to 1881
(Alexander Nunn's *Yesterdays*, page 22).
Rebecca soon removed to Birmingham, Alabama. A
deed relating to the settlement of her father's
estate in Lee County establishes she was a
widow by 4 February 1897. Rebecca died in
Birmingham on 17 October 1913. Since she was
alive at the time, it is not clear why her name
does not appear on a remission of release of 6
June 1911 relating to the settlement of her
father's estate.

Rebecca married at the same ceremony that
united Mary Trawick, sister of her stepmother,
Georgia Trawick, with Ben's brother, W. H.
Reynolds. William B. Neal officiated for the
ceremony, held at the home of W. Hiram Trawick.

Benjamin Reynolds, son of Jeptha and Adelia
Harris (Turner) Reynolds, was born on 12 April
1838. Ben died on 4 October 1887 and is buried
in Oak Hill Cemetery in Birmingham. Ben and
Rebecca had eight children, six of whom
survived infancy. They were William Henry
Vinon (1214a1), born 20 September 1866 and died
24 September 1867; Mary Adelia (1214aa), born 8
January 1868, married 18 October 1888 to James
Thomas McCrorey, and died 13 May 1961; Walter
Augustus (1214a2), born 18 March 1869, married
Eugenia Buckingham Crain on 2 November 1898 and
died 6 December 1918; George Dowdell (1214a3),
born 9 January 1871, married 1) 15 June 1897
Jennie Jones, 2) 7 October 1915 Laura Brown
(Morgan) and died 8 December 1956; Herbert

Eugene (1214a4), born 5 February 1872, married
15 April 1903 to Ida Mae Beavers and died on 14
November 1958; Luther Early (1214a5), born 19
November 1873, married 19 February 1897 to
Daisey Catherine Sparkman; Benjamin Arthur
(1214a6), born on 18 August 1876, married 8
January 1907 to Bessie LeGrand and died 24
December 1936; and Elizabeth Camilla Maybelle
(1214ab), born 20 January 1878 and died 17
August 1878.

Children of James and Mary Adelia McCrorey were
Nettie Yongue (1214aaa), born on 17 September
1889, married on 15 June 1910 to John Sanders
Counselman and died 29 November 1972; a
stillborn child (date uncertain); Maude Willa
(1214aac), born 1 May 1894 and died on 20 March
1896; Verna Ailine (1214aad), born 23 October
1897, married 12 November 1919 to Charles
Gordon McDowell.

Children of Walter A. and Eugenia Reynolds were
Ralph Walter (1214a21), born 23 September 1899
and died October 1901, and Walter Willard
(1214a22), born 2 February 1902, married 6 June
1936 to Helen Janak and died 2 July 1961.

George Reynolds had no children by either of
his wives.

Herbert E. and Ida Reynolds' children were
Annie Eloise (1214a4a), born on 23 October
1905; Jennie May (1214a4b), born 5 January 1909
and married Sigurd Hogsbro; and Herbert Eugene,
Jr. (1214a41), born 12 December 1912, married
but had no children.

Luther E. and Daisey Reynolds' children were
Earlyne (1214a5a), born 16 September 1898,
married to Houston Brice, and died on 16 July
1981; Marguerite (1214a5b), born 7 December
1900 and married to James Adams; and Luther
Early, Jr. (1214a51), born 23 May 1903 and
married to Magdalen.

Children of Benjamin A. and Bessie Reynolds
were Benjamin Clark (1214a61), born 14 May 1908
and died 24 May 1910; Elizabeth LeGrand

(1214a6a), born 29 March 1911, married July 1930 to Thomas McConnell Ellisor; and Catherine Jane (1214a6b), born 8 March 1914.

John S. and Nettie Counselman had one child: Mary Elizabeth (1214aaaa), born 19 November 1911 and married on 13 November 1941 to Horace Benton Vinyard.

Children of Charles G. and Verna Ailine McDowell were Verna Allene (1214aada), born 11 February 1922 and married on 24 February 1944 to James Charles Fitzpatrick, Jr.; and Charles G., Jr. (1214aadl), born 1 May 1925 and married to Vivian Frances Delmar on 15 February 1951.

Children of Walter Willard and Helen Reynolds were Donald Durward (1214a221), born 14 February 1941 and married on 25 July 1964 to Margie May Cummins; and Walter Willard, Jr. (1214a222), who had no children.

Sigurd and Jennie Hogsbro had one child, Richard (1214a4b1).

Children of Thomas M. and Elizabeth Ellisor were Thomas M., Jr. (1214a6a1), born 20 July 1932 and married to Ella Dean Bates; David Reynolds (1214a6a2), born 8 October 1933 and married to Myra Camp; John LeGrand (1214a6a3), born 21 January 1935 and married 1) Carolyn Kelly, 2) Glenda Thomas; and William Blakely (1214a6a4), born 14 November 1936 and married 1) Sandra Adair and 2) Marjorie Helt Hastings, a widow.

Horace B. and Mary Vinyard had one child: William Sanders (1214aaaal), born on 22 December 1943, married 1) on 5 November 1967 to Betty McCary (Phillips) and 2) on 6 November 1973 to Rebecca Rose Thompson (Baker).

Children of James C. and Verna Fitzpatrick are Thomas Michael (1214aadal), born 25 January 1948; James C. III (1214aada2), born 14 November 1950 and married on 8 August 1970 to Patricia Alveta Davis; Mary Margaret (1214aadaa), born 30 November 1954 and married

248

on 15 March 1980 to Donald Lamar Douglas; and
Stephen Kerry (1214aada3), born on 27 December
1964.

Children of Charles G. and Vivian McDowell are
Randolph Curtis (1214aad11), born 4 February
1952 and married 1) on 15 October 1971 to
Deborah Sirmon, 2) on 2 January 1976 to Mariko
Turner; Katherine Elizabeth (1214aad1a), born
on 14 August 1957 and married 8 July 1978 to
Michael T. Freedman; and Charles G. III
(1214aad12), born on 16 September 1963.

Children of Donald D. and Margie Reynolds are
Stephanie Ann (1214a221a), born 25 September
1965; Walter Clay (1214a2211), born 16 November
1966; Elizabeth Leigh (1214a221b), born 25
December 1967; and Donald Cummins (1214a2212),
born 27 August 1969.

Most of the above information on the
descendants of Rebecca Vaughan Reynolds comes
from Mrs. Verna Fitzpatrick, member 1214aada
above.

GEORGE LOUIS VAUGHAN (12143)

George Louis was born on 29 September 1847 (29 December according to a list of Fannie P. Vaughan). He married Ida Taylor, called Betty in some accounts, postmistress at Betty, Texas. Stories in the family say Ida attended Auburn University. George and Ida lived in Corsicana, Texas, and were visited there by Hosea Vaughan in the early 1900's. George and Ida are known to have lived in Jefferson County, Arkansas in 1874.

In the settlement of the estate of Henry J. Vaughan, George and his wife delegated power of attorney to William Miles Vaughan. Their residence in the document was Shelby County, Texas. A list of pensioners in Texas carries George's name on it. George is believed to have died about 1919. Known children of George Louis were G. H. (121431), of Garrison, Nacogdoches County, Texas, and David Arthur (121432) of Corsicana, Texas.

G. H. VAUGHAN (121431)

The only information available on G. H. is that he resided at one time in Garrison, Nacogdoches, Texas.

BIBLES ASSOCIATED WITH THIS HISTORY

1) The Bible of Noel Anguish Vaughan was passed down to Noel's daughter Mary Anna Vaughan Gann. Copies of pages obtained through Pat Weber, who presumably got them from Mrs. Gann.

2) Jackson Harrison's Bible was last known to be in possession of Mrs. Jesse King Harrison of Pulaski, Virginia. Information conveyed through Verna Fitzpatrick.

3) Bible of Rebecca A. Reynolds in possession of Catherine Reynolds and Elizabeth Reynolds Ellisor of Mobile, Alabama. Copies of pages obtained through Verna Fitzpatrick. This has been said to be referred to by Rebecca as the small Bible. Both of the last two may have belonged originally to Rebecca's parents.

DAVID ARTHUR VAUGHAN (121432)

David Arthur lived in Corsicana, Texas. Texas marriage records show he married in July 1906 at Emhouse, Navarro County, Texas, Barbara Elizabeth Allen.

BIBLES (CONT'D)

4) Lettie Thomas had a Bible last known to be in possession of her son William S. Thomas. Mrs. Weber was presumably able to access this material.

5) The Rutherford Family Bible in possession of Mrs. C. H. Gunter. I accessed through an article in Taproots.

6) Bible of Henry, Sr. and Elizabeth Vaughan was purchased by John and Frances Reynolds at estate sale. Whereabouts unknown.

7) Bible passed down from Vermelle Vaughan Rees-Bradford to her great-granddaughter Virginia Reynolds Hodges. May have originally belonged to Henry Vaughan, Jr. Information accessed through Vermelle Galbreath.

WALTER H. VAUGHAN (12144)

Walter H. was born on 24 November 1849. He has proven an enigmatic family member to trace. He married Ida E. Rutherford on 3 December 1872, J. D. Roby officiating. W. D. Coker went bond with Walter for the license. This information comes from both Lee County Marriage Records and the Rutherford Bible, still in possession of Rutherford descendants. The Bible lists this member as Walter H.; however, the marriage records list him as Wallace W.

The variable references to this personage is here summarized: The 1850 Macon County census shows him as a one-year-old named D. William; the 1870 Chambers County census lists him as twenty-one-year old Wallace William, in the household of his uncle, Noel Anguish Vaughan; estate papers on Henry J. Vaughan's estate give an inheritance to Walter H. Day, daughter of Walter H. Vaughan, deceased; Henry J.'s obituary in The Alabama Christian Advocate states Henry had one son who preceded him in death and was represented by a daughter; a list of children of Henry J. by one of his grandchildren, Mary Adelia (Reynolds) McCrorey, names Walter Wallace as an uncle and states he married Ida Rutherford [This list was found on an envelope postmarked 1930]; a list of children of Henry J. from Pat Weber, who received the same from Fannie Vaughan, another granddaughter of Henry J., in about 1958, names him as Wallace Walton. Additionally, when Jackson Harrison, Walter's mother's brother, administrated the estate of Josiah Parmer, he listed among the heirs a Wallace W. Vaughan, son of Mary A. Vaughan, but, this document being dated December 1874, a notation was made that Wallace had died recently, leaving a widow. All sources for a death date for Walter H. give 8 January 1874.

The Rutherford Bible, mentioned above, was as of about 1990 in the possession of Mrs. C. H. Gunter of Phenix City, Alabama. In Bobby Lindsey's Reason for the Tears (page 167) is

listed a Jesse Day, who married a lady of
unknown name, all of whose children lived in
Texas and one of whom was Wm. H. Day.

BIBLES (CONT'D)

8) The Bible of Isham Vaughan in possession of
Mary Jennings Terry of Columbia, South Carolina
in 1983. Information accessed through
McClesky's New Limbs from Old Roots.

WALTER H. VAUGHAN (12144a)

Walter H. was the only child of her father of
the same name. She was a participant in the
settlement of the estate of Henry J. Vaughan,
sole heir to her father's share of the estate.
She had married a Mr. Day by 6 June 1911 and is
referred to by that name in deed items. The
Rutherford Bible gives 2 February 1874 as the
birth date for Walter Henry Vaughan, thus
posthumous to her father. She resided in Texas
at the time of settlement of the estate and
with George Louis Vaughan signed over power of
attorney to William Miles Vaughan in said
settlement. Documents were apparently
notarized in Shelby County, Texas in 1899, for
the continuing transactions related to the
estate settlement.

LETTETIA VERMELLE VAUGHAN (1214e)

Lettetia Vermelle was born on 5 June 1861. In reminiscences of Mary Adelia (Reynolds) McCrorey she tells of Lettie living with her family. Lettie was about fourteen to eighteen years of age at that time, but the writer suspects she may have spent much time with her sister's family in her youth. Lettie was Mary's aunt; her sister Rebecca, Mary's mother. Lee County Estate Records establish Lettie received a bequeath from the estate of Josiah Parmer. Ben H. Reynolds was to administrate the bequeathal, so long as Lettie was a minor. These papers, for the years of 1867-1872 and arranged alphabetically in the papers of the Probate Court, indicate Mr. Reynolds was more the caretaker for her than the father or stepmother. Since all the other children were so much older than Lettie, the family probably felt she was better off with her sister's family.

According to Lee County Marriage Records (Book A, page 546) Lettie married Josephus N. Thomas (known as Seph) on 14 December 1886. Another source, a Bible said to have belonged to Lettie that has come through Pat Weber, gives 22 December 1886 as the date. John R. Peavy, MG, presided at the ceremony uniting her with Seph. Seph was born in 1858 in Georgia, son of John L. and Belinda F. Thomas. Lettie is said to have attended Auburn University for a while before her marriage.

By 1896 Seph and Lettie had moved to Corsicana, Texas. There they presented their petition for the probate of the will of Miles Edwin Vaughan. This document may be found in the 1892-1904 Macon County Wills and Appraisement Record, page 271. On page 272 is the will, in which Lettie was bequeathed half-interest in Miles' mill and gin and half-interest in ten acres of land on which the mill and gin were situated.

Lettie died on 6 August 1909 (9 August per Bible) and Seph died on 31 January 1940. The

256

Thomases had three children: Claud E.
(1214e1); Lettie (1214ea); and William Sanford
(1214e2), born 2 October 1900 in Corsicana,
Texas. All the children were born in Texas and
in 1940 the two older children still lived
there, while William was living in Denver,
Colorado. Seph died in Dallas, Texas.

One grandson of Josephus and Lettie was also
named William S. He died about 1941 and was
survived by a son named Bill.

CAROLINA REMNANTS

NOEL VAUGHAN, JR. (122)

Noel, Jr. was the son of Noel and Winnie Vaughan. Census records indicate he was born before 1775. He married Hannah W_____?. Although no document is available to him with her last name, this writer thinks she was a White. Her estate was administrated by Anthony White and Noel's lands were surrounded by that of Whites.

Noel appears in several land transactions in Sumter County and was co-administrator of his father's estate in 1829. The Sumter Gazette of 5 November 1831 lists Noel as a member of the States Rights and Free Trade Party. The Columbia Telescope of 11 July 1829, referring to the Fourth of July celebration, attributes this toast to Noel: "To the memory of Major General Jacob Brown, lamb in peace, thunderbolt in war." A sketch of Brown appears in Draper's Kings Mountain and Its Heroes (page 424), although he is there referred to as Major: Jacob Brown was born in South Carolina, December eleventh, 1736; settled on Nolachucky, in 1772, purchasing lands of the Cherokees. He served in the Indian Wars, at the head of his Company in Sevier's regiment at King's Mountain, and then on Arthur Campbell's expedition. He was made a Major, defeated a party of Indians in the fall of 1781, and died, June twenty-eighth, 1785, from an accidental wound received while out hunting."

Children of Noel and Hannah, taken from their wills, probated on 2 June 1848 and 15 May 1850 were: Sarah W. (122a), who married James J. L. Allen; Christopher D. (1221), born in 1815, who married Martha E. _____; James H. (1222), born in 1820, married to Mary E. Britton and died in February of 1887; Mary E. (122b), born in 1822 and married to Oliver P. McRoy; and Charlotte A. (122c), born in 1826 and married to J. Francis Bradford. The 1830 census indicates a

son born between 1800-1810, but perhaps this was a relative or other household member.

Noel, Jr. died on 2 May 1848. Quoting the Sumter Banner of 5 May 1848: Died 05/02/1848 at his nearby residence, Mr. Noel Vaughan, in the 68th year of his age. [This would make him born in late 1780 or early 1781.]

Noel's will, dated 8 October 1846, was probated on 2 June 1848. Hannah died about the first of May in 1850. Her will, dated 24 April 1850, was probated on 15 May 1850. Besides the census records, Noel's signature as witness on deed transactions, which supposedly required him to be twenty-one years of age, indicate he was older than indicated in the death notice.

PLAT OF NOEL'S AND HANNAH'S LAND AT SETTLEMENT OF HANNAH'S WILL

CHRISTOPHER D. VAUGHAN (1221)

Christopher D. was the elder son of Noel and Hannah Vaughan. The Sumter County census of 1850 indicates he was born about 1815. Christopher married Martha E. _____. The census lists Christopher as a planter. He stood as a witness for Victoria A. Vaughan in her deed transaction of 17 December 1833.

The only child of Christopher and Martha known to the writer is Noel (12211), born in 1850.

NOEL VAUGHAN III (12211)

Noel, son of Christopher and Martha Vaughan,
was born in 1850.   This information comes from
the 1850 Sumter County census.

JAMES H. VAUGHAN (1222)

James H. was the younger son of Noel and Hannah Vaughan. He was born about 1820. James was a coachmaker and storeowner in Sumter. James married Mary H. Britton, as related by the Sumter Banner of 29 March 1848: Married by Rev. J. H. Zimmery [Zimmerman], J. H. Vaughan to M. H. Britton, on the 23rd instant, all of this place. An article on page 188 of volume 54, South Carolina Historical and Genealogical Magazine states that the office of the Sumter Banner was removed "to the new building next to the lot of Mr. James H. Vaughan on the Stateburg Road." [Soon after 1846].

James' known children are Charlotte (1222a); John Francis (12221); Mary Elizabeth (1222b); Sally (1222c); Pickens P. (12222); and Caroline H. (1222d). Dates of birth are not known on the last two. An article in the Sumter Banner of 1849 gives vital but tragic information on the first four: "Died in this district on Friday, 31 August, Charlotte, aged 11 years, John Francis, aged eight years, On Wednesday night, September 5th, Mary Elizabeth, aged 6 years and on Tuesday, 11th September, Sally, aged 2 years, children of Leatha [?] Vaughan." This article demonstrates the disastrous outcome of many epidemics of the period. The article also serves as an indication that James had been previously married to a wife who died about 1847. The last two children were probably a product of the second marriage.

Sometime after the above events James and his family moved to McClellan County [Writer thinks McLennan County], Texas, where he died in 1887. The Sumter Banner and Southron of 4 May 1887 states that Pickens P. was on a visit to Sumter and that his father had died in February of that year. Vol. II, 1871-1881 of McLennan County, Texas, Marriage Records records the marriage of P. P. Vaughan to A. E. Connally on 11 January 1877.

PICKENS P. VAUGHAN (12222)

Pickens P. appears to have been the second son of James H. Vaughan, probably born after 1848 to Mary H. (Britton) Vaughan. He lived in Texas, probably in McLennan County, and he probably married A. E. Connally in 1877. See article on James H. for citations.

CAROLINE H. VAUGHAN (1222d)

Caroline H. was the last daughter of James H. Vaughan. Her mother was probably Mary H. (Britton) Vaughan.

SARAH W. VAUGHAN (122a)

Sarah W. was a daughter, probably the oldest,
of Noel and Hannah Vaughan. She married James
J. L. Allen, son of Ezra Allen. Sarah was
administratrix of the estate of Ezra Allen,
which was appraised in December of 1842. In
the papers it is stated that Ezra Allen died 21
October of 1842. Since Sarah was made
administratrix, perhaps her husband was
deceased by the above date. While a James J.
L. Allen (in one place listed as J. J. S.
Allen--probably an error of transcription) is
listed in the papers, this could have been the
son of the Allens. The one known child of
James and Sarah Allen was James J. L., Jr.
(122a1).

MARY E. VAUGHAN (122b)

Mary E. was a daughter of Noel and Hannah Vaughan. She was born in 1822 and was probably the second daughter, as her sister Sarah would have had to be twenty-one to administrate her father-in-law's estate. On 12 June 1850 Mary married Oliver P. McRoy, a farmer and recent immigrant to Sumter.

CHARLOTTE ANN VAUGHAN (122c)

Charlotte Ann, daughter of Noel and Hannah, was born in 1826. This comes from her tombstone in Madisonville, Texas. On 20 September 1849 Charlotte married J. Francis Bradford (Sumter Banner of 29 September 1849). Children of J. Francis, known in some records as James Franklin Bradford, and Charlotte were James Noel (122c1), born 2 September 1850; Albertus (122c2); Benjamin Franklin Witherspoon (122c3); F. O. W. (122c4); and Arthur (122c5).

According to her tombstone Charlotte died on 15 October 1886. She is buried in County Cemetery, Madisonville, Texas.

268

ISHAM VAUGHAN (123)

Isham was the third son of Noel and Winnie Vaughan. According to his Bible, in possession of Mrs. Terry, he was born on 25 February 1788. Isham married Frances Bradford, daughter of John Angel and Mary Bradford. Frances was born on 16 March 1789. One source says Frances died on 22 March 1845 of cancer of the head and face. Isham's Bible, however, says she died on 23 March 1845. Isham died on 11 October 1865.

Information on the children of Isham and Frances is somewhat confusing. At one time the writer was using census information for vital statistics on the children, but they seem to contain errors. The 1850 Sumter County census, for example, has an incorrect age for Rebecca Caroline and even incorrect sex codes for three members of the family. I thus use information from the Bible for authority. Rebecca Caroline (123a) was born on 5 December 1817 and died 27 September 1885. The other children were Leonora Harriot (123b), born 6 September 1819, married G. W. Brunson and died 25 July 1875; Rufus E. (1231), born on 8 May 1821 and died on 23 September 1848; Waid [Wade?] Hampton (1232), born on 10 May 1823 and died 15 October 1861; Edgar J. Washington (1233), born on 21 February 1825 and died in 1862; Francis Oliver (1234), born on 30 September 1827 and died on 11 June 1861; Mary Susan Vermelle (123c), born on 15 June 1830; and Robert James Hamilton (1235), born on 4 April 1832.

REBECCA CAROLINE VAUGHAN (123a)

Rebecca Caroline was born on 5 December 1817, daughter and first child of Isham and Frances Vaughan. She died on 27 September 1885. Isham's Bible has the notation that she was 67 years and 8 months old. My mathematics indicates she would have been more like 67 years and 10 months old, but we will consider the dates as valid. Rebecca probably died unmarried since the Bible usually carries the decedent's married name where applicable.

LEONORA HARRIOT VAUGHAN (123b)

Leonora Harriot was the second child of Isham and Frances Vaughan. She was born on 6 September 1819. Probate Court records for Sumter County state that she married George Washington Brunson and removed to Early County, Georgia. She died in Early County on 25 July 1875 according to Isham's Bible in which she is listed as both Leonora Harriot and Harriot Leonora.

RUFUS E. VAUGHAN (1231)

Rufus E. was the first son of Isham and Frances
Vaughan. He was born on 8 May 1821 and died on
23 September 1848.

WADE HAMPTON VAUGHAN (1232)

Wade Hampton was the son of Isham and Frances Vaughan. According to Isham's Bible Wade Hampton (spelled also as Waid Hampton) was born on 10 May 1823 and died on 15 October 1861 near Blakely, Georgia, situated in Early County. This writer does not know whether he lived there or perhaps was visiting his sister Leonora's family. The will of Hampton Vaughan of 1887 in Sumter County does not seem to be a relative of this family of Vaughans.

EDGAR J. WASHINGTON VAUGHAN (1233)

Edgar J. Washington was the third son of Isham and Frances Vaughan. He appears in censuses, Probate Court and Equity Court records. Edgar was an overseer by profession.

Edgar was born on 21 February 1825. He was a casualty at the Second Battle of Manassas, according to Isham's Bible, which therefore means he died on either 29 or 30 August of 1862. This would have put him in his thirty-eighth, not thirty-seventh year (that is, he was already thirty-seven), as the Bible states.

FRANCIS OLIVER VAUGHAN (1234)

Francis Oliver, son of Isham and Frances
Vaughan, was born on 30 September 1827. He
married Susan B. _____ and was an overseer on
his father's farm in 1860. Isham's Bible
states he died on 11 June 1861 in Culpepper,
Virginia in service under General Beauregard in
the 2nd Palmetto Brigade of the Sumter
Volunteers.

SUSAN VERMELLE VAUGHAN (123c)

Susan Vermelle, daughter of Isham and Frances Vaughan, was born on 15 June 1830. She is listed as Mary Susan Vermelle in Isham's Bible. Susan married John James Jennings, son of Eliza Jennings. The Sumter Watchman and Southron of March 1887 carries a notice that John committed suicide because he was plagued by a malady that caused recurrent pains. Susan died on 9 November 1907.

Children of Mr. and Mrs. Jennings were William H. (123c1), born in 1863; Nora A. (123ca), born in 1865; Francis (123c2), born in 1868; and E. Estell (123cb), born in 1871.

Isham's Bible doesn't carry Susan's death date, but has entries for the children of Willie and Viola Jennings/Ollie and Essie Jennings. The conclusion this writer would draw is that, after her father's death, the Bible came into Susan's possession and she made the notations until it passed on down after her death, with no one making any further notations. The handwriting seems to be the same until the entry on Francis' death. Entries on the deaths of Francis, Edgar, Isham, Leonora and Rebecca are in different handwriting. Actually the handwriting for the entry on Rufus' death is different and possibly the Bible passed hands earlier. All the entries on the Jennings children are in the same hand and all entries are prior to 1907, so the writer reasons as above. Willie and Viola were probably William H. and wife. Ollie and Essie could have been Francis (123c2), if named Francis Oliver for Susan's brother (1234), or perhaps E. Estill was Essie, who married a relative. This is offered by the writer for those who may wish to pursue this line. Perhaps this could be clarified by Mrs. Terry.

ROBERT JAMES HAMILTON VAUGHAN (1235)

Robert James Hamilton, last child of Isham and Frances Vaughan, was born on 4 April 1832.

APPENDICES

APPENDIX I
OTHER SUMTER COUNTY VAUGHANS

One John Vaughan left a will, probated on 17 November 1800, in Sumter County. In the will he named his wife Jane, a son John, Jr. and a daughter Gineia [Virginia]. John, Jr. married Martha _____. Two transactions involving John, Jr. are on record in Sumter County: one of February 1800 involving a conveyance from Henry, Sr. to John, Jr. and one of 2 January 1808 involving John, Jr., his wife Martha and his mother Jane. No relationship has been established between this John and the line subject to this treatise, although transactions involving other Vaughans tend to make one suspect kinship. Two John Vaughans are carried on the 1800 Sumter County census, one of whom would be John B. Vaughan.

Wilie Vaughan, who married Miss Champion, and his son John Champion Vaughan lived in the Camden area. Both were lawyers. They were also financiers and had dealings in Sumter, although they didn't live there. Wilie came from Virginia. His wife Sarah was the daughter of Richard Champion. Mr. Champion emigrated to Camden from Bristol, England, where he was a potter, making "Bristol Ware" produced under the Cookworthy patent at Castle Green Pottery in Bristol. A son of Mr. Champion, born in 1771 and died in 1813, married in 1810, Mary Dubose, daughter of Captain Isaac Dubose, and widow of Dr. John Trent. Their daughter married Major John deSaussure. Champion Vaughan, son of John Champion Vaughan and grandson of Richard Champion, was a distinguished officer under Custer. For more biography on Champions, see South Carolina Historical and Genealogical Magazine, Vol. 39, page 155. These Vaughans are unrelated to other Sumter County Vaughans and, after Wilie died in 1820, John removed in 1834 to Ohio.

Two Robert Vaughans of questionable identity appear in Sumter records. Robert C. appears in the 1840 census and was married to Ann E. Robert E. appears in the 1860 census and was also married to Ann E. Comparing the ages, they would appear to be the same person. Robert C. is known to have lived around Bishopville and Lancaster County in the middle 1840's.

Hampton Vaughan, who left an 1887 will in Sumter County, does not appear related to any of the Vaughans subject to this treatise.

APPENDIX II
MAPS

1) SUMTER DISTRICT FROM MILLS' ATLAS (1821)

2) LEE, MACON, CHAMBERS COUNTIES, ALABAMA, TROUP, GEORGIA

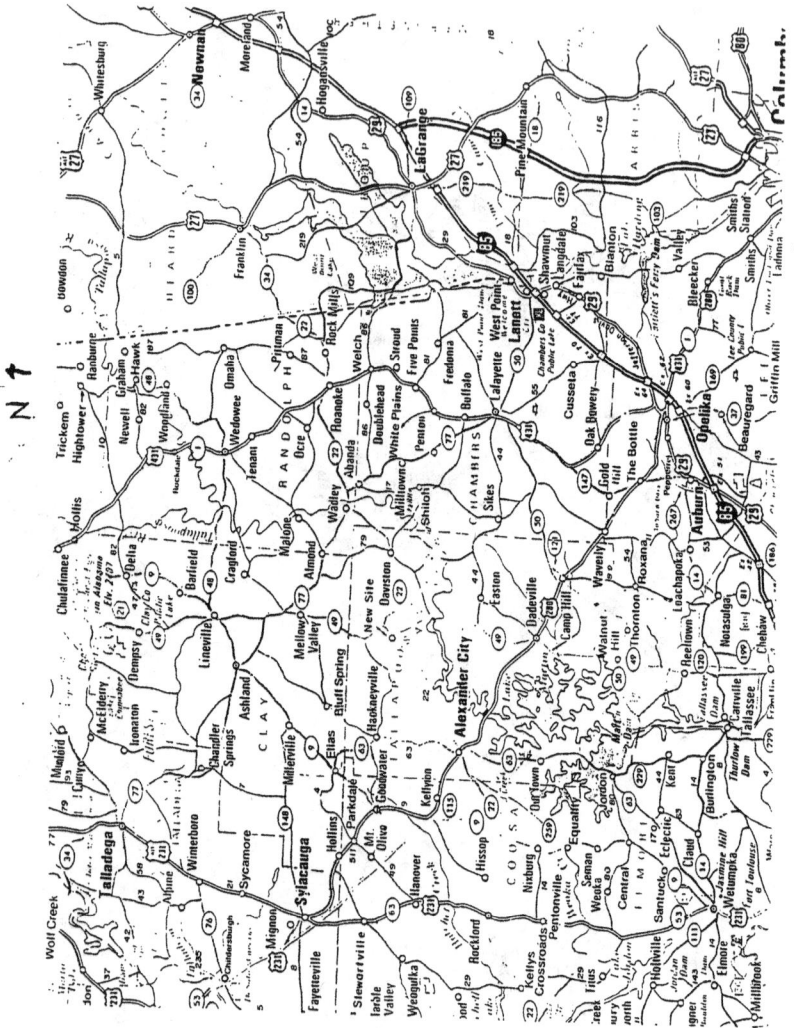

A HORIZONTAL (GENERATIONAL) INDEX OF VAUGHANS

FIRST GENERATION

Vincent (1): Naomi, Henry, Noel

SECOND GENERATION

Henry (11): William, Sr., Henry, Jr., Frances, Elizabeth, Vincent, John B., Richard

Noel (12): Mary, William, Jr., Noel, Jr., Isham

THIRD GENERATION

William, Sr. (111): Kiturah, Emily, James A., John H., Alice, Leonora, Mary H., Martha, Frances

Henry, Jr. (112): Julia, Mary M., Henry III, John A., Vermelle

Vincent (113): Unknown

John B. (114): Elizabeth, John S., Beverly, Vincent, Henry, Mathew, Robert

Richard (115): Richard, Jr.

William, Jr. (121): Mary C., Harriett, Elvira, William C., Noel A., Miles, Henry J.

Noel, Jr. (122): Sarah, Christopher, James H., Mary E., Charlotte

Isham (123): Rebecca, Rufus, Wade/Waid, Edgar, Francis, Mary S. V., Robert

FOURTH GENERATION

James A. (1111): None

John H. (1112): Mary T., Elizabeth A.

Henry III (1121): Mary S., Margaret, Betsey,
    Henry IV, John A., Charles B., Hugh, James
    B., Alice, Emma, Francis, William R.

John A. (1122): None

John S. (1141): Sarah, Mary C., Caladonia,
    John S., Jr., Livingston, Joseph H.,
    Abernathy

Beverly (1142): Unknown

Vincent (1143): Unknown

Henry (1144): Unknown

Mathew (1145): Laura, Andrew, Mathew, Jr.,
    Mary L., Savena, Elizabeth

Richard, Jr. (1151): Unknown

William C. (1211): Mary C., William A.,
    Charles C., Virginia, California, Joseph
    B.

Noel A. (1212): Noel A. C., Harriett, Joanna,
    Noel H. A. C., Mary A. L.

Miles (1213): None

Henry J. (1214): William M., Henry K.,
    Rebecca, George, Walter, Mary S., Martha,
    James M., Exenia, Jackson, Ora, Lettetia

Christopher (1221): Noel

James H. (1222): Charlotte, John F., Mary E.,
    Sally, Pickens P., Caroline

Rufus (1231): Unknown

Wade (1232): Unknown

Edgar (1233): Unknown

Francis (1234): Unknown

Robert (1235): Unknown

FIFTH GENERATION

Henry IV (11211): Emma M., Henry V, Wesley

John A. (11212): None

Charles B. (11213): Charlie Muteth, William

Hugh (11214): None

James B. (11215): Emma, James, Samuel, Henry
    Y., Mary, Charles, John A.

Francis (11216): Unknown

William R. (11217): William R., Alice

John S., Jr. (11411): Unknown

Livingston (11412): Unknown

Joseph H. (11413): Unknown

Abernathy (11414): Unknown

Andrew (11451): Unknown

Mathew, Jr. (11452): Unknown

William A. (12111): Unknown

Charles C. (12112): None

Joseph B. (12113): William T., Cecil, Jessie,
    Mary E., Nettie, Lois, B. H.

Noel A. C. (12121): None

Noel H. A. C. (12122): Charlie, Bessie,
    Arthur, Claude

William M. (12141): Mary L., Ida L., Annie,
    Walton, Willie (daughter), Hosea

Henry K. (12142): Wilemma, Mary L., Sarah A.,
    Ora, John, Fannie, William R.

George (12143): G. H., David

Walter (12144): Walter (daughter)

James M. (12145): None

Jackson (12146): None

Ora (12147): None

Noel (12211): Unknown

John F. (12221): None

Pickens P. (12222): Unknown

SIXTH GENERATION

Henry V (112111): Unknown

Wesley (112112): Unknown

James (112151): Unknown

Samuel (112152): Unknown

Henry Y. (112153): Richard, Henry Y., Jr.,
     Carrie, Nolan, Claiborne

Charles (112154): Charles B.

John A. (112155): Unknown

William R. (112171): William A., Ida, Hugh,
     Merle, Aubrey

William T. (121131): None

Cecil (121132): None

B. H. (121133): Unknown

Charlie (121221): Unknown

Arthur (121222). Unknown

Claude (121223): Unknown

Walton (121411): Edgar, Herbert, Bernard, Otis

Hosea (121412): Hosea, Jr., Miles, Edna, Mary
    E., Eva, Homer, James D., Barbara

Ora (121421): Ora

John (121422): None

William R. (121423): None

G. H. (121431): Unknown

David (121432): Unknown

SEVENTH GENERATION

Richard (1121531): Unknown

Henry Y., Jr. (1121532): Unknown

Nolan (1121533): Carolyn, Nolan, Jr., Cynthia,
    Lucy

Claiborne (1121534): Unknown

Charles B. (1121541): Unknown

Hugh (1121711): Hugh, Jr., William L., Mary
    M., Lydia, three more daughters

Merle (1121712): None

William A. (1121713): William A., Jr., Thomas

Aubrey (1121714): Susan

Edgar (1214111): Unknown

Herbert (1214112): Marylyn, Herbert, Jr.,
    Susie

Bernard (1214113): Mary E., Frances, William
    W., Michael, Sarah L., Bernard, Jr.

Otis (1214114): Unknown

Hosea, Jr. (1214121): None

286

Miles (1214122):   Miles, Jr., William T.,
     Robert

Homer (1214123):   Frederick, Karel, Vlasta,
     Pamela

James D. (1214124):   Elizabeth, Nancy, Joy

Ora (1214211):   Unknown

EIGHTH GENERATION

Nolan, Jr. (11215331):   Unknown

Hugh, Jr. (11217111):   Unknown

William L. (11217112):   William R.

William A., Jr. (11217131):   Unknown

Thomas (11217132):   Unknown

Herbert, Jr. (12141121):   Unknown

William W. (12141131):   Unknown

Michael (12141132):   Unknown

Bernard, Jr. (12141133):   Unknown

Miles, Jr. (12141221):   Kristin, Amy, Miles

William T. (12141222):   None

Robert (12141223):   Jeffrey, Keith

Frederick (12141231):   Unknown

Karel (12141232):   Jesse

NINTH GENERATION

William R. (112171121):   William R., Jr.

Miles (121412211):   None

Jeffrey (12141231):   None

Keith (121412232): None

Jesse (121412321): None

TENTH GENERATION

William R., Jr. (1121711211): None

APPENDIX IV

WILL OF VINSON VAUGHAN

In the Name of God, Amen: I, Vinson Vaughan,
of the County of Northampton in the Province of
North Carolina, being in a very sick, week
condition and knowing it is appointed for all
men once to die, I hereby make and ordain this
my last will and testament and manner and force
following: Viz.

First: I recommend my soul to Almighty God,
the giver, and as for my worldly goods I give
and bequeaths as follows:

Item: I give and bequeath unto my son, Vinson
Vaughan three hundred and fifty acres of land
and to (him?) one negro girl named Lucy and one
negro boy named Hary.

Item: I give and bequeath unto my Daughter,
Margaret Breathen one Negro girl named Jean.

Item: I give and bequeath unto my Daughter,
Sarah Vaughan, a Negro girl named Bety.

Item: I give and bequeath unto my son John
Vaughan, one Negro girl named Gillie and one
goon [?] and my waring cloaths and my stock to
be divided and cattel, one half to my son
Vinson Vaughan, the other half I lend to my wif
(sic) and one Negro wench named   during her
widderhood.

Item: I give and bequeath unto my Daughter,
Naomy Vaughan Clador, the first child the said
Negro wench brings.

Item: I give and bequeath unto my son, Henry
Clador, the second child the wench brings.

Item: I give and bequeath unto my son, Noel
Huchens, the third child the said Negro wench
brings.

Item: I lend to my wif one bed and furniture
during her natural life and one bed I give to
my son Vinson Vaughan and all the other
household goods to be divided one half to my
son Vinson Vaughan and the other I lend my wife
during her natural life.

And I do solemnly appoint John Brethen and
Frances Vaughan my whole and sole Executors to
this my last will and testament and I do hereby

revoke all others made heretofore either by word or wrighting. In witness whereof I have hereunto set my hand and fixt my seal this 29th. day of June in the Year of our Lord God 1749.

Test: Richard Brown Vinson (V) Vaughan
      John Breeding (his mark is very shaky)
      John Brown Junr.

Northampton County August Court 1749
The within written will of Vinson Vaughan Deceased was proved in open Court by oath of John Brown one of the subscribing witnesses thereto which was ordered to be certified and at same time John Brethen and Frances Vaughan were duly qualified Executors thereof.

29th. Aug. 1749 Test: (name blurred)
    Recorded in the Secy
    Office in No. (wording very dim)
    Page 229 23--
    231--------- Northampton (county)

The following is a copy of Major Dargan's narrative, the original of which is possessed by Mr. Raymond Dick of Glendale, California:

A history of the Vaughan family.

Henry Vaughan married Francis Elizabeth Bradford. She was a descendent of the Rolfe family—consequently of Indian extraction. History informs us that Pocahontas, the heroic daughter of the old Chief Powhatan, became a christian, married a young Virginian, Thomas Rolfe. She died young, leaving an only child - a son, from whom have sprung some of the best families of Va. The Bradfords the Randolphs & Mordaunts stand conspicuous among those families — So the early traditions inform us. Henry Vaughan with his wife and an only brother of hers, Richard Bradford emigrated to South Carolina some years previous to the Revolution of /75 — and settled on Reese Swamp about six miles above the town of Sumter. (The writer of this sketch was born on the old place, and from early life took much delight in gathering up all the old traditions of the family. Only four children reached maturity Viz. William Elizabeth, Henry, Francis— John the youngest died in early life. William Vaughan, the eldest, altho' a youth, was one of Gen. Sumter's bravest soldiers in the old war of Independence. I will give the names of the entire family - but they may not be in correct order.

William Vaughan married Alice Cook
Elizabeth   "   "   Amos DuBose afterwards married James Dwyer no children
Fensy   "   "   forgotten
Francis   "   "   John Reynolds.

290

The following is to the best of recollection.
William Vaughan's children and whom they married viz.
Kitty married a cousin Bradford — had a large family
Emily " John M. Dargan - " "
James died unmarried. Was Col. James Vaughan.
Alice married Benjamin Mitchel 2 children
Horace " Victoria Dargan.) 2 children
Leonora " Samuel Mitchel) After Horace's death, Horace
Mary " Timothy Jones) having also died about
Francis " -- Castles) the same time Victoria
                              married Timothy Jones.
                              a large family

Elizabeth Vaughan DuBose's children
Henry DuBose married Eliza McKewn. 2 children
Amos " " Martha Paris. 1 child
Francis " " Isaac Michau after wife's death married Philip Bower
Elizabeth " " John Robinson. 2 children
Vincent " " Winnie Days. 3 "
Martha " " Ralph Diers. 8 "
Hampton " left his home — fate unknown.
Mary " married Philip Bower after her sister's death

Henry Vaughan's children viz.	Francis Vaughan Reynolds children viz.
Henry married Miss Keese.	Col. William Reynolds died unmarried
Julia " John Frisson.	Elizabeth " married Florence Spann
Vermeille " Wentworth Keese	Ellen " " Lucius James
John died at University Va.	Ellen became deranged died some years ago in the Asylum Columbia

After Wentworth Keese died
Vermeille married a cousin
John Bradford — and is
again a widow

From Sumter County Miscellaneous Records, Vol. XX, page 242:

State of South Carolina, High Hills of Santee, June 9, 1787. To all whom it may concern, we the subscribers do hereby certify that we have long been acquainted with the bearer, Amy Cornet and her mother, Margaret Cornet who formerly lived in the State of North Carolina near the Roanoke River, Northampton County, and do further certify that they the said Margaret and Amy Cornet and all others of that family are a free born People and as far as we know have behaved themselves honestly and industriously. Given under our hands, etc.--

JAMES SCOTT   HENRY CLARKE
CHARITY SCOTT   AMY CLARKE
WILLIAM BRADFORD   NOEL VAUGHAN
WILLIAM REAMES   WINEFRED VAUGHAN
CHARLES SPANN   NATHENIEL BRADFORD
ISHAM MOORE   JOHN BRADFORD
WILLIAM MCCONNICO   CELIA BRADFORD
              SHADRACH HATCHER

Recorded the 9th. day of April, 1788.

Note that William and Nathaniel Bradford, as well as a Richard Span, appear in a Northampton County will of Thomas Bradford (abstracted in another appendix). A Naomi Vaughan is known to have married a William Reames in Brunswick County, Virginia (although not the Naomi Vaughan of this treatise). Reamses and Spanns were prominent citizens of Sumter County. Henry Clark witnessed Wm. Spence's deed to Henry Vaughan, Sr. in 1763. At least three John Bradfords are known to have settled in Sumter County (then District) in the 1770's, although the only one whose wife's name is known was John Angel (wife Mary). The grandmother of William Vaughan, Sr.'s wife Alice was Ann Clark; she had descendants named Couliette who were tied to Bradfords and

McConnicos; McConnicos were also tied to Couliettes and Bradfords. This information comes from estate settlements 'far too voluminous to enumerate here. Isham Moore had descendants in Sumter named John Isham Moore and indeed he may have had that first name himself. He was probably the progenitor of the entire Moore clan prominent in the Manchester area of the district. All of this is mentioned to give the reader an idea of where some of these prominent families came from and to show how they often came in groups, keeping a bond after arrival as before it; also why these names tend to show up with one another in the area's documents.

ABSTRACT OF WILL OF THOMAS BRADFORD

Northampton, North Carolina, Will Book One, 1759-1792

Will 50, page 75---THOMAS BRADFORD 23 May 1761 November Court 1762--to my loving wife MARY BRADFORD I lend my plantation whereon I now live with 2 negroes, cows, calves, bed, furniture, etc. and at her death or marriage the same to be divided between my sons WILLIAM and HENRY BRADFORD to son WILLIAM BRADFORD my plantation where I now live, joining the river, my son NATHANIEL BRADFORD and RICHARD SPAN with my negro boy Peter, my still, bed, furniture, etc. to my son HENRY BRADFORD a parcel of land containing 200 acres more or less, joining RICHARD SPAN, WILLIAM BRADFORD and the sd. HENRY with one negro girl to my daughters EDITH BRADFORD, SARAH BRADFORD and ELIZABETH BRADFORD negroes, money son NATHANIEL BRADFORD 100 acres more or less, joining his own (line?) and the county road where JOHN RICHARDSON now lives and I also give him my white coat and one negro fellow named Tim son RICHARD BRADFORD 400 acres in Orange County on Lick Creek and 2 negro boys to son THOMAS BRADFORD all my Island land
Extrs.: my loving wife and my son NATHANIEL
Wits.:   JOHN AVENT, WILLIAM BROOCKS

APPENDIX VIII

CENSUSES

1790 Claremont, Camden District, S. C.

Head of HH	Free White Males		Females	Others	Slaves
	16+	16-			
Nathaniel Vaughan	1	0	5	0	0
William Vaughan	2	3	2	0	2
Henry Vaughan	2	4	3	0	10
Noel Vaughan	1	2	3	0	3
William Vaughan	1	3	4	0	2
Henry Vaughan, Jr.	1	1	1	0	2
Miles Potter	1	1	3	0	3

1800 Brunswick County, Wilmington District, N. C.

Head of HH	Free White Males					Free White Females					Slaves
	10-	16	26	45	45+	10-	16	26	45	45+	
Miles Potter	2	2	0	1	0	2	0	0	1	1	3
John Potter	0	1	0	0	0	0	0	0	0	0	6
Robert Potter	0	1	0	0	0	0	0	0	0	0	4
James Potter	0	1	0	1	0	2	0	0	0	0	7

Key: Beginning page 369, 5- means under 5; 10 means 5-10; 20 means 15-20, etc. M on the left means Male and F on right means Female.

1800 Claremont County, Sumter District, S. C.

Head of HH	Free	White	Males			Free	White	Females			Slaves
	10-	16	26	45	45+	10-	16	26	45	45+	
Henry Vaughan	1	0	1	1	0	2	0	2	0	0	2#
William Vaughan	1	1	1	1	0	2	0	1	0	1	6
John Vaughan	3	0	1	2	0	1	0	0	1	0	8
John Vaughan	4	0	2	1	0	1	0	0	1	0	4
Henry Vaughan, Sr	0	0	1	0	1	0	0	1	0	1	17#
William Vaughan	1	0	1	1	0	3	0	0	1	0	9
Miles Potter	0	1	3	0	1	0	0	0	0	1	3
Nicholas Vaughan	0	1	1	0	1	0	1	0	0	1	8*

- May be 2 other free and 1 slave for Henry, Jr. and 1 other free and 7 slaves for Henry, Sr. instead of 21 and 17, respectively, depending on source you use.
* - Also 1 other free person in household.

1810 Sumter County (formerly Claremont) County, S. C.

Head of HH	Free	White	Males			Free	White	Females			Slaves
	10-	16	26	45	45+	10-	16	26	45	45+	
William Vaughan	2	2	1	0	1	3	1	2	1	1	25
Henry J(r) Vaughan	2	0	0	1	0	1	2	0	1	0	84 or 87
Nowell Vaughan(Sr)	0	0	1	0	1	0	0	0	0	1	10 or 100
Nowell Vaughan(Jr)	1	0	0	1	0	0	0	1	0	0	4
William Vaughan(J)	1	0	0	1	0	3	0	0	1	0	2 or 5
Vincent Vaughan	2	0	0	1	0	0	0	1	0	1	14

1820 Sumter County, S. C.

Head of HH	Free White Males					Free White Females					Slaves *	#
	10-	16	26	45	45+	10-	16	26	45	45+		
William Vaughan(j)	1	0	0	1	0	2	1	0	1	0	13 6	0

1820 Sumter County, S. C. (Cont'd)

Head of HH	Free White Males					Free White Females					Slaves	*	#
	10-	16	26	45	45+	10-	16	26	45	45+			
Isaac Norton	1	0	0	1	0	2	0	1	0	0	0	1	0
Robert Potter	0	0	0	1	0	1	0	1	1	1	0	1	0
Levi Potter	1	0	0	1	0	0	0	0	0	0	1	0	1
Isham Vaughan	0	0	0	1	0	2	0	0	1	0	3	2	0
Noel Vaughan	2	1	0	1	1	3	0	0	1	0	14	7	0
Miles Potter	0	0	0	1	0	0	0	0	0	0	10	4	0
William Vaughan	0	2	0	1	3	3	0	0	1	2	31	4	0
Margaret Vaughan	0	0	2	0	0	1	0	0	1	0		84	50
	0												

*Engaged in agriculture.   #Engaged in manufacture.

**** *for the following 2 censuses you said "same code scheme as above", but there are only 10 numbers across to enter* ***

1820 Amite County, Mississippi

Head of HH	Free White Males					Free White Females					Slaves	*	#
	10-	16	26	45	45+	10-	16	26	45	45+			
Elizabeth Spears	1	1	2	0	0	0	0	0	0	0			
Auston Spears	0	0	1	0	0	0	0	1	0	0			

1820 Greene County, Mississippi

Head of HH	Free White Males					Free White Females					Slaves	*	#
	10-	16	26	45	45+	10-	16	26	45	45+			
Lauchlin McKay	3	0	0	1	0	0	0	1	1	0			

1830 Sumter County, S. C.

Name	M	5-10	15-20	30-40	50-60	70-80	F	5-10	15-20	30-40	50-60	70-80	Slaves
James A. Vaughan		0 0	0 0	1 0	0 0	0 0		0 0	0 0	0 0	0 0	0 0	2
Margaret Vaughan		0 0	0 0	0 0	0 0	0		0 0	0 0	1 0	0 0	0 0	(err?)34 (84?)
Isham Vaughan		2 2	0 0	0 0	1 0	0 0		0 0	2 0	0 0	1 0	0 0	4
Isaac Norton		1 0	1 0	0 1	0 0	0 0		1 1	0 0	1 0	0 0	0 0	1
William Vaughan		0 0	1 2	1 0	0 1	0 0		0 0	0 0	0 0	1 0	0 0	21
William, Sr Vaughan		0 0	0 0	0 0	0 1	0		0 0	0 4	1 0	0 1	0 0	19
Henry Vaughan		0 0	0 0	0 1	0 0	0 0		2 0	0 0	1 0	0 0	0 0	71
Knowel Vaughan		0 0	1 1	1 0	0 1	0 0		0 0	1 1	0 0	1 0	0 0	23
James Norton		1 0	0 0	1 0	0 0	0 0		1 0	0 0	1 0	0 0	0 0	0
Hugh Norton		0 0	0 0	1 0	0 1	0		0 0	0 0	0 0	1 0	0 0	0
John C(hamp) Vaughan		0 0	0 0	2 0	0 0	0 0		1 0	0 1	0 0	0 0	0 0	22
John H. Vaughan		0 0	0 0	1 0	0 0	0 0		1 0	0 0	1 0	0 0	0 0	8

1830 Greene County, Mississippi

Name	M	5-10	15-20	30-40	50-60	70-80	F	5-10	15-20	30-40	50-60	70-80	Slaves
Lauchlin McKay		1 1	3 0	0 1	0 1	0 0		2 1	0 0	0 2	0 0	0 0	0

1830 Jackson County, Mississippi

Name	M	5-10	15-20	40	50	60+	F	5-10	20	30	40	50	60+	Slaves
John Vaughan		0 0	0 0	1	0	0 1		1 0		0 0	0 0	0	1	4

1830 Jackson County, Mississippi (cont'd)

Name	M	5-10 20 40 60+	50	F	5-10 20 40 60+	30 50	Slaves

Name	M 5-10/20/40/60+ 50	F 5-10/20/40/60+ 30/50	Slaves
Vincent Vaughan	1 0 0 0 1 0 0 0	0 0 1 0 0 0 0 O	3
Henry Vaughan	0 0 0 0 I 0 0 0	0 0 1 0 0 0 0 0	2

1840 Sumter County, S. C.

Name	M 5-10/20/40/60/80	F 5-10/20/40/60/80	Slaves
C. D. Vaughan	0 0 0010 0000	00 00000000	5
Noel Vaughan	0 0 0010 0010	00 02100100	40
Wm. Vaughan	0 0 0010 0001	00 00000100	14
Isham Vaughan	0 2 1200 0100	00 12000100	15
Robert C. Vaughan	0 0 0010 0000	00 00100000	8
John S. Bradford	0 0 0020 0000	11 10010000	142
John N. Frierson	1 1 1010 0000	00 00001000	169
John M. Dargan	1 0 2000 1000	11 13001000	25
Amos D. Nettles	1 1 1000 1000	11 00010000	13
Mrs. Mary Richardson	0 0 0010 0000	00 00000010	15
John Reynolds	0 0 0000 0010	00 01100010	34
Wm. J. Reynolds	0 0 0010 0000	00 00000000	14

1830 Lowndes County, Mississippi

Name	M 5-10/20/40/60/80	F 5-10/20/40/60/80	Slaves
James T. Barnard	0 0 1 1 0 0 1 0 0 0	0 0 1 0 0 1 0 0 0 0	0

1840 Clarke County, Alabama

Name	M	5-10	15 20	30 40	50 60	70 80	F	5-10	15 20	30 40	50 60	70 80	Slaves
John S. Vaughan		0	0 0	0 0	0 2	0 0 0		1 2	0 0	1 0	0 0	0 0 0	0

1850 Clarke County, Alabama

Name	Age	Sex	Occ.	R. Estate	P. Estate	POB
John S. Vaughan	52	M				SC
Luticia	34	F				NC
Sarah	17	F				AL
Mary	12	F				AL
Caladonia	12	F				AL
John	8	M				AL
Livingston	4	M				AL
Joseph	1/12	M				AL

1840 Mobile County, Alabama

Name	M	5-10	15 20	30 40	50 60	70 80	F	5-10	15 20	30 40	50 60	70 80	Slaves
John Vaughan		0	0 0	0 0	0 0	0 0 1		0	0 0	0 0	1 0	0 0	James Magee's District
Matthew J. Vaughan		1	0 0	0 0	1 0	0 0 0		0 0	0 0	1 0	0 0	0 0	

1840 Macon County, Alabama

Name	M	5-10	15 20	30 40	50 60	70 80	F	5-10	15 20	30 40	50 60	70 80	Slaves	Occup
Henry* Vaughan		1	2 0	0 0	1 0	0 0 0		0	1 0	0 0	1 0	0 0 0	2	Farmer
M. E. Vaughan		0	0 0	0 1	0 0	0 0 0		0	0 0	1 0	0 0	0 0 0	18	Merchant

* Not Henry J., but rather another Henry Vaughan, descended from the John Vaughan line of Northampton County Vaughans

1840 Chambers County, Alabama

Name	M	5-10	15-20	30-40	50-60	70-80	F	5-10	15-20	30-40	50-60	70-80	Slaves
Isaac Norton	0 2	1 0	0 0	1 0	0 0		2 1	1 0	0 1	0 0	0 0		1
Henry Gilmore	1 0	0 0	1 0	0 0	0 0		0 0	0 0	1 0	0 0	0 0		1
John Gilmore	0 0	0 0	1 0	0 0	1 0		0 0	0 0	0 0	1 0	1 0		2
John T. Goldsmith	0 1	0 2	0 0	1 0	0 0		0 2	2 0	1 0	0 0	0 0		15

1840 Lowndes County, Mississippi

Name	M	5-10	15-20	30-40	50-60	70-80	F	5-10	15-20	30-40	50-60	70-80	Slaves
William C. Vaughan	0 0	0 0	1 0	0 0	0 0		0 1	0 0	1 1	0 0	0 0		
Felicia Vaughan	0 0	0 1	6 0	0 0	0 0		0 0	1 1	1 0	3 0	0 0		
Allen R. Vaughan	0 1	0 1	0 0	0 1	0 0		0 1	0 1	0 0	0 1	0 0		
James Vaughan	0 0	0 0	0 0	0 0	0 1		0 0	1 2	0 0	0 1	0 0		
George Vaughan	0 2	2 1	1 0	1 0	0 0		0 0	0 2	1 0	1 0	0 0		
William W. Vaughan	1 1	0 0	1 0	0 0	0 0		1 1	1 0	0 1	0 0	0 0		
Gabriel Vaughan	0 0	0 0	1 0	0 0	0 0		0 0	0 0	1 0	0 0	0 0		
John Vaughan	0 0	1 1	0 0	0 1	0 0		0 0	0 0	1 0	0 1	0 0		

Besides William Christopher the other Vaughans listed in Lowndes County, Mississippi are carried in the event they may turn up to be related on an as yet untraced line. There may have been a reason for William C. going to Lowndes County (instead of somewhere else) and the large number of Vaughans there. See narrative for story on William's relocation.

1850 Sumter County, S. C.

Name	Age	Sex	Occ.	R. Estate	POB	Notes
Edgar Vaughan	23	M	Overseer	--	SC	
Elizabeth A. Vaughan	18	F		--	SC	Yes*
Wm. Vaughan	85	M	Planter	$6000	VA	
Alice	77	F		--	SC	
C. D. Vaughan	35	M	Planter	$1200	SC	
Martha E.	24	F		--	SC	
Noel	2 mo	M		--	SC	
Isham Vaughan	60	F(err)	Planter	$1600	SC	
Caroline	20	M(err)		--	SC	
Francis 0.	21	F(err)	Laborer	--	SC	
Susan Vermelle	20	F		--	SC	
Hamilton	17	M	Laborer	--	SC	
James H. Vaughan	30	M	Coachmaker	$2500	SC	
Mary H.	25	F		--	SC	

Note: Elizabeth A., daughter of John H. Vaughan was living with H. Stith and wife.

1850 Gadsden County, Florida

Name	Age	Sex	Occ.	R. Estate	POB	Notes
Joseph Sylvester	43	M	Farmer	$6000	SC	
Violet	44	F			NC	
Sarah	20	F			FL	
Isabella	18	F			FL	
Joseph	17	M	Clerk		FL	
Emma	14	F			FL	
James	10	M			FL	
Augusta	8	F			FL	
William	6	M			FL	
Mary	4	F			FL	
Rebecca	0	F			FL	

1850 Jackson County, Mississippi

Name	Age	Sex	Occ.	R. Estate	POB	Notes
Matthew J. Vaughan	42	M	Farmer		SC	
Celitta A.	36	F			GA	
Andrew A.	12	M			AL	
Matthew J.	10	M			AL	
Mary S.	7	F			AL	
Savina	4	F			MS	
Elizabeth	10/12	F			MS	
Henry	45	M	Schoolteacher		SC	

1850 Macon County, Alabama

Name	Age	Sex	Occ.	R. Estate	POB	Notes
William C. Vaughan	42	M	Farmer		SC	
Irena	33	F			VA	
Mary	10	F			MS	
Alexander	8	M			MS	
Charles	7	M			MS	
Virginia	5	F			MS	
California	1	F			AL	
William Vaughan	77	M	Farmer	$1600	VA	Dtd 9 Oct.
Miles E. Vaughan	36	M	Merchant		SC	
Mary L.	26	F			SC	
Emaley Hayley	8	F			AL	
John W. Par	16	M	Clerk		GA	
Henry J. Vaughan	32	M	Farmer		SC	
Mary	23	F			AL	
Miles	8	M			AL	
Henry K.	6	M			AL	
Rebecca	4	F			AL	
George	3	M			AL	
D. William(?)	1	M			AL	
Isom Trawick	36	M	Farmer		GA	
Sarah	32	F			SC	
Georgia	8	F			GA	
Harrison H.	5	F(err)			AL	
Mary C.	3	F			AL	

1850 Macon County, Alabama (cont'd)

Name	Age	Sex	Occ.	R. Estate	POB	Notes
Sarah	70	F			SC	
Isaac Norton	59	M	Farmer		SC	
Harriett	45	F			SC	
William	24	M	Carpenter		SC	
Harriett	19	F			SC	
Joseph	18	M	Farmer		GA	
Robert	16	M			GA	
Eivira	14	F			GA	
Martha	10	F			AL	
Henry Vaughan	48	M	Farmer	$2100	NC	see note
Nancipa	45	F			SC	with 1840
John W.	13	M			GA	Macon
Gillam	14	M			GA	County
Thomas	12	M			AL	Census
Amanda	9	F			AL	concerning
James H.	6	M			AL	this Henry
Nancy	3	F			AL	

1850 Chambers County, Alabama

Name	Age	Sex	Occ.	R. Estate	POB	Notes
Noel A. Vaughan	38	M	Physician	$1000	SC	
Sara A.	30	F			GA	
George M. Goldsmith	9	M			AL	
Amanda Permelia	8	F			AL	
Frances Logenia	5	F			AL	
Caroline S.	3	F			AL	

1850 Mobile County, Alabama

Name	Age	Sex	Occ.	R. Estate	POB	Notes
B. Vaughan	45	M	Merchant		SC	Note*
Mrs.	45	F			SC	
Emma	15	F			AL	

* These members were in a household of 2 merchants, 9 clerks (6 females and 3 underage males.. Could be Beverly ?)

1860 Sumter County, S. C.

Name	Age	Sex	Occ.	R. Estate	POB	Notes
Robert E. Vaughan	46	M	Farmer	$12000(P)	SC	Idiotic
Ann E.	45	F			SC	
Laurence	39	M		$25000(P)	SC	Idiotic
Isham Vaughan	75	M	Farmer	$2400(R)	SC	$7000(P)
Rebecca C.	35	F			SC	
Francis 0	30	M	Overseer		SC	
Susan B.	26	F			SC	
Robert H.	24	M	Laborer		SC	

Note: (P) = Personal and (R) = Real

1860 Macon County, Alabama

Name	Age	Sex	Occ.	R. Estate	POB	Notes
Jerry Vaughan	19	M	Overseer	$800(R)	GA	
Henry Vaughan	56	M	Farmer	$8000(R)	NC	
Nancipa	54	F			SC	
Gillam	23	M			GA	
Thomas	22	M			AL	
Amanda	19	F			AL	
James	15	M			AL	
Nancy	12	F			AL	
Frank	8	M			AL	
John Vaughan	35	M	Mason	$400	GA	Son of
Sarah	35	F			GA	preceding
Albert	11	M			GA	Henry
George	9	M			GA	
W. C. Vaughan	51	M	Farmer	$700	SC	
Irena	38	F			SC(?)	
Mary	20	F			MS	
Alexander	18	M			MS	
Charles	16	M			MS	
Virginia	14	F			MS	

306

1860 Macon County, Alabama (cont'd)

Name	Age	Sex	Occ.	R. Estate	POB	Notes
California	11	F			AL	
Joseph	5	M			AL	

1860 Tallapoosa County, Alabama

Name	Age	Sex	Occ.	R. Estate	POB	Notes
Henry Gilmore	49	M	Farmer	$7360	GA	
Emily A	25	F			GA	
Joseph Norton	28	M	Farmer	$6540	GA	Son of
Susan B.	34	F			GA	Harriett
Harriett	3	F			AL	
Lewis J.	3/12	M			AL	
James Chevers	14	M			MS	(See Below)
Isaac Norton	69	M	Farmer	$16120	SC	
Harriett S.	56	F			SC	
Martha	18	F			AL	
Ann Chevers	33	F			SC	
Jame(s) Chevers	13	M			MS	
Bruce Chevers	11	M			MS	
Sarah Chevers	9	F			MS	

1860 Clarke County, Alabama

Name	Age	Sex	Occ.	R. Estate	POB	Notes
Letitia Vaughan	45	F	Farmer		NC	
John S.	18	M	Student		AL	
Livingston	15	M	Student		AL	
Joseph H.	10	M			AL	
Abernathy	6	M			AL	

1860 Yazoo County, Mississippi

Name	Age	Sex	Occ.	R. Estate	POB	Notes
Henry Vaughan Sr.	60	M	Planter	$235827(P)	SC	
E. M.	50	F		$115500(R)	SC	
H. R.	21	M	Planter		MS	
James	18	M			MS	
Frank	11	M			MS	
William	6	M			MS	
Alice	15	F			MS	
Emma	13	F			MS	
Elizabeth M Reilly	23	F	Teacher		MS	
W. N. Langford	25	M	Overseer		AL	
C. B. Vaughan	23	M	Planter	$27000(R)	MS	
M. L.	21	F		$47000(P)	MS	
N. B. Street	22	M	Overseer		AL	

1870 Macon County, Alabama - Notasulga Beat

Name	Age	Sex	Occ.	R. Estate	POB	Notes
William C. Vaughan	60	M	Act Grocer Merchant	$350(R) $175(P)	SC	
Irena	50	F	Keep House		VA	
California	19	F			AL	
Joseph	16	M	Farm Hand		AL	
Ida Linsey	10	F	At Home		AL	
Robert Linsey	8	M			AL	
Mary	1	F			AL	
Minnie L.	1	F			AL	

1870 Chambers County, Alabama - Beat #10

Name	Age	Sex	Occ.	R. Estate	POB	Notes
N. A. Vaughan	59	M	Farmer	$1800(R)	SC	
Sarah A. M.	57(51)	F	Keep House	$900(P)	GA	
Harriet E.	18	F			AL	

1870 Chambers County, Alabama - Beat #10 (cont'd)

Name	Age	Sex	Occ.	R. Estate	POB	Notes
James V.	15	M(err)			AL	(Joanna?)
Noel H.	12	M			AL	
Mary A. L.	8	F			AL	
Wallace William	21	M			AL	

NOTE: (P) = Personal and (R) = Real

1870 Lee County, Alabama - Loachapoka Beat

Name	Age	Sex	Occ.	R. Estate	POB	Notes
H. J. Vaughan	50	M	Miller	$5000(R)	SC	$100(P)
G. A.	27	F	Keeps House		GA	
W.	19	M	Clerk in Store		AL	
L.	9	F			AL	
B. H. Reynolds	30	M	Farmer	$2000(R)	AL	$500(P)
R.	24	F	Keeps House		AL	
M. A.	2	F			AL	
W. A.	1	M			AL	

NOTE: (P) = Personal and (R) = Real

1880 Macon County, Alabama - Notasulga Beat

Name	Age	Sex	Occ.	R. Estate	POB	Notes
W. Vaughan	71	M	Farmer		SC	
Irena	60	F	Wife		VA	
Joseph	23	M	Son		AL	
Minnie Trot	10	F	Housekeeper		AL	
Robert Lindsey	19	M	Grandson (Linsey?)		AL	

1880 Chambers County, Alabama - Beat #10

Name	Age	Sex	Occ.	R. Estate	P. Estate	POB
Nowell Vaughan	69	M	Farmer			SC
Sarah Ann	61	F	Wife			GA
Annie L.	18	F	Daughter			AL
William M. Vaughan	38	M	Farmer			AL
Mary E.	34	F	Wife			AL
Lillie M.	12	F	Daughter			AL
Ida	10	F	Daughter			AL
Annie	8	F	Daughter			AL
Walton H.	6	M	Son			AL

1880 Lee County, Alabama - Loachapoka Beat

Name	Age	Sex	Occ.	R. Estate	P. Estate	POB
Henry Vaughan	61	M	Miller			SC
Georgia	37	F	Wife			GA
Robert Lindsey	32	M	Farmer			AL
California	30	F	Wife			AL
Marvin	2	M	Son			AL
Miles Vaughan	62(?)	M	Miller			GA(err)
Allen Robinson*	75	M	Uncle and Visitor			GA
Horatio	40	M	Cousin and Farmer			GA
Mary	57	F	Aunt and Boarder			GA

*Spelling should be Robison.

APPENDIX IX DEED RECORDS

The following is a listing of deed records referenced by the researcher in compiling this work. It is not all inclusive. In some instances abstracts are given. Deeds used as proof are cited in the text and can usually be found here; hopefully they will also serve as a resource all researchers.

NORTHAMPTON COUNTY, NORTH CAROLINA

1. Deed Book 3, page 266--Spence to Vaughan: This indenture made the thirty first day of October in the Year of our Lord One Thousand Seven Hundred and Sixty three between William Spence of Northampton County, Province of No. Carolina of the one part and Henry Vaughan of the said County and Province of the other part. Witnesseth that the said William Spence for and in consideration the sum of five Shillings sterling to him in hand paid by the said Henry Vaughan before the Execution of these presents the receipt whereof he doth hereby Acknowledge and of every part and parcel thereof, doth acquit and Discharge the said Henry Vaughan his heirs, Est. and Administ. forever by these presents, hath granted, Bargained, sold and conveyed, confirmed and by these presents doth fully, freely and absolutely grant Bargain, sell when Enfeoffe, Convey and Confirm unto the said Henry Vaughan, his heirs and assigns forever: a Tract or parcel of land Situate, lying and being in the County of No.Hampton on the east side of Glovors Spring Branch containing by estimation two hundred acres, be the same more or less, and bounded as follows: to wit: Beginning at a corner red oak in Thomas Bradford's line: thence along his line So. 75, W. 40 poles to James Taylor's line North 45, West 120 poles to Taylor's red oak on the Spring Branch thence thru the prong of said Branch to five corner pines then along a line of Chopt trees to a corner white oak on a small branch then up the said Branch to a corner pine, thence along a line of Chopped Trees to the first station being part of a tract taken

up and surveyed by Capt. John Moore and granted
by patent to Mark Moore bearing date the first
day of February 1760, Together with all houses,
orchards ways waters hereditaments and
appurtenances to the said land belonging or in
anywise appertaining with the reversion and
Reversions, Remainder and Remainders, Rents,
issues and profits thereof and of every part
and parcel thereof: To Have and To Hold the
said two hundred Acres of land with all and
singular the premises hereby granted unto the
said Henry Vaughan to the only proper use,
Benefit and Behoof of him the said Henry
Vaughan, his heirs and assigns forever and the
said William Spence for himself, his heirs and
Est. Administ. doth covenant and agree to and
with the said Henry Vaughan, his heirs and
assigns that at the time of delivery hereof he
is lawfully seized and possessed of all and
Singular the above granted premises an absolute
Estate of Inheritance in fee Simple, and that
the said land and premises is free and clear
from all manner of former and other gifts
Bargains, sales, leans, Mortgages and all other
incumbrances whatsoever and that the said Henry
Vaughan, his heirs and assigns shall and may
from time to time and at all times forever
hereafter peaceably and quietly have, hold and
occupy, possess and enjoy the same without the
            or molestation of the said William
Spence, his heirs Est. or Administ. or any
other person or persons claiming by from or
under them or any of them or further that he
the said William Spence, his heirs Etc. (?) the
said land and premises and every part and
parcel thereof unto the said Henry Vaughan, his
heirs and assigns, shall and will warrant and
forever defend against all claims and demands
of all and every person or persons whomsoever.
In Testimony whereof the said William Spence
hath herewith set his Hand and Seal the day and
year first above written.   (Oct. 31, 1763)
Signed, sealed and delivered in presence of--
James Clark-- Northampton Co.   his
Henry Clark-- November Court 1763
John Crittenden--   William X Spence (seal)
Preceeding deed proved in open court on
Oath of Henry Clark CLERK, L. Edwards   mark

312

2. Deed Book 5, pages 279-81--Vaughan to Love:
THIS INDENTURE made this 26th. day of November
in the year of our Lord One Thousand Seven
Hundred and seventy two Between Henry Vaughan
and Elizabeth, his Wife of Northampton County
and province of North Carolina of the one part
and William Love of Brunswick County in the
Colony of Virginia of the other part,
Witnesseth that the said Henry Vaughan and
Elizabeth his Wife for and in Consideration of
the sum of Eighty pounds Current money of
Virginia to them in hand paid by the said
William Love before the Execution of these
presents the receipt whereof he doth hereby
acknowledge and of every part and parcel doth
acquit and Discharge the said William Love, his
heirs, Executors and Adminis. forever by these
presents hath Granted, Bargained, Conveyed and
Confirmed and by these presents Doth fully,
freely and absolutely Grant. Bargain, Sell and
Convey and Confirm unto the said William Love
his heirs and assigns forever a Tract or parcel
of land--[description exactly as in previous]--
hereby granted unto the said William Love to
the only Benefit and Behoof of him, the said
Love, his heirs and assigns forever and the
said Henry Vaughan and Elizabeth, his wife, do
for themselves, their heirs, Executors and
Administrators doth Covenant and agree to and
with the said William Love, his heirs and
assigns, that the time of the sealing and
delivery hereof, he is lawfully seized,
possessed of all and singular the above granted
premises absolute Estate of inheritance in fee
Simple and that the said land and premises is
free and clear from all manner of former and
other gifts, Bargains, sails, leans, Mortgages
and all other Incumberances whatsoever-and that
the said William Love, his heirs and assigns
shall and may from time to time and at all
times forever hereafter peaceably and quietly
have, hold and occupy, possess and enjoy the
same without the molestation of the said Henry
Vaughan and Elizabeth, his Wife, their heirs.
Executors, Adminis. nor assigns or any other
person or persons whatsoever and further that
the said Henry Vaughan and Elizabeth, his Wife,
their heirs, etc., the said land and premises

and Every part and parcel thereof unto the said
William Love his heirs and assigns shall and
will warrant and forever defend against the
claims and demands of all and every person
whatsoever.   In Testimony we the said Henry
Vaughan and Elizabeth have set our hands and
affixed our Seal this day and year first above
written-(Nov. 26, 1772)   HENRY VAUGHAN Seal
William Garner)
Thomas Williams)   Northampton County for June
Susan Richards)   Court 1774
          This deed was proved by the Oath of
          Wm. Garner; ordered to be registered
                     Willie Jones, C. C.
This deed was duly Registered Aug. 1st. 1774-

SUMTER COUNTY, SOUTH CAROLINA

1. Deed of gift--Deed dated 12 March 1761, but recorded in Sumter County on 26 April 1805-- From Noel Waddell of New Kent County, Colony of Virginia, to his sister, Frances Johnson's children, namely: Naomi Jones (Sones?), Henry Clader and Noel Hutchens Clader, as follows: To Naomi Jones and her children, one Negro girl named "Sal" and her increase, now in possession of William Johnson of Northampton Co. in the Province of North Carolina; and to Henry Clader and Noel Hutchens Clader, two Negro slaves, "Patt" and her daughter, "Judith" now in possession of said Wm. Johnson; their mother, my said sister, Frances Johnson to have use of said "Patt" during her natural lifetime: In consideration of love and affection.

Signed, Noel Waddill
Witnesses: John Waddill, Jr.   before
William Irby   J. Edwards, Pub. Reg.

2. Book A, page 41--Know all men by these presents that I, Henry Vaughan, Sr. of . . . in consideration of three hundred dollars to me paid by William Vaughan, Sr. . . . do grant . . . all those two plantations parcells or tracts of land . . . one plantation . . . two hundred acres situated in Camden . . . originally granted to Henry Vaughan on 21 January 1785 . . . Office Grant Book AAAA, p. 413 . . . Also another plantation containing 64 acres . . . situate and adjoining to the above . . . part of a tract of 150 acres originally granted to John Flin on 2 June 1769 recorded in grant book DDD, p. 198 . . . To have and to hold . . .
Wit: John J. Bradford
Samuel Hatfield

3. Book A, page 52--Land sale from Timothy Dargan, Jr. to Henry Vaughan, Jr.

4. Book A, page 312--I, William Vaughan, Sr. . . . in consideration of two hundred dollars to me paid by John B. Vaughan . . . have granted bargained sold and released . . . containing 51 acres situate in Claremont County near Big Swamp comprehending part of a tract originally

granted to David Neilson and part of a tract granted to William Vaughan, Sr. on February 1803 . . . recorded in Book ABXXX (?), #5, p. 276. Dated June 1803.

5. Book A, page 319--Sale of three slaves by John Bradford Vaughan to William Jones (Sones) for $600: Cafsey (Cassie), George and Sophey. Dated 4 May 1803.

6. Book AA, page 138--For thirteen (hundred?) Spanish milled dollars John Peck mortgaged three negroes (Subiner, Saul and James) to Miles Potter.
　　　　Wit: P. Potter
　　　　　　William Vaughan, Jr.
A further entry notes that the mortgage was satisfied 26 April 1803 and the negroes returned to Peck.
　　　　Wit: Robt. Potter, son of Miles Potter.

7. Book AA, page 256--Amos Dubose grants for 100 pounds sterling from Noel Vaughan, Sr. 250 acres . . . granted to Benjamin O'Neal 7 May 1787 containing 540 acres, lying on the North side of Green Swamp, bounded on SW by land of Henry Wheeler. Land conveyed from B. O'Neal to John Cater, to George Cater, Sr. to Thomas Jackson, to Amos Dubose.
Dated 3 November 1803.
　　　　Wit: Henry Vaughan
　　　　　　Vincent Vaughan
Following the above is a statement of release by Elizabeth Dubose, wife of Amos.

8. Book B, page 64--Purchase of land tract by John B. Vaughan.

9. Book B, page 66----) Sale of land tract by
　　Book BB, page 247--) John B. Vaughan.

10. Book B, page 93--Land grant from Miles Potter to his daughter Lettetia Vaughan.

11. Book B, page 139--Land grant from John B. Vaughan to his niece, Frances Dubose, daughter of Amos and Elizabeth Dubose.

12.   Book B, page 343--Land grant to Henry Vaughan, Jr.

13.   Book C, page 317--Forfeiture of dower rights by Elizabeth (Bradford) Vaughan, wife of Henry Vaughan, Sr.

14.   Book H, page 4--Reference to a land grant to Noel Vaughan in 1784.

15.   Book H, page 29--Julia F. Frierson petitions John B. Miller, trustee, for estate partition. (Error in text--17 May 1827 should read 1817.)

16.   Book H, page 46--Deed from John A. Bradford to William W. Bradford as trustee for Frances Vaughan.

17.   Book H, page 107--Sale of land from Thomas Sumter to John Colclough, original grant to Vaughan.

18.   Book H, page 300--Slaves deeded to Henry Vaughan III by John M. Dargan.

19.   Book H, page 360--Henry Vaughan III sells land inherited by Victoria Vaughan after death of her parents, Mr. and Mrs. John M. Dargan.

20.   Book HH, page 41--William Vaughan, Jr. sells land to John Witherspoon.

21.   Book HH, page 43--Renunciation of dower rights by children of William Vaughan, Jr.

22.   Book HH, page 273--Noel Vaughan, Jr. sells slave to J. B. White.

23.   Book HH, page 330--Conveyance from Henry Vaughan III to John J. Frierson.

24.   Book HH, page 335--Names of some slaves bought by Henry Vaughan III.

25.   Book I, page 70--Sale of land by Victoria A. Vaughan.

26. Book I, page 104--Sale of land by Margaret Vaughan to J. Caldwell. (This deed contains a good early map of Sumter.)

27. Book I, page 243--Henry Vaughan III delegates power of attorney to John B. Miller; Vaughan states that he plans to remove to another state. [Mississippi]

28. Book I, page 254--A deed involving Vaughans, Friersons and Rees'.

29. Book I, page 327--Sale of land from Noel Vaughan, Jr. to Thomas Sumter. Deed involves inherent trusteeship.

30. Book A, page 154--John B. Vaughan to Joseph Singleton for $500, a negro boy Antony. Dated 9 June 1802. Wit: Robert Singleton.

31. Book AA, page 13--Thomas Sumter to Mason Spears for $400, 972 acres on Mulberry Branch, part of a 14,288 acre tract granted to Sumter in 1787. Dated 1 November 1801.
     Wit: William Jones

32. Book AA, page 71--Thomas Sumter to Henry Vaughan, Jr. for $500, a parcel of 68 3/4 acres and one of 21 acres, bounded by William Rees, William Murrell and Henry Vaughan on the south, William Rees on the west and lands of Greens and Jameses on the north.
Dated 14 October 1802.

33. Book AA, page 101--William Jones and wife Elizabeth grant to Moses Gordon for $200, 200 acres of land granted to William Jones on 8 July 1774.

34. Book AA, page 103--Thomas Sumter grants to Henry Jones for 400 pounds, 432 acres on Raften [Rafting] Creek part of a tract of 700 acres originally granted to Robert Dearington and 103 acres granted to John Wheeler and conveyed by Wheeler to Thomas Sumter.

35. Book AA, page 179--Transaction between Hubert Rees, Sheriff and Henry Vaughan.

Charles Pinckney had 700 acres of land and became indebted to Susanah Carnes for somewhat over $700. After Pinckney's death his estate was auctioned by order of judge and bought by Henry Vaughan for $3050. 700 acres in High Hills of Santee bordered by vacant lands. This parcel was part of an original 1000 acre tract. Dated 7 March 1803.

Wit: Thomas Dearington
J. B. Vaughan

36. Book AA, page 193--Grant from Thomas Sumter to Henry Vaughan, Jr.; 64 acres bounded by Henry Vaughan, Anthony Lee, Thomas Sumter and James Spann and originally granted to William Richardson on 9 June 1775 by William Bull, governor, as part of 200 acres. Dated 29 September 1803.

37. Equity Court Records: The following list concerns documents pertaining to Vaughans, Friersons, Rees', Nortons, DuBoses, Bradfords, Hamptons, Andersons and others subject to this treatise. The Sumter catalogue system has been used and (at latest knowledge of this writer) can also be used in looking up references in South Carolina Archives.

A) Package 4, Roll 360.   M) P. 19, R. 357.
B) P. 6, R. 98.   N) P. 24, R. 435.
C) P. 7, R. 114.   O) P. 25, R. 447.
D) P. 9, R. 151.   P) P. 25, R. 451.
E) P. 9, R. 155.   Q) P. 26, R. 482.
F) P. 10, R. 160.   R) P. 32, R. 550.
G) P. 10, R. 164.   S) P. 36, R. 602.
H) P. 10, R. 174.   T) P. 2, R. 45.
I) P. 12, R. 195.   U) P. 2, R. 47.
J) P. 12, R. 199.   V) P. 2, R. 70.
K) P. 16, R. 197.
L) P. 18, R. 329.

TROUP COUNTY, GEORGIA

1. Book D, page 197--Sale of Lot #287, District #5 to William Vaughan by Sinik Gilder. Dated 26 December 1833.

2.   Book E, page 55--Sale of same lot to Lazarus Atkins by William Vaughan. Dated 29 December 1834.

MACON COUNTY, ALABAMA

Macon County records include items from Will Book, Probate Records and County Minutes, as well as those from Deed Books.

1.   1851-'55, Will Book, page 52--Inventory of notes and accounts due William Vaughan, Deceased.

page 53--Bill of appraisement of William Vaughan, Deceased

page 54--Statement of commissioners as to how estate was divided. Commissioners found that the portion of Mary Cummings' children could not be divided equitably and those heirs should further divide their share among themselves or, if that did not satisfy the court, the estate be sold. Probate Judge adds his attestation that the estate has been divided to the court's satisfaction.

page 110--Statement of personal property belonging to the estate of William Vaughan, deceased, sold on 2 January 1854. M. E. Vaughan's statement that the sale was advertised three weeks in advance of sale.

pages 110 & 111-- Statement by Miles E. Vaughan that he sold two bales of cotton from William Vaughan's estate for $111.50 after handling charges.

page 128--A list of perishables of the estate of William Vaughan, deceased, sold on 5 December 1853 by M. E. Vaughan.

page 147--Statement of tract of land sold from estate of William Vaughan, deceased to Isaac Norton for $535.50.

2.   1850-'52, Probate Record--Henry J. Vaughan petitions for guardianship of Alfred M. and Joseph W. Cummings as he, M. E. Vaughan and Henry Gilmore have stood security for the children.

3.   1852-'82, Probate Record, page 51--M. E.
Vaughan swears oath as administrator of William
Vaughan estate.

4.   1852-'54, County Minutes, page 473--Miles
E. Vaughan petitions to administrate estate of
William Vaughan. Dated 6 October 1853. States
William died 15 days earlier.   Powers of
administration were granted and Miles entered
into bond for $90,000, William Wood and Thomas
Ingram standing security.   B. S. Johnson,
William Tally, John Crawford, John Tally and H.
F. Cowans appointed appraisers to return within
60 days.
                        page 493--Inventory
returned; Johnson, Crawford, Wm. Tally, Davis
P. Durr and L. T. Wimberly to divide the
estate.
                        page 503--M. E.
Vaughan petitions court to sell tract of land
from estate (see above).

5.   2 December 1850--Sale of items from estate
of Alexander C. McLeod to Henry Vaughan: 1
smoothing plow, 2 pointed plows, 1 oil stove.

DEEDS

Book G, page 716, 8 December 1848--Purchase of
tract of land by William Vaughan from George
Segrest.

Book H, page 181, 27 December 1851--Sale of
land by William Vaughan to David Lowry.

Book O, page 194, 25 April 1869--Purchase of
land by Miles E. Vaughan from Helen M. Ferrell
with mill and usage of mill supplies.

Book O, page 293, 5 March 1870--Miles E.
Vaughan purchases one-fifth interest in estate
of William and Mary Ferrell.

Book O, page 733, 1870--Purchase of further
interest in Ferrell estate from W. B. and Sally
Ferrell.

Book F, page 209, 18 December 1846--Sale of land by Henry J. Vaughan to Elijah Davidson.

CHAMBERS COUNTY, ALABAMA
(Deed Records Only)

1. Book 10, page 575, 13 December 1851--Noel Vaughan purchases land from Joshua Staples.

2. Book 10, page 577, 22 December 1851--Noel Vaughan purchases land from Henry Williamson.

3. Book 11, page 671, 27 April 1854--Noel Vaughan purchases land from estate of Henry N. Spinks, R. R. Spinks administrator.

4. Book 12, page 274, 25 July 1855--Sale of land to N. A. Vaughan by John A. Goldsmith, son of John T. Goldsmith.

5. Book 12, page 294, 31 August 1855--Sale of land to N. A. Vaughan by Jonathan and Ann Stamps.

6. Book 14, page 38, 30 November 1860--Gift of land (for $1) to Sarah A. Goldsmith [Vaughan] by Michael Loveless, whose wife Martha was a daughter of John T. Goldsmith.

7. Book 14, page 442, 21 August 1863--Sale of land to N. A. Vaughan by W. B. Gross.

8. Book 14, page 449, 1 April 1864--Sale of house and lot to M. L. Vaughan [Mary Lucretia?] by B. A. Hill.

9. Book 14, page 625, 14 September 1866--Gift of land from N. A. Vaughan to Harriett, Joanna, Noel H. A. C. to revert if grantee dies before marriage.

10. Book 15, page 601, 13 January 1872--Gift of land from N. A. Vaughan and wife to M. A. L. Vaughan, to revert if grantee dies before marriage.

11. Book 15, page 600, 15 January 1872--Gift of 120 acres to N. J. and Hattie Barber from N. A. Vaughan.

12. "M" Book 10, page 313, 15 February 1876--Promise by N. J. Barber and N. A. Vaughan to pay Renfro & Andrews $75.30 on 15 October 1876 for farming necessities loaned to them. Waiver of homestead rights and promise to present two bales of cotton free of charge.

13. "M" Book 14, page 210, 25 April 1879--Promise to pay to bearer of note to Crayton & Harwell $50, borrowed for the purpose of making a crop, without which note, crop could not be made. To pay on 1 November 1879 with waiver of homestead rights by W. M. Vaughan.

LEE COUNTY, ALABAMA
(Deed Records Only)

1. Vol. 89, page 361, November 1910--Sale of 25 acres by M. E. and W. M. Vaughan to O. O. Hinkle.

2. Vol. 89, page 611, January 1907--Sale of 1 acre to S. E. [Q?] Hales by Georgia Vaughan originally bought in 1903 [?] from W. T. & E. H. Webb and known as the S. E. Hales Place. [Note: There are documents on file in Sumter County, S. C., concerning the settlement of an estate of a White in which an S. Q. Hale acted as a trustee for minors in Alabama.]

3. Vol. 89, page 363, 20 December 1905--Purchase of 25 acres by W. M. Vaughan from William and Phala Graves.

4. Vol. 94, page 240, August 1893--Sale of 54 acres from W. T. and E. H. Webb to Henry Vaughan.

5. Vol. 94, page 240, 4 February 1897--"This indenture, made and entered into this, the 4th day of February 1897, by and between W. Miles Vaughan and wife, Mary E. Vaughan, H. King Vaughan and wife, Lou C. Vaughan, Rebecca A. Reynolds widow over the age of twenty-one

years, George L. Vaughan and wife Betty
Vaughan, Lettie V. Thomas and husband J. N.
Thomas, Walter H. Vaughan, over the age of
twenty-one years and only heir of Walter H.
Vaughan deceased, (the said W. Miles Vaughan,
H. King Vaughan, Rebecca A. Reynolds, George L.
Vaughan, Lettie V. Thomas, and Walter Vaughan
being all the children of Henry J. Vaughan,
deceased) Grantors and Mrs. Georgia A. Vaughan,
widow of said Henry J. Vaughan, deceased.
Grantee, witnesseth: That for and in
consideration of the conditions of an agreement
entered into this day between the said Grantors
and Grantee and the release of the Grantee by
quit-claim deed in certain other property; and
$1 to us paid, the said grantors have remissed
and released, and by these presents do quit-
claim and do convey unto the said Grantee
certain property in said County and State,
described as follows: A certain tract of land
with the improvements thereon, the same being
in Lee County, and State of Alabama, and more
particularly described as follows, to-wit:
Fifty-four (54) acres of land, more or less,
part of Section twenty-five (25), Township
nineteen (19) and Range (24) twenty-four, and
part of Section Twenty-six (26) Township
nineteen (19) and Range Twenty-four (24) known
as the S. Q. Hale place and lying in the
western part of the town of Loachapoka, Lee
County, and State of Alabama, bounded on the
north and west by the T. F. Mahone place, and
on the south and east by the J. F. Yarbrough
place. To Have and To Hold the Same unto the
said Grantee, her heirs and assigns in fee
simple forever. In Testimony Whereof the said
grantors have hereunto set our hands and seals
the day and year first above written."

6. Vol. 94, pages 341-2, 6 June 1911--A
statement from George L. Vaughan and Walter H.
Vaughan, now Walter H. Day, that they appoint
W. M. Vaughan their attorney in fact and have
received their parts of the settlement and
reaffirm the previous remission.

7. Vol. 94, page 203, 11 January 1911--Sale of 289.06 acres to Walton H. and William M. Vaughan by J. H. & E. E. Cooper.

8. Vol. 60, page 405, 16 August 1902--Sale of 115 acres to W. H. Vaughan by Frank and Lula Booker.

9. Vol. 60, page 485, 2 December 1903--Sale of 200 acres to W. H. Vaughan by C. G. and Minnie Williams.

10. Vol. 98, page 244, 9 April 1912--Sale of a lot and house on Clanton St. to W. M. Vaughan by W. H. Vaughan and wife Lena.

11. Vol 57, page 544, 6 October 1900--"Know all men by these presents, that for and in consideration of ($105.00) One hundred and five 00/100 dollars to the undersigned grantors W. M. Vaughan, M. E. Vaughan, H. K. Vaughan, Lou Vaughan, Rebecca Reynolds, Walter H. Vaughan, George L. Vaughan, do grant, bargain, sell and convey unto the said John Harmon, the following described real estate, to-wit: Five twenty-fourths (5/24) interest in a certain tract or parcel of land ten (10) acres more or less known as the mill tract, it being a part of the western portion of the east half (1/2) of Section (14) Fourteen Township (19) Nineteen, Range (24) Twenty-four all of which is in the county of Lee and State of Alabama including the mills Gin and machinery and all belonging thereto to run the said mill and gin together with all mill and water privileges on both sides of the creek commencing at the southwest corner of said ten acres of land more or less at a certain white oak and running a northwest direction so as to throw the millers house on the said mill tract, thence north on to the pond leaving a certain spring on the said mill lot and from same white oak along the road to the corner of fence and thence across the creek then up the creek to the east line lying on a public road from Loachapoka to Dadeville. To have and to hold to the said John Harmon, heirs and assigns forever.

And we do for his heirs, executors, and
administrators covenant with the said John
Harmon, his heirs and assigns that we are
lawfully seized in fee simple of said premises;
that they are free from all incumbrances and
that we have a good right to convey the same as
aforesaid; that we will, and our heirs,
executors, and administrators shall, warrant
and defend the same to the said John Harmon,
his heirs, executors, and assigns forever,
against the lawful claims of all persons." The
names of Josephus and Lettie Thomas were erased
from the conveyance, notarized by H. T. Dent.
M. A. Pinson, N. P., Chilton County witnessed
the signatures of H. K. and L. C. Vaughan. T.
B. Alford of Jefferson County, N. P., witnessed
the signature of Rebecca Reynolds, widow.

12. Vol. 40, pages 443-4, 4 February 1897--
Release of one-quarter interest in mill tract
to Georgia A. Vaughan by heirs of Henry J.
Vaughan, deceased for one dollar in hand paid.
Same tract as in previous deed.

13. Vol. A5, pages 358-9, 16 November 1870--
Sale of 160 acres to Henry Vaughan, William
Reynolds, Harrison and Sarah Trawick by Mark
and S. J. Phillips. (The Trawicks sold their
share to Colonel Jim Thornton in 1874, who, in
1875, sold to S. R. Armstrong.)

14. Vol. 52, page 149, 28 March 1896--Sale of
20 acres to J. B. Fielder from M. E. Vaughan.

15. Vol. 26, page 53, 1 January 1894--Sale of
22 acres known as the Miles Vaughan House Place
and 278 other acres south of Loachapoka to J.
L. Wise.

16. Book OO, page 205, 15 December 1883--Sale
of 336 1/2 acres to Miles E. Vaughan by Mary W.
Allen.

17. Book C, pages 182-3, 5 November 1867--Gift
of 3 acres to J. R. McGhee from M. E. and Mary
L. Vaughan.

18.   Book E, page 312, 14 May 1870--Grant of half-interest in mill and tract of land from Orrin D. Cox to Mary L. Vaughan.

19.   Vol. 123, page 61, 20 November 1917--Sale of house and lot on Clanton St. to Hosea and Eva Vaughan by W. M. and Mary E. Vaughan.

20.   Probate Minutes, Vol. Q, page 531, 29 July 1930--Property of Georgia A. Vaughan at death was 53 acre "Hale Place." Heirs were William S. Reynolds (53) Birmingham; Sally A. Edmond, Birmingham; Cemmie Montgomery, Birmingham; Mrs. W. O. Livingston, Oxford, Mississippi; Mrs. Reesie Trawick, Oxford, Mississippi; Harrison Trawick, Memphis, Tennessee.   She died insolvent.   Note that 53 acres is the acreage of the August 1893 purchase from the Webbs, less the 1 acre sold in 1907 to Mr. Hales.

APPENDIX X SOME PLATS AND LAND BOOKS PERTINENT TO PROPERTY OF THOSE IN THIS TREATISE

A. Land Plats in Sumter County Land Records:
   1. Henry Vaughan: A39, A138, B104, D101, AA72, AA181, AA194, O220, O224.
   2. Henry Vaughan, Jr.: B345, CC175.
   3. Henry, Jr's. heirs: ZZ5.
   4. John Vaughan: CC113.
   5. John B. Vaughan: A313.
   6. Julia Finetta Frierson: DD7.
   7. Margaret Vaughan: DD32, DD36, DD492, EE350, EE353.
   8. Noel Vaughan: F371, I328, GG286.
   9. William Vaughan: F60.
   10. William, Sr.: Misc. 159.

B. Property Designations from 1890-'93 Chambers Land Book:
   Miss A. L. Vaughan:
   NE1/4 of NW1/4 of S17 T21 R25 '90-'92
   SE1/4 of NW1/4 of S17 T21 R25 '90-'92
   NE1/4 of NE1/4 of S17 T21 R25 '90-'92
   N. A. Vaughan:
   SE1/4 of NE1/4 of S18 T21 R25 '90-'91
   NW1/4 of SW1/4 of S19 T21 R25 '90-'93
   W. M. Vaughan:
   NE1/4 of SW1/4 of S29 T21 R25 '90-'93
   NE1/4 of NW1/4 of S29 T21 R25 '90-'92
   NW1/4 of NW1/4 of S29 T21 R25 '90-'92
   SW1/4 of NW1/4 of S29 T21 R25 '90-'92
   SE1/4 of NW1/4 of S29 T21 R25 '90-'92

APPENDIX XI REFERENCES FOR UNRESEARCHED RECORDS

SUMTER COUNTY EQUITY COURT RECORDS

1. Package 1, Roll 9--Elizabeth Vaughan
2. P. 1, R. 16--Beverly, Matthew Vaughan
3. P. 1, R. 41--Victoria Vaughan
4. P. 2, R. 46--Elizabeth DuBose
5. P. 2, R. 47--Henry Vaughan
6. P. 2, R. 62--Margaret Vaughan
7. P. 2, R. 71--Vermelle (Rees)
8. P. 2, R. 72--John A. Vaughan
9. P. 3, R. 59--Margaret Vaughan
10. P. 3, R. 61--Henry Vaughan
11. P. 3, R. 62--Julia Frierson
12. P. 3, R. 111--Julia Frierson
13. P. 3, R. 131--Vermelle (Rees)
14. P. 3, R. 141--Julia Frierson
15. P. 5, R. 232--Henry Vaughan
16. P. 6, R. 100--William Vaughan
17. P. 6, R. 257--Vermelle (Rees)
18. P. 6, R. 268--Leonora Mitchell
19. P. 7, R. 285--Henry Vaughan
20. P. 14, R. 259--Elizabeth DuBose

SUMTER COUNTY, SOUTH CAROLINA
BILLS AND PETITIONS (1795-1840)

	ARCHIVES #	SUMTER CO. #
A. Vincent Vaughan:		
	29, 35, 218, 308	Package 5, #84; P. 8, #122; P. 1, #9
B. Matthew Vaughan:		
	218	--
C. John Bradford Vaughan:		
	40, 43, 48, 218	P. 7, #114
D. John Horace Vaughan:		
	121, 314	P. 1, #47
E. John Vaughan:		
	218	--
F. James Alexander Vaughan:		
	266	--
G. Elizabeth Vaughan:		
	218, 308	--
H. Beverly Vaughan:		
	218	P. 1, #10

I. Henry Vaughan:
                21, 66, 112,   P. 4; #60, P. 12,
                153, 154,   #195; P. 18, #329;
                228, 251,   P. 25, #447; P. 25,
                260, 269,   #451; P. 5, #232;
                289, 292   P. 5, #235; P. 7,
                                #286; P. 2, #47;
                                P. 3, # 61; P. 3, #62
J. Margaret Vaughan:
                34, 35, 43,   P. 2, #45; P. 2,
                45, 60, 101,   #62; P. 2, #70;
                224, 228,   P. 2, #72; P. 3,
                229, 230,   #59; P. 6, #98;
                240, 291,   P. 6, #100
                303
K. William Vaughan, Jr.:
                53, 54, 57   P. 7, #15; P. 9,
                                #155; P. 10, #164
L. William Vaughan, Sr.:
                29, 35, 40,   P. 9, #137; P. 12,
                43, 48, 68,   #199
                308
M. Noel Vaughan:
                191   P. 32, #550
N. Martha E. Vaughan:
                266   P. 6, #268
O. Richard Vaughan:
                43   --
P. Robert Vaughan:
                218   --
Q. Alice Vaughan:
                266   --
R. Leonora C. Vaughan:
                266   --
S. Mary Theodosia Vaughan:
                266   --
T. Victoria Vaughan:
                121, 314   P. 19, #351
U. Vermelle Vaughan:
                34, 43, 48,   P. 2, #71; P. 3,
                60, 101,   #60; P. 3, #131;
                230, 240,   P. 10, #74; P. 16,
                251   #267

NEW SERIES (1840-1870)

V. Alice Vaughan:
                Bill 42; Petition 152   #201

330

W. Christopher D. Vaughan:
Bills 33, 37 #156, #178
X. Elizabeth Alice Vaughan:
Petition 159 1853-#327
Y. Edgar J. W. Vaughan:
Petitions 196, 1852-#534;
204   1858-#584
Z. Frances, w. of Isham Vaughan:
Petition 140 1844-#101
AA. Henry/J. Champion/John P. Vaughan:
Bills 4, 10 P. 1, #14; P. 1,
#43
AB. Isham Vaughan:
Petitions 140, --
196
AC. James H. Vaughan:
Bill 37   --
AD. Noel Vaughan:
Bill 23,   #107, 1846-#13
Petition 142
AE. William Vaughan [Sr.]:
Bill 42   --
AF. William Vaughan, Sr.:
Petition 152 1850-#283

SUMTER COUNTY, SOUTH CAROLINA, MINUTES

A. William Vaughan: Book B, page 154, dated
1836 (Security for J. & M. Gibson,
guardians of J. H. & M. J. Sylvester)
B. Isaac Norton: Book B, pages 238 & 247
(Concerning his daughter Jane)

SUMTER COUNTY, SOUTH CAROLINA,
DECREES BOOK

Isaac Norton: Book C, pages 34-43
(Concerning his daughter Jane)

TALLAPOOSA COUNTY, ALABAMA DEED BOOKS

Book	Page	Book	Page	Book	Page	Book	Page
1. 69	84	4. 70	11	7. 73	146	10. 304	419
2. 69	299	5. 71	77	8. 299	216	11. 317	86
3. 69	391	6. 71	132	9. 301	105	12. H	181

APPENDIX XII THE EVERPRESENT
VINCENT VAUGHAN

Since many Vincent (Vinson) Vaughans appear in this volume, it seems appropriate to sort them out. In some instances Vincents discussed separately may be identical. Perhaps the reader may have additional information.

Vincent did sawyer work for St. Peter's Parish Church in New Kent County, Virginia, in 1701. He was paid in 1702 and 1704.

Vincent Vaughan married Frances Waddill and left a 1749 will in Northampton County, North Carolina. He was likely the same as above, but possibly a relative, perhaps even son, to the same.

Vincent Vaughan, son of the above, is mentioned in the 1749 will and left one of his own in Northampton County, dated 10 December 1764 and probated May 1765 (Book 1, page 127 of Northampton County Wills). The deceased named as an heir a cousin William Vaughan, indicating the elder Vincent may have had a brother in the area. He also lists as heirs Vinson Vaughan, William Vaughan, Martha Vaughan and Susannah Vaughan, children of John Vaughan, whom we should probably take to be his brother named in the 1749 will.

A Vincent Vaughan left a will of 1750 in Granville County, North Carolina (Will Book 6, page 229). It names a nephew, Vincent Vaughan, son of John Vaughan. Note similarity to above will, although clearly a different person.

Patent Book 14, page 322--a book of Granville County Land Grants, 1748-1763--Vinson Vaughan 1 August 1762, 91 acres in Northampton County, joining Robert Warren, William Vincent, John Boude, a pond and James Denton. Witness: Wm. Gay, Jno. Haywood; J. Edwards, surveyor. This grant could have been made to Vincent of the 1764 will or either of the Vinsons mentioned as

a nephew in the previous two wills. See also following paragraph.

Vincent Vaughan of Granville County, North Carolina, states in military pension application that he was born 8 February 1761 in New Kent County, Virginia, and removed in early infancy to Northampton County, North Carolina. Removed across Roanoke River to Halifax County at school age and remained until age 27. Removed to western Warren County for twenty years, then moved a few miles to Granville County and married Martha _____, born 27 February 1771. Child of this Vincent of same name, born 15 November 1814. [The author has a copy of the application narrative from the National Archives. Could this Vincent be the son of John? He could have been a child in Northampton County in 1764, but only if presumed father John returned to New Kent before going back to Northampton County.]

Vincent Vaughan, son of Henry Vaughan, Sr., was probably born in 1760's; he died between 1814 and 1820, after going to Alabama.

Vincent Vaughan was a son of John Bradford Vaughan and removed to Mississippi and Alabama with him.

In Northampton County we find a grant from William Acock to Richard Brown on 20 January 1747, witnessed by Vincent Vaughan, and including a piece of land set aside for Vincent Vaughan for use of a mill. This land was on the upper side of Stony Creek. On 21 February 1747 William Acock granted a tract on the north side of Roanoak [sic] River to Vincent Vaughan. On 24 February 1747 Thomas Avent granted a tract to Vinson Vaughan, said grant seeming to have abutted the above land. Both were on north side of Roanoke River at Arthur's Creek. This land passed around among several families thereafter. Some of them, besides the above, were Raglands, Moores, John Bradford and Thomas Bradford. The Bradfords are also involved in land deals in another area called the Moratuck/Morratock/Morratoke River area. The

names Richard Pace, William Pace and Thomas Pace occur in most of these deeds. From Pace Family we know that John Bradford married Rebeckah Pace, daughter of Richard Pace, notwithstanding the fact that Rebeckah's daughter Winnefred (Acock) Lane said Rebeckah married William Bradford. Winnefred's father, Mr. Acock, was her mother's second husband. We can thus get some idea what the Vaughan and Bradford association was at this time. In listings in the IGI and county records for at least five counties in Virginia and two in North Carolina one finds John Bradfords and Rebecca Paces; however, one would probably best look to the Pace Family to sort them out. At any rate, it is obvious the Bradfords and Paces had a long and close association. But that is another story, best left to the reader. Suffice it to say, if there was a Pocahontas connection to the Vaughan Family through Frances Elizabeth Bradford (as Major Dargan states), it probably went through these Bradfords and possibly the Paces, who were known to have been in Jamestown at the time of the marriage of Pocahontas and John Rolfe, who left one son.

APPENDIX XIII THE BRADFORD FILES

It has already been noted that a Thomas Bradford left a will of 22 march 1785 in Granville County, North Carolina, and that a John Bradford lived in Northampton County of the same state and had children there in the 1720's and 1730's whose names correspond to many of the Bradfords found early on in Sumter District. The writer prefers, however, to believe the Sumter District Bradfords were (at least mostly) children of the Thomas Bradford who left a will (in an earlier Appendix) of May 1761 in Northampton County.

The reader may note the land Henry Vaughan, Sr., acquired in Northampton County from William Spence bounded that of Thomas Bradford. By this date (1763) the elder Thomas was deceased, but his land may have still been known as Thomas Bradford lands (or perhaps it was then in possession of his son of the same name).

The first Bradford we know was resident in Sumter District was Nathaniel. An article concerning him appears on the last page of this vignette. Nathaniel and two other Bradfords signed the Amy Cornet document. A Thomas Bradford received an early land grant in Sumter District according to Janie Revill's Sumter District (page 31). He sold the land before 1800 for the offices of Salem County to be housed thereon. Did this Thomas possibly move back to Granville County, North Carolina (or perhaps he only possessed property in Sumter District and never actually lived there)?

Nathaniel's son John A. had a cousin John James Bradford, sometimes designated Sr., in Sumter District. In the attached article William Vaughan, Sr., states the two Johns were cousins, but the older's parentage is not given. Likely he was a son of one of the other two Bradfords of the Amy Cornet document. If so, Celia was probably his wife, which would

334

make Margaret, named as John J's. wife in later documents, a second wife.

Nathaniel married Elizabeth Hicks (Nicks in some documents). Their children were Nathaniel, Jr., John Angel, Richard, Mary (married Mr. Drake) and Sarah (married Mr. Rheames).

John A. was born on 16 September 1764, married Mary Mitchell and died 5 December 1829. Mary was born on 20 August 1768 and died 19 May 1848. Sumter Banner of 05/25/1848: Died near Sumterville on 05/19/1848, Mrs. Mary Bradford, in the 80th year of her age. Mother of 11 children, 6 boys and 5 girls. Member of Methodist Episcopal Church for 35 years.

The children were Frances, who married Isham Vaughan, Middleton, Susan, Mary Mercy A., William Wade, Nathaniel, Winnie, John Mitchell, Robert Rivers, Tom W. and Heriot (Harriett?).

Middleton married firstly Martha G. Moody of Charleston. He moved to Madison County, Tennessee. By Moody he had Lidia, William and Frances. Martha died in 1837 and he married Lydia Belle McCollum, by whom he had Jane and Malcomb. After Lydia's death in 1860 Middleton married Elizabeth Anne Kuykendall Moore in Yalobusha County, Mississippi, where he himself died in 1866. Winnie married Edward Wingate. William Wade was born in 1804 and married Matilda R. Wilson. Sumter Banner of 02/06/1850: Died near Sumterville, Mrs. Matilda R. Bradford, daughter of Robert Matthews Wilson of Middle Salem, consort of William Wade Bradford, in the 35th year of her life. She left one son and 5 daughters. Robert Rivers died in 1839, leaving a wife and children (Estate Settlements, Bundle 9, Package 7).

Richard, son of Nathaniel and Elizabeth Bradford, married Elizabeth Singleton and died about 1825. Elizabeth died in 1806 or 1807. Their children were Richard, Jr., who was dead by 1813, Robert, Matthew, Elizabeth, Sarah and

Mary. Richard, Jr., married Elizabeth Brunson [writer thinks she was daughter of Isaac Brunson, since she married Warner Macon after Richard, Jr's. death and Macon administrated Isaac's estate]. She would have been Richard's cousin as the daughter of Brunson and Mary Singleton. Richard's only other heir was Natala (or Nately) Eliza, who married James Nettles, son of William and Mary (Mathis) Nettles. One source has stated that Richard, Jr., had a son Robert, but the writer has found no substantiation of this claim.

Robert, son of Richard, married Nancy Singleton, also a cousin and daughter of his uncle, Major John Singleton. Robert married secondly Nancy Brunson. Robert's children were John Singleton (by his first wife) and Mary Ann Elizabeth. John Singleton Bradford was the second husband of Vermelle Vaughan and their children are listed in the passage on Vermelle. Cassie Nicholes states that Robert was coroner and later sheriff of Sumter County, but the writer seems to remember seeing Richard, Sr., listed as sheriff in deeds involving fieri faciae (reneging on debt). Mary A. E. married her cousin, Gabriel Wesley Bradford, for which see below.

Matthew, son of Richard, married Harriet Dingle. Their children were Gabriel Wesley, Robert Dingle and Mary Louise. Gabriel Wesley married his cousin, Mary Ann Elizabeth Bradford, daughter of Robert. Their daughter Sally Bradford married Joseph R. Singleton, son of Major Joseph Singleton. A second daughter married Mr. Singleton after her sister's death. Their only child died at 10 months. The Sumter Banner of 03/23/1849 carries a notice that Robert H. Bradford married Mary Ann McKnight, daughter of A. C. McKnight, but writer thinks this is Robert D. Mary L. married William Eldridge Mellett.

Elizabeth, daughter of Richard, married Thomas James Wilder. They had nine children. Mr. Wilder was clerk of the Court of Common Pleas.

Daughters of Richard, Sr., and Elizabeth Bradford, Sarah and Mary, married Adam Ervin Brown and Jeremiah Brown, respectively. The writer does not know if the Browns were related. Ervin Brown left a will of 1864 in which he left an estate in trust for his wife, Caroline M. Brown, to Gabriel W. Bradford.

Some Sumter County Bradfords are not readily identifiable. One is John James Bradford, previously mentioned, and a cousin to John A., probably nephew to Nathaniel. One Nathaniel married Sarah Howard. This could have been either the son of Nathaniel or John A. Both resided in Sumter District and the former was probably Sarah's husband. The estate settlement of Nathaniel's son Nathaniel was conducted between 1824 and 1829 and does not mention a wife. It does mention William and Martha Boone, John W. and Sarah McIntosh, Warner, Louisa and Hele Bradford (who appears in several deed transactions) and these were presumably children (and spouses thereof) of Nathaniel. Samuel J. Bradford, who married Kiturah Vaughan, was said to be her cousin by Major Dargan, but he does not mention parentage of Samuel. In Thomas Britton's will of 10 June 1807, he calls Richard Bradford, son of Nathaniel, a half-brother, which would make sense only if Elizabeth Hicks had been married prior to her marriage to Nathaniel. Charlotte Vaughan, daughter of Noel Vaughan, Jr., married J. Francis (some places J. Franklin) Bradford. He is unidentifiable other than that he might possibly be that son of Samuel J. and Kiturah Bradford named John F. Bradford.

Clarke County, Alabama records show the marriage of a Nathanel Bradford on 23 February 1826 to Maria Blackwell. Also in that county, near Amity Church and the Choctaw County line, is a memorial to Thomas Bradford, revolutionary soldier of South Carolina. He had sons Brasil and Nathan. One of the witnesses to Thomas Darrington's South Carolina will, probated in Sumter on 28 July 1800 and dated 1793 is John Bradford, said will also recorded 5 January 1836 in Clarke County. This is the county John

Bradford Vaughan came to and his descendants
settled in.

From <u>South Carolina Magazine of Ancestral
Research</u> (Vol. 6, page 31 and taken from
<u>Wesleyan Journal</u> of 15 July 1826)--"Departed
this life, the 21st June 1826, near
Sumterville, the venerable Richard Bradford,
about 82 years of age . . . a member of the
Methodist Episcopal Church about 40 yrs."

Hopefully this sketch will assist any who are
interested in researching this line.
Undoubtedly there are those who know much more
in this area than I.

BRADFORD ARTICLE CONVEYED TO WRITER
FROM UNKNOWN SOURCE

56.

1836 being noted from time to time as they afterwards happened. Said Almanack and other Bible are lost or destroyed, as being considered useless.
(Signed)   W.W. BRADFORD

--

S. C., Sumter District..15 Aug.1854..
WILLIAM WADE BRADFORD, abt 50 yrs old, son of John A. & Mary Bradford made affidavit. Abt 25 yrs old when his father died. His father related many incidents of his connection with the Army, such as: "His father (deponent's grandfather) was an old and infirm man who procured parole from the Army to remain at home. That deponent's grandfather was opposed to his father going into the service but in consequence of the enemy having taken from him a sack of meal which deponent's father was conveying home from the mill, it so exasperated his said father that he was induced to steal his Grandfather's horse "Boots & Spurs" and proceeded to join General Marion's army and continued to serve during hostilities under Captain Joseph Hill, Warren R. Davis and others . . . Abt seven years ago deponent received a formal deposition proving his father's service signed by the late John China, a Revolutionary pensioner,. similar affidavit made by William Vaughan a fellow soldier of his father.

S.C., Sumter Dist..15 July 1854,William Vaughan, aged 89 and upwards, Rev. Pensioner, resident said district... His father emigrated from Virginia to S.C. 1772. Lived within 2 miles of Nathaniel Bradford and family in Sumter District, who were also Virginians. Knew John A. Bradford from earliest childhood, etc.. (Testifies as to his service.) Two Bradfords served at same time with this deponent- John Bradford and the aforesaid John A. Bradford, cousins, and designated as "Senior" and "Junio",said John A. being the younger, but 8 or 9 mos. older than this deponent. John A. Bradford married Mary Mitchell. Deponent did not attend marriage, but was at the infare- now upward of 65 years ago.

S.C., Sumter District..19 Nov. 1854... NATHANIEL BRADFORD made affidavit that he found an old pocket book of his

father. Among papers in it was a certificate of Obediah Spears, late of Sumter Dist, dated 13 Oct.1827, testifying to his father's service. He remembers that his father went and spent the day with Obediah Spears, returning with this certificate which he intended to get John China and William Vaughan to sign; was taken sick and unable to attend to it before his death.

--

Sumter, Dist..19 Dec. 1854, Joshua Spears makes affidavit that the above referred to certificate was his father's writing. Gave his age as 54 years.

Note: In the testimony of William Wade Bradshaw it is not quite clear as to whether the horse "Boots & Spurs" belonged to John A. Bradford"s father, Nathaniel or to his grandfather; apparently the latter. Therefore, in making further investigations it would be well to consider the possibility of Nathaniel's father (unnamed) being still alive and in Sumter District about 1783.
Mary (Mitchell) Bradford's tombstone inscription reads that she was the mother of eleven children, but on ten were recorded on original page from Bible, or the list presented in court.--KPWE

S.C. Memorials (Land Grants)- Esker (1946) Robert Singleton exhibted Memorial to be registered..250 a..Craven County..high hilss of Santee, St. Marks Parish; bounding on NW by Matthew Singleton & John Dargan; NE on sd Matthew Singleton; SE on THOMAS BRADFORD & William Moore; SW on Ann Bodeley. Survey..12th Novr.1771; granted 16th Jany 1772, etc., etc.

Richard Bradford m. Elizabeth, dau. of Robert Singleton, before Nov. 1798, Sumter Co. (Ref: Will of Robert Singleton)

Yalabusha Co., Mississippi-Census 1850
P.O. Oakland

BRADFORD,	Middleton	56 m Planter	S.C.
"	Lidia	28 f	N.C.
"	William	21 m	Tenn.
"	Frances	17 f	Tenn.
"	Jane	4 f	Miss.
"	Malcomb	8/12 m	Miss

Note: Lydia was undoubtedly a second wife and mother of only Jane & Malcomb

APPENDIX XIV MILITARY PAPERS

In this Appendix are copies of military records from the National Archives. Most of the information therein has already been extracted and may be found in the narrative concerning the subject thereof.

CHARLES B. VAUGHAN (11213)

Card 1

(Confederate.)

| 1 L. Arty. | Miss. |

C. B. Vaughn

Priv., Co. ____, { 1 Reg't Mississippi Light Artillery.

Appears on a

Regimental Return.

of the organization named above,

for the month of _August_ 1862

Return Not Signed.

Commissioned officers present and absent: ____

Station ____

Remarks: ____

Enl'std men on Extra or Daily Duty: ____

Pace ____

Remarks ____

Alterations since last return among the enlisted men: ____

Pace ____

Absent enlisted men accounted for: ____

(44) ____ J. N. Franciser, Copyist.

Card 2

(Confederate.)

| 1 L. Arty. | Miss. |

C. B. Vaughn

Priv., Co. ol, { 1 Reg't Mississippi L. Art'y.

Appears on a

Descriptive List

and account of pay and clothing of deceased members of the organization named above.

List dated _Gallatin, Miss._ Dec. 17, 1862.

Description: Age 24; height 5-8½;
Complexion dark; hair dark; eyes gray.

Where Enlisted: _Yazoo City_
When: _May 7, 1862_
By whom: _Capt. Vaughn_
Period: _3 years_

Occupation: _Farmer_
Nativity: _Yalla Co. Miss._

Last paid: _Capt. Mill._
By whom: ____
To what time: _Oct. 31, 1862_

Bounty: Paid, $ 50 ____ due, $ ____

When died: _Nov. 27, 1863_
Where: _Hazel Hayer Co._
Cause: _of Measles_
Nearest living relative: _Mrs. E. B. Vaughn_
How related: _Wife_
P. O. address: _Hesper Co. Miss._
Remarks: ____

Book mark: ____

(402) ____ A. Murchison, Copyist.

Card 3

(Confederate.)

| 1 L. Arty. | Miss. |

C. B. Vaughn

Priv., Co. ol, { 1 Reg't Mississippi Light Artillery.

Appears on

Regimental Return.

of the organization named above,

for the month of _Jan._ 186 3.

Return Not Signed.

Commissioned officers present and absent: ____

Station ____

Remarks: ____

Alterations since last return among the enlisted men:
Date: _Jan. 21_ 1863.
Place: _Warren County_
Remarks: _Died_

Enl'sted men on Extra or Daily Duty: ____
Place ____
Remarks ____

Absent enlisted men accounted for: ____

(44) ____ A. Murchison, Copyist.

Card 4

(Confederate.)

| 1 L. Arty. | Miss. |

C. B. Vaughn

Priv., Co. ol, { 1 Reg't Mississippi Light Artillery.

Appears on

Regimental Return

of the organization named above,

for the month of _December_, 186 2.

Commissioned officers present and absent: ____

Station ____

Remarks: ____

Alterations since last return among the enlisted men:
Date ____ 186 :
Place ____
Remarks: ____

Enl'sted men on Extra or Daily Duty: ____

Absent enlisted men accounted for:
_Nov. 27 Hospital at Vicks-
burg Since Nov. 13_

(44) ____ A. Murchison, Copyist.

CERTIFICATE OF DISABILITY FOR FURLOUGH.

We certify that we have carefully examined _Colo B. Vaughan_ of Captain _____

Company (I.) Regiment of _Withers Artillery_ ____ and find him incap ble of performing the duties of a soldier, because of _Syphilis Primaria — Ut Hunter_ _____

Recommend that he be granted a furlough for 30 Days

Petersburg, 27 Feby 1863

{ Examino Ioann. }

APPROVED BY _____

STATION _____

DATE _____

HUGH REES VAUGHAN (11214)

Richmond Va. Feby 21st Oct 1816 3

I hereby [appoint] Lieut W. Baskin Co. "C" 18th Va. Regt. —
Pay Master in fact and authorize him to receive the
within account of one hundred and [fifty] dollars (150.00)
for me.

Hugh W. Vaughan
Capt Co. "B" 18th Va. Regt

[I hereby Certify] that Vaughan is a private of
the Baskin Co. of said Command
[Officers]

Aug 22d 67   Col ... Bjone
... Sergeon member of Board

THE CONFEDERATE STATES OF AMERICA,

To _____, Dr.

ON WHAT ACCOUNT.	COMMENCEMENT AND EXPIRATION.		TERM OF SERVICE Charged in.		PAY PER MONTH.		AMOUNT.		REMARKS.
	From—	To—	Months.	Days.	Dollars.	Cts.	Dollars.	Cts.	
Pay—	1862	1862							
For myself,	April 27	May 31	1	4	130		147	29	
For _____ year's service,									
Forage for _____ horses.								$147 29	

I hereby certify that the foregoing account is accurate and just; that I have not been absent, without leave, during any part of the time charged for; that I have not received pay, forage, or received money in lieu of any part thereof, for any part of the time therein charged; that the horses were actually kept in service and were mustered for the whole of the time charged; that for the whole of the time charged for my staff appointment, I actually and legally held the appointment and did duty in the department; that I am not in arrears with the Confederate States on any account whatsoever; and that the last payment I received was from _____ Confederate States, the ____ day of ____

and to the ____ day of ____ 186_

I, at the same time, acknowledge that I have received of ____ the sum of ____

this ____ day of ____ 186_, the sum of ____ Dollars

being the amount in full of said account.

Pay, - - - $ 147 00
Forage, - - $ ____

Amount, $ 147 00

(Signed Duplicates.)

Card 1

(Confederate.)

9 | 18 | Miss.

H. Vaughan.

Capt., Co. B, 18 Reg't Mississippi Vols.

Appears on a

Roster

of the Eighteenth (18th) Regiment Mississippi Volunteers, Humphreys' Brigade, Kershaw's Division, Longstreet's Corps, Army Northern Virginia; organized June 7, 1861; mustered into Confederate service June 7, 1861.

Roster dated .... *Qva.* ....

Date of entry or muster } .... , 186 .
into State service,

Date of entry or muster } .... , 186 .
into Confederate service,

Date of rank, and whether } *Apl. 26, 186 2.*
by appointment, election *Election*
or promotion,

Date and cause } *d. Capt. Vach. .... 1864.*
of vacancy,

Name of successor ....

Remarks: ....

Book mark: ....

Pan Cuchley, Copyist.

(608)

Card 2

(Confederate.)

9 | 18 | Miss.

H. A. Vaughan.

Capt., Co. B, 18 Reg't Mississippi Vols.

Appears on a

Roster

of the 18th Regiment of Mississippi Volunteers, Humphreys' Brigade, Kershaw's Division, Longstreet's Corps, Army of N. Va.; organized June 7, 1861; mustered into Confederate service June 7, 1861.

Roster dated .... *Sept. dated, 186* .

Date of entry or muster } .... , 186 .
into State service,

Date of entry or muster } .... , 186 .
into Confederate service,

Date of rank, and whether } *C.*
by appointment, election *Apl. 26 .*
or promotion,

Date and cause } *per back. .. , 186 4.*
of vacancy,

Name of successor ....

Remarks: ....

Book mark: ....

Pett Buchley, Copyist.

(608)

Card 3

(Confederate.)

9 | 18 | Miss.

Hugh R. Vaughan

Capt., Co. B (Benton Rifles),
18 Regiment Mississippi Infantry.

Appears on a

"Record"

of the organization named above, from April 27, 1861, to Feb. 24, 1865.

Record dated .... *Not stated* ...... , 186 .

Enlisted:

When .... *Apl. 27* ..... , 186 1 .

Where ...... *Benton, Miss.* ......

Period .... *12 mos.* ....

Occupation ...... *Farmer* ......

Born—(State) ...... *Miss.* ......

Residence.—(Nearest P.O.) *Benton, Miss.*

Age when enlisted ....

Married or single. *S*

Remarks: *Died March 5, 1864 in*
effects returned received at
Hai. of Shachalie, Sept. 17, 1864.

Book mark: ....

Ale Black, Copyist.

[872]

(884)

Card 4

(Confederate.)

9 | 18 | Miss.

H. R. Vaughan.

Capt., Co. B (Benton Rifles),
18 Mississippi Regiment.

Appears on a

"Record".

of the organization named above, from April 27, 1861 to Feb. 22, 1865, (under the head of, "Roster of Commissioned Officers.")

Record dated .... *Not stated* ...... , 186 .

Appointment: ....

Date of .... *Apl. 26* .... , 186_ .

Authority of .... *Confed. States.* ....

Commission Expired: ....

When ...... *Mar. 5* .... , 186 4 .

Cause ...... *Died at Turnwill* ......

Remarks: ....

Book mark: ....

Ale Black, Copyist.

(884)

JAMES B. VAUGHAN (11215)

18 | Miss.

J. B. Vaughan

Co. B, 18 Reg't Mississippi Vols.

Appears on a

Report of Sick and Wounded

of the organization named above,

for .... 186 .

.... Vicksburg, Va.

Surgeon's Certificate and Deaths:

Date of death .... 186 .

Remarks: ....

(448) .... Copyist.

---

18 | Miss.

James Vaughan
Sergt. Co. B, 18 Miss.

Appears on a

Register

of Payments to Discharged Soldiers.

Date of discharge 20 Nov., 186 / .
Date of payment 20 Mar., 186 / .
By whom ....
Remarks: ....

Confed. Arch., Chap. 5, File No. 110, page ......

Book mark: ....

(685) .... Copyist.

---

18 | Miss.

Samuel Vaughan

Capt. Wm. H. Kinet's Company
(Benton titles),
18 Reg't Mississippi Infantry.

Appears on a

Company Muster-in Roll

of the organization named above, called into the service of the Confederate States. Roll dated
.... 186 / .
Muster-in to date .... 186 / .
Joined for duty and enrolled:
When .... , 186 / .
Where ....
By whom ....
Period ....

Traveling to place of rendezvous ...... miles.
Remarks: ....

Book mark: ....

(688) .... Copyist.

---

18 | Miss.

Samuel Vaughan

Co. B (Benton Rise),
18 Regiment Mississippi Infantry.

Appears on a

"Record"

of the organization named above,
from April 27, 1861, to Feb. 24, 1865.

Recom'd. dated .... , 186

Enlisted .... , 186
When .... , 186
Where ....
Period ....
Born—(State) ....
Occupation ....
Residence—(Nearest P. O.) ....
Age when enlisted ....
Married or single .... S
Remarks: ....

Book mark: ....

(684) .... Copyist.

MAR 15 47644393 NO. 506

ENGAGEMENTS.*

Manassas, July 21, 1861.

Leesburg, Va., Oct. 21, 1861.

Savage Station

Malvern Hill

Maryland Heights

Sharpsburg

Fredericksburg, Va., Dec. 11

Fredericksburg, May 3

Gettysburg

Chickamauga

Knoxville

Bean's Station

Wilderness, May 6, 1864

Spotsylvania, May 8

Spottsylvania, May 12

Hanover Junction

Cold Harbor, — days

Petersburg — ten days

Deep Bottom

Berryville

Cedar Creek

*The following characters mean: P, present and unhurt; w. wounded; s. w. severely wounded; k. killed; a. absent without leave; a. f. absent on furlough or satisfactorily; a. d. absent on detail or duty by order; a. s. absent sick; a. w. absent wounded; a. c. absent captured; a. a. absent under arrest; c. captured; x. deserted; m. missing; p. d. present detailed; m. w. mortally wounded. Those marked thus (*) in column of names, re-enlisted under Act of December 11, 1861, or were held in service by Act of April 16, 1862.

CHARLES C. VAUGHAN (12112)

V	6	Ala.

Charles C Vaughan

P't, { (Old) Co. B, 6 Reg't Alabama Infantry.*

Appears on

Company Muster Roll

of the organization named above,

for May 15 to Jun 30 , 186 1 .

Enlisted: mustered in

When May 15 , 186 1 .

Where Montgomery, Ala

By whom Maj. McLean

Period 12 mos

Last paid:

By whom no pay since mustered in

To what time , 186 .

Present or absent Present

Remarks:

Name appears in column names present as Charles C Vaughn

*This company subsequently became (New) Company L, 6th Regiment Alabama Infantry.

Book mark:

(042) W. R. Lee Copyist.

V	6	Ala.

Charles C Vaughan

P't, { (Old) Co. B, 6 Reg't Alabama Infantry.*

Appears on

Company Muster Roll

of the organization named above,

for July & Aug , 186 1 .

Enlisted:

When May 7 , 186 1 .

Where Loachapoka Ala

By whom Jno. M. Kennedy

Period

Last paid:

By whom E. H. Harris

To what time June 30 , 186 1 .

Present or absent Present

Remarks:

*This company subsequently became (New) Company L, 6th Regiment Alabama Infantry.

Book mark:

(042) W. R. Lee Copyist.

(CONFEDERATE.)

	6	Ala.

Charles C. Vaughan

Co. B, 6. Reg't.

Name appears on a

Register

of Claims of deceased Officers and Soldiers from Alabama which were filed for settlement in the Office of the Confederate States Auditor for the War Department.

By whom presented: Thomas Berdin

When filed .... July 28, 1862.

Where born ....

Where died ....

Comptroller:

When reported to .... May 21, 1863

When returned .... June 24, 1863

Number of settlements 3587

Certificates ....

Report ....

Amount found due $26.76

By whom paid ....

No. of Paymasters' Settlements ....

Abstract and No. of Voucher ....

Confed. Arch., Chap. 10, File No. 26, page 254

(999)   J. Gay   Copyist.

(Confederate.)

N	G	Ala.

.... Vaughan.

.... Co. B, 6 Reg't Alabama Infantry.

Appears on a

Report of Sick and Wounded

of the 6th Regiment Alabama Infantry,

for .... , 186

Station Gainsburg x Sicks

Disease ....

Discharges on Surgeon's Certificate and Deaths:

Diseaase, Typhoid Fever.

Date of discharge } from service, } 186

Date of death ....} Sept 5. 186

Remarks:

Book mark: ....

(666)   .... Copyist.

Adjutant and Inspector General's Office,

Richmond, Va. Dec. 15 1862

It appears from the Muster Roll of Capt. P. Canedy's ....Company

(.... B ...) of the .... 6 .. Regiment ..... Ala ....Volunteers,

on file in this office, that Chas C. Vaughan (private) of his Company

was enlisted ... May 7 ..186 2 and for 12 mos. Died

Sept. 5 186 .

Ida Halfin

350

PAGE THREE

Declaration for Pay &c
Fathers Claim

The State of Alabama } On this 22nd day of
Montgomery County } July 1862. Before me
Thomas Duncan an Acting Justice of the Peace
within and for said County Personally came
William C. Vaughan aged fifty five years a
resident of the County of Macon and State of
Alabama who being duly sworn Declares that
he is the reputed Father of Charlie C Vaughan
who was a Private in Co (B) commanded by
Captain Kennedy. in the 6th Regiment of Ala
Volunteers during the War with the United States
in 1861, That his Son the said Charlie C Vaughan
enlisted at Lochapoka Ala on the 7th day of
May 1861 for the term of Twelve Months and
continued in actual service in said war
until he died; That he died on the 5th day
of September 1861 at Fairfax Station Va from
sickness contracted while in the service of
the Confederate States and while in the line
of his duty as a Soldier & that he left no
Widow or Child surviving him and that
the Declarant is the only Legal heir & claimant
  He makes this Declaration for the purpose
of Obtaining from the Government of the Con
federate States the Arrearages of Pay Com
mutation retained pay & all other allowancy
that may be found due the said Charlie C Vaugh
up to the time of his death as well as the
proceeds of all or any Effect he may have left.
And he claims that in case the Claim
is allowed that the Warrant be sent

Th. Whereas Darden Montgomery Ala
Sworn to and subscribed before me
this day and year first above written

William C, Vaughan

Th. Darden JP.

We the undersigned resident of the counties
of Macon & Montgomery and State of Alabama
do upon our oaths declare that we
knew Charles C Vaughan in his lifetime
and always understood from him that he
was the son of Wm C Vaughan whose
signature we have subscribed to the foregoing declaration. And we know that the
declarant is the reputed father of the said
Charles C Vaughan and that the said Charles
C Vaughan died leaving no widow nor
child surviving him, and that the declarant is the only legal heir of the deceased
and that we are disinterested
Sworn to and subscribed before me this
22d July 1862   Henry J. Vaughan

Th. Darden JP   M. E. Vaughan

The State of Alabama } It is hereby
Montgomery County } certified that
satisfactory proof has been exhibited
before me by affidavits of H J Vaughan
and M E Vaughan two credible witnesses
that Wm C Vaughan is the reputed father
of Charles C Vaughan deceased and
that I am disinterested
Given under my hand at office   Th. Darden JP
this 22d July 1862

HENRY JACKSON VAUGHAN (1214)

	(CONFEDERATE)	
V	46	Ala

H. J. Vaughan

Co. F. 46 Ala. Regt.

Appears on a
RECEIPT ROLL

for clothing,

for .... 2 qr ...., 1864 .

Date of issue.... Apr. 30 ..., 1864 .
Signature ......
Remarks:.....

Roll No.
53

Copyist.

(CONFEDERATE.)

V | 46 | Ala.

H. J. Vaughan
Prt. Co. F 46 Ala. Regt.

Appears on a Register of

St. Mary's Hospital,
La Grange, Ga.

Date _Not shown_ ..., 1864

Remarks: .....

June 6, 1864. Transferred
to Montalga.

Henry J. Vaughan, June 6.

Confed. Arch., Chap. 6, File No. 274, page

(C85) Copyist.

WILLIAM MILES VAUGHAN (12141)

(Confederate.)

| U | 1 | Ala. |

William Vaughan

Pv't, { (New) Co. H., 1 Reg't Alabama
Infantry.*

Appears on

Company Muster Roll

of the organization named above,

for ..Jan'y & Feb'y...., 186 3.

Enlisted:
When ..22 Jan'y..., 186 3.
Where ..Mauget....
By whom ..Billups....
Period ..3 yrs....
Last paid:
By whom ....
To what time ....Been paid..., 186 .
Present or absent ..Present....
Remarks: Received clothing $93.00
....Shoes ,....

Book mark: ....

(642) .... Copyist.

(Confederate.)

| U | 1 | Ala. |

Wm M. Vaughan +

Pv't, { (New) Co. H., 1 Reg't Alabama
Infantry.*

Died

Appears on

Company Muster Roll

of the organization named above,

for ..April 30 to Nov 30 ', 1865.

Enlisted:
When ..22 Jan'y...... 186 3.
Where ..Macon Co....
By whom ..Billups....
Period ..3 yrs....
Last paid:
By whom ..Capt Billups....
To what time ..30 April..., 186 3.
Present or absent ..Present....
Remarks: Clothing since Oct 5 6 2
..to Oct 1'63 $47.00 ,....

Book mark: ....

(642) .... Copyist.

(Confederate.)

| U | 1 | Ala. |

William Vaughan

Pv't, { (New) Co. H., 1 Reg't Alabama
Infantry.*

Appears on

Company Muster Roll

of the organization named above,

for ..March & April..., 186 3.

Enlisted:
When ..22 Jan'y...... 186 3.
Where ..Macon Co....
By whom ..Billups....
Period ..3 yrs....
Last paid:
By whom ..Capt Billups....
To what time ..25 Feb'y..., 186 3.
Present or absent ..Present....
Remarks:

Book mark: ....

(642) .... Copyist.

(Confederate.)

| U | 1 | Ala. |

Wm M. Vaughan

Pv't, { (New) Co. H., 1 Reg't Alabama
Infantry.*

Appears on

Company Muster Roll

of the organization named above,

for ..Nov & Dec '62, '63.

Enlisted:
When ..22 Jan......., 186 3.
Where ..Macon Co....
By whom ..Billups....
Period ..3 yrs....
Last paid:
By whom ..Capt Billups....
To what time ..Oct 31..., 186 3.
Present or absent ..Absent....
Remarks: Detailed Selma Arsenal
..Oct 1'63 ,....

Book mark: ....

(642) .... Copyist.

(Confederate.) 1 Ala.

Wm J. Vaughan

Pri.{ (New) Company K, 1 Regiment
Alabama Infantry.

Appears on a

Roll

of "Capt. J. F. Whitfield's Company 'K', 1st
Reg't Ala. Vols., Army of the Confederate
States, Col. I. G. W. Steedman, in compliance
with Par. III, Genl. Orders No. 27, A. & I.
G. O., Richmond, Va."

Roll dated Fort Gaines Ala.
April 16 ", 1864.

Remarks: Detached in Selma
Railroad

(652)   Copyist.

(Confederate.) 1 Ala.

W. M. Vaughn

Pri., Co. K., 1 Reg't Alabama Infantry.

Appears on a

Report

of "detailed men of 1st Ala. Regiment, January
31st, 1864."

Report dated _____
_____ Jun. 31 _____, 1864.

By whose order detailed _____
When detailed _____, 1863.
Where stationed _____

Remarks: _____

Book mark: _____

(654)   Copyist.

(Confederate.) 1 Ala.

Wm Vaugher ×

Pri., Co. K, 1 Alabama Regiment.

Appears on a

List

of non-commissioned officers and privates, prisoners
of war, who have been this day released upon
their paroles.

List dated Port Hudson, July _____, 1863.

Remarks: _____

× Name appears on Roll as of departure, et
_____ W. M. Vaughan _____

Number of roll
15   October
(652)   Copyist.

(Confederate.) 1 Ala.

William Vaughran

Pri. Co. K, 1 Reg't Alabama
Infantry.

Appears on a

Roll of Prisoners of War

paroled at Port Hudson, La., July 12 and 13,
1863.

Roll not dated.

Where captured Port Hudson
When captured July 7, 1863.

Remarks: _____

Number of roll
167; sheet 18

(650)   Copyist.

Card 1

(CONFEDERATE)

W. M. Vaughan

Co. K, 1st Cala.

Appears on a

RECEIPT ROLL

for pay

for

Date _Jan_ ...., 186 †.

Occupation _S. Arinient_

PERIOD OF SERVICE:

From ...., 186

To ...., 186

Months ....

Days 31

Rate of pay 3.0.0

Signature ....

Remarks: _Subsistence Cook_

Roll No. 579

Will., Copyist.

Card 2

(CONFEDERATE.)

W. M. Vaughn

Pvt. Co. K, 1st Ala.

Appears on a

RECEIPT ROLL

for pay .... Doo

for

Date ...., 186 3.

Occupation _Laborer_

Salem Arsenal

PERIOD OF SERVICE:

From ...., 186

To ...., 186

Months ....

Days 20

Rate of pay ....

Signature ....

Remarks: ....

Roll No. ....

McIntosh, Copyist.

Card 3

(CONFEDERATE.)

Appears on a Register of

Way Hospital,

Meridian, Miss.

Complaint ...... _Fever B_ ......, 1865

Admitted ...., 186

Returned to duty ...., 186

Transferred ...., 186

Furloughed ...., 186

Remarks: _Paroled Selma_

Confed. Arch., Chap. 6, File No. 665, page 112.

(623) .... A. McIlwain, Copyist.

Card 4

(CONFEDERATE.)

W. M. Vaughn

Black. 1st Rgt Ala.

Appears on a consolidated

Report

of Officers and Men absent on Detached service
belonging to French's Division.

Report dated _Meridian, Miss_ ......, 186 4

Where stationed ...... _Selma, Ala._

By whose order ...... _Genl Johnston._

No. and date of order ...... _Dec. 1_, 186 3

Remarks: ....

(741) .... Copyist.

HENRY KING VAUGHAN (12142)

(Confederate.)

V | 46 | Ala.

H. K. Vaughan

Pvt. Capt. Baggett's Company,* 46 Regiment Alabama Infantry.*

Appears on a

Muster Roll

for Bounty of the organization named above,

for .... May 7, 1862

Station Chattahoochee, Ala.

Enlisted:

When .... May 7, 1862

Where .... Tallapoosa, Ala.

By whom ....

Period .... 3 yrs or the War

Last paid:

By whom ....

To what time 186

Present or absent .... Present

Remarks:

*This company subsequently became Company F, 8th Regiment Alabama Infantry.

Book mark: ....

(850) Copyist.

(Confederate.)

V | 46 | ? | Ala.

Sgt Maj.- H. K. Vaughan

F & S 46 Ala Regt

Appears on a

RECEIPT ROLL

for clothing,

for .... 2 Qr 186

Date of issue APR 30, 1864.

Signature

Remarks:

Roll No. ....

Copyist.

(Confederate.)

V | 46 | Ala.

H. K. Vaughn

Sergt F Co. ......, 46 Reg't. Ala. Inf.

Appears on a

LIST

of officers and men, of the 46th Alabama Regiment, who will be effective at the expiration of their furlough.*

List not dated.

* Other records indicate men were furloughed at Enterprise, Miss., about July 22, 1863.

Shepherd

Copyist.

357

PAGE TWO

Roll of Prisoners of War

Co. ..... 46 Reg't Alabama Infantry.

Appears on a

Roll of Prisoners of War

paroled at Vicksburg, Miss., according to the
terms of capitulation entered into by the commanding Generals of the United States and
Confederate forces July 4, 1863.

Roll dated. *Not dated.*

Paroled at Vicksburg, Miss., July 10, 1863.

When captured

Where captured *Vicksburg Miss*
July 4, 1863.

Remarks:

Duplicate Roll above.

H. K. Vaughan.

VICKSBURG, MISSISSIPPI, JULY ....9...... 1863.

To all Whom it may Concern, Know Ye That:

I...*H. K. Vaughan*.........a *Serg't Maj* of Co. *Co (B) 46* Reg't *Ala*
Vols. C. S. A., being a prisoner of War, in the hands of the United States Forces, in virtue
of the capitulation of the city of Vicksburg and its Garrison, by Lieut. Gen. John C. Pemberton, C. S. A., Commanding, on the 4th day of July, 1863, do in pursuance of the terms
of said capitulation, give this my solemn parole under oath————
That I will not take up arms again against the United States, nor serve in any military, police,
or constabulary force in any Fort, Garrison or field work, held by the Confederate States of
America, against the United States of America, nor as guard of any prisons, depots or stores
nor discharge any duties usually performed by Officers or soldiers against the United States
of America, until duly exchanged by the proper authorities.

H. K. Vaughan Sergt mja

Sworn to and subscribed before me at Vicksburg, Miss., this *9* day of July 1863.

25 Reg't *Ohio* Vols
maj AND PAROLING OFFICER.

BIBLIOGRAPHY

BOOKS

Avant, David A., Jr. _Illustrated Index of J. Randall Stanley's History of Gadsden County, 1948_. Tallahassee: L'Avant Studios, 1985.

Boatner, Mark M. III. _Encyclopedia of the American Revolution_. New York: David McKay Co., Inc., c1974.

Brown, C. C. _History of the First Baptist Church of Sumter_.

Cain, Cyril E. _Four Centuries on the Pascagoula_. 2 vols. Spartanburg, S. C.: The Reprint Company, 1983.

Cook, Harvey Toliver. _Rambles in the Pee Dee Basin, South Carolina_. Columbia, S. C.: The State Company, 1926.

DeCell, Harriet and JoAnne Prichard. _Yazoo: Its Legends and Legacies_. Yazoo City: Yazoo Delta Press, 1976.

Frierson, John L. _The Friersons of Stateburg_. Camden: Self-published, 1972.

Fulton, William Frierson. _Family Record and War Reminiscences_. Place unknown: Self-published, 1919.

Gillis, Norman E. _Mississippi Genealogical Notes_. Vol. 1, 105.

Goodspeed, Thomas W. _Biographical and Historical Memoirs of Mississippi_. Vol 2. Chicago: The Goodspeed Publishing Company, 1891.

Gregg, Alexander. _History of the Old Cheraws_. New York: Richardson and Company, 1867. Reprint. Spartanburg, S. C.: The Reprint Company, 1965.

358

Gregorie, Anne King. History of Sumter County. Sumter, S. C.: Osteen Davis Publishing Co., 1954.

Hathaway, James Robert Bent. Register of North Carolina. 3 vols. Edenton: Self-published, 1903. (Books in Print lists a reprint edition of 1979.)

Kirkland, Thomas J. and Robert M. Kennedy. Historic Camden. 2 vols. Columbia: The State Company, 1905.

McCleskey, Delores B. New Limbs from Old Roots. 2 vols. Indianapolis: Self-published, 1988.

Nicholes, Cassie. Historical Sketches of Sumter County: Its Birth and Growth. 2 vols. Sumter: Sumter County Historical Society, 1975.

Nunn, Dr. Alexander, ed. Lee County and Her Forebears. Montgomery, AL: Herff Jones, 1983.

Nunn, Dr. Alexander. Yesterdays in and around Loachapoka. Opelika, AL: Loachapoka Homecoming Association, 1968.

Revill, Janie. Sumter District. Columbia: The State Printing Co., 1968.

South Carolina Historical Society. South Carolina Genealogies. Spartanburg: The Reprint Company, 1983.

Townsend, Leah. South Carolina Baptists. Baltimore: Genealogical Publishing Co., Inc., 1974.

Womack, Miles Keenan. Gadsden: A Florida County in Word and Pictures. 1st ed. Dallas: Taylor Publishing Co., c1976.

Wright, John Peavy. Glimpses into the Past from My Grandfather's Trunk. Alexander City, AL: Outlook Publishing Co., 1969.

PERIODICALS

Deep South Genealogical Quarterly 9 (507) and
18 (66).

Dorman, John Frederick, ed. Virginia
Genealogist 6, no. 2 (April 1962-June
1962).

East Alabama Historical Society. Taproots 1-
13.

Neuffer, Claude H., ed. Names in South
Carolina 1, no 2 (2) and 13 (32-33).

South Carolina Historical South Society. South
Carolina Historical and Genealogical
Magazine (1949 and 1953).

Warren, Mary B., ed. Family Puzzlers 584 (18-
19).

OTHERS

Alabama Archives Microfilms, Roll M-70 (Minutes
of the Notasulga Baptist Church).

Alabama Military records, Military Division,
Alabama Archives.

Census records of Sumter, County, South
Carolina; Chambers, Clarke, Lee, Macon,
Mobile and Tallapoosa Counties, Alabama;
Gadsden County, Florida; Amite, Green,
Jackson, Lowndes and Yazoo Counties,
Mississippi.

Marriage, will and cemetery records of W. P. A.

Military, bounty land and pension records of
the National Archives, Washington, D. C.

Newspapers. Alabama Christian Advocate,
Grenada (Miss.) Herald, Macon Republican,
Montgomery Advertiser, Opelika Daily News,
Opelika Democrat, Opelika Industrial News,
Southern Whig, Sumter Banner, Sumter
Gazette and States Rights Advocate, Sumter

Watchman, _Yazoo City Weekly Whig_, _Yazoo City Whig & Political Register_ and _Yazoo Democrat_.

Probate Court records of Chambers, Lee, Macon, Russell, and Tallapoosa Counties, Alabama; Troup County, Georgia; and Sumter County, South Carolina.

United States Senate Document 514, 1st Session, 23rd Congress, 1833 (for roll of South Carolina College).

Vaughan and Robison Family Bible records. Robison taken from Alabama Archives file.

Yale Obituary (1816-1884).

Also correspondence with those mentioned in the preface.

INDEX

The index is a tool in itself. By using it the reader can assemble material on given individuals when, in the text, they were not the sole focus of the passages in which they appear. I have attempted to list each individual so they are distinguishable, even though their name be identical. If the reader has more information than I, he may find some individuals the same, although unknowingly listed as separate individuals. Feature sections on individuals are indicated by italics.

```
Anderson, Walter            204
         William            53
         Dr. William Wallace  47, 48, 53, 97
Antony, a slave             317
Armstrong, Capt.             26
         S. R.              325
Arthur, Mary (Reese)         52
Atkins, C. J.               169
         Elizabeth (Nettles)    29
         Lazarus            121, 319
Atkinson, Elizabeth (Spears)  8-10
         Littleton           10
Austin, J. S.               357
Avant, David A., Jr.          9
Avent, John                 294
         Thomas             332

Baggett, Capt.              231
Bagnal, Isaac                65
Baker, Albert Brewer        208, 211, 213
         Albert Love        213
         Benajah            212
         Carlton            213
         Frances (Zuber)    211, 212
         Freddie (Wright)   208, 211, 213
         J.                 354
         J. A.              213
         James Noel         213
         John J.            212
         Julia (Gilmore)    212
         Julius R.          211, 212
         R. H.              213
         Seth L.            213
         Tabitha (Voss/Vance)   212
         Willie B.          213
Ballard, John R.            259
Bancroft, Rev. J.           162
         J. W.              342
Bannister, John              46
Barber, Comfort Ann         151
         Elizabeth (Hardin)     151
         Harriett (Vaughan)     142, 151, 282,
                             307, 321, 322
         Ira (Oliver)       151
         John               151
         Margaret           151
         Nathaniel C.       151
         Nathaniel J.       142, 151, 322
```

Bradford, Malcomb   335, 339
Margaret   335
Maria (Blackwell)   337
Martha (Moody) 335
Mary (of Granville) 12
Mary, Jr. (of Granville) 12
Mary (of Northampton) 13, 294
Mary (Bradford) 336
Mary (Dargan) 29
Mary (McKnight) 336
Mary (Mitchell) 268, 292, 335, 339
Mary Mercy   335
Matilda (Wilson)   335
Matthew   335, 336
Middleton   31, 335, 339
Nancy (Brunson) 336
Nancy (Singleton)   336
Nathan   337
Nathanel   337
Nathaniel   12, 13, 292, 294,
334, 335, 337, 339
Nathaniel (son of 12
John of Brunswick)
Nathaniel (son of 335, 337, 339
John A.)
Nathaniel, Jr. 335, 337
Philemon   12
Rebecca (Pace) 12, 333
Richard (son of John 12
of Brunswick)
Richard (of Northampton 294
and son of Thomas)
Richard (brother of 290, 338 (?)
Frances Elizabeth)
Richard (venerable) 338
Richard (son of 335-337, 339
Nathaniel)
Richard, Jr. 32, 335, 336
Robert   96
Robert (son of Richard) 335, 336
Robert D.   31, 259, 336
Robert H. (sic) 336
Robert R.   335
Samuel J. 15, 28, 29, 337
Sarah   12, 294
Sarah (of Granville) 12
Sarah (Howard) 337
Susan   335

Clark(e), Ann	13, 14, 292
Clark(e), Henry	292, 311
James	311
Clayton, P.	147, 168
Clopton, James	165, 166
Clower, Agnes (Bennett)	162
George W.	162
Louise (Warren)	162
Thomas M.	162
Tom	158, 162
Coate, Burr J.	110
Liningston	111
Mary (Vaughan)	110, 111, 282, 300
Cobb, Captain James P.	127-130, 147, 148, 165, 166, 168, 174-176, 178, 181
Coker, W. D.	252
Colclough, John	316
Converse, Augustus L.	46
Mary (Kellogg)	46
Cook, Alice	14, 38
Samuel	14, 38
Cooper, E. E.	324
J. H.	324
Katharine	v
Cornet, Amy	4, 12, 115, 292, 334
Margaret	4, 292
Couliette Family	292, 293
Counselman, John S.	246, 247
Nettie (McCrorey)	246, 247
Cousins, A. J.	139
Cowan, Louisa (McKay)	109, 110
Oliver C.	109, 110
Cowans, H. F.	320
Cox, Orrin D.	326
Crawford, Eleanor	v
John	320
Linda	v
Crayton & Harwell	322
Crittenden, A. M.	311
Crosby, A. M.	341
Cruger, Lt.	25
Crump, Sarah (Vaughan)	1, 2, 288
Culbreath, Eunice	211
Thomas	211
Culpepper, Rev. Mr.	141
Cummings Family	121
Alfred M.	122, 159, 319

```
Lindsey, Marvin              138, 309
        Robert               125, 138, 309
        Robert father        131
        of Isaac Linsey)
        Thomas               131
Linsey, Ida                  131, 307
        Isaac                125, 131, 138
        Mary (Vaughan)       125, 131, 138, 282,
                             303, 305
        Robert (son of Isaac)   131, 307, 308
Livingston, Mrs. W. O.       326
Longstreet, General James 85
Lossing                      25
Love, William                4, 13, 312, 313
Lovejoy, Amanda (Goldsmith)     142, 304
        Frank                142
        Jeremiah F.          142
Loveless, Martha (Goldsmith)    321
           Michael              321
Lowry, David                 320
Lucy, a slave                288
Ludden, Forest E.            235
Luse, Captain William H.     85, 86, 346
Lyons, Peter                 343

McBath, Edgar B.             177
McCleskey, Ruth              vi, 110, 253
McConnico Family             293
         William             292
McCoy, H. R.                 231
McCrorey, James T.           245, 246
         Mary (Reynolds) 245, 246, 252, 255,
                             308
         Maude Willa         246
McDonald, Rachel (Davis)     46
         Sgt.                25
         Willis              46
McDowell, Charles G.         246, 247
         Charles G., Jr.  247, 248
         Charles G. III   248
         Deborah (Sirmon)       248
         Mariko (Turner) 248
         Randolph C.         248
         Verna (McCrorey)       246, 247
         Vivian (Delmar) 247, 248
McElveen, Margaret           v
McGeorge, Captain Skenery 166
McGhee, J. R.                325
```

```
Moore, Elizabeth (Kuykendall)    335
       James Sinkler        79, 85, 96, 97
       Isham                292, 293
       Col. John (same as Isham?) 10
       Capt. John (same as above?)  311
       John Isham           vi, 97, 293
       John Isham (son of James)  97
       Kent                 226, 228
       Margaret (Rees)      53, 96-98, 282
       Margaret (Vaughan)   75, 79, 85
       Margaret Mary, Jr.   97
       Mark                 311
       Marylyn (Vaughan)    201, 285
       Matthew H.           70
       Mr.                  201
       Nancy (Vaughan)      226, 228, 286
       Sarah (Sylvester)    10
       William              339
Mordaunt Family            290
Moseley, Margaret (Vann)   183
        Robert D.          183
Moses, O. D.               352
Moss, Arlina               vii
Motte, Rebecca             24, 25
Murrell, William           317
Myers, William             70

Neal, William B.           245
Neilson/Nelson, David      315
Nettles, Abigail S.        31
        Amos A.            29, 30
        Amos D.            299
        Amy (Alexander)    32
        Ann (Stroud)       29
        Caroline           30
        Elijah             31
        Elizabeth (d. of Mary Mathis)  31
        Elizabeth (w. of Solomon)  31
        Elizabeth (Miller)     32
        Elizabeth Perdue       32
        Frances (McCoy)    30
        Hariet             30
        Harvey             30
        Hezekiah           29, 30
        Huldah             30
        Isham              31
        Israel             31
        Jacob              31
```

```
Scroggins, Allison          175
Segrest, George             320
        Reuben              183
Sevier, General John        257
Shakelford, Emily (Burruss)     90
            Mr.             90
Shorter, E. S.              147
Silliman, Dr. Andrew        42, 43
Simmons, Louise             238
        Sarah (Vaughan)     232, 238, 283
        Sarah, Jr.          238
        Tommy               238
        Vaughan             238
        William H.          232, 238
        William H., Jr.     238
Singleton, Major John       336
        Joseph              317, 336
        Matthew             339
        Robert              107, 317, 339
        Sally (Bradford)        336
        Sarah (Gayle)       107
Smith, Barbara (Thompson)   212
        Lt. Daniel P.       185
        Dink                212
Sneed, Eliza (Burruss)      90
        Mr.                 90
Sones, Hall/Henry           7
        Hall/Henry, Jr.     7, 317
        Mr.                 4, 7
        Naomi (Vaughan)     viii, 1, 4, 7-11, 14,
                            120, 281, 288, 292,
                            313
        William             7, 10, 315, 317
Sophey, a slave             315
Spann, Anna                 100
        Bettie              100
        Charles             100, 292
        Elizabeth (Reynolds)    100, 291
        Ella                100
        Harriet             100
        James, Sr.          55, 100, 318
        James (son of Lawrence) 100
        James G.            100
        Lawrence M.         100, 291
Span(n), Richard            13, 292, 294
Spann, Timothy H.           100
        Tyre I.             100
        William T.          100
```

398

Marguerite (Lewis) 94
Marion (Hazelwood) 210, 215
Marni (Kallis)   221, 223
Martha (d. of John of Northampton) 331
Martha (w. of John, Jr.) 277
Martha (w. of Vincent of Granville) 93, 94
Martha (O'Reilly) 93, 94
Martha E.   15, *40*, 281, 329
Martha E. (w. of Christopher) 257, 260, 261,
                                 302
Martha Elmira   170, 282
Mary   137, 307
Mary (d. of James B.)   88, 283
Mary (Anderson)   87, 93
Mary (Britton)   257, 262-264
Mary (Burks)   92
Mary (Clark)   83, 84, 307, 341
Mary (Fisher)   93
Mary (Goff)   111
Mary (Harrison)   120, 169, 171, 177, 179,
                   180, 182, 185, 231, 235,
                   245, 252, 303
Mary (Robeson)   120, 155, 158, 303, 321,
                   325, 326
Mary (Spear)   125, 139
Mary (Walton)   170, 185-187, 198, 309, 322,
                   324, 326
Mary Elizabeth   202, 285
Mary Elizabeth (d. of James H.) 262, 282
Mary Ellen   140, 283
Mary Lou   232, *237*, 283
Mary Louise   111, 282, 303
Mary Margaret (Anderson) 13, 42-44, 46, 47,
                   67, 69, 95, 96, 297,
                   298, 316, 327-329
Mary Margaret, Jr. 42, *44*, 67, 281
Mary Merle   93, 285
Mary Saphronia   170, 282
Mathew J.   108, 109, 111, 281, 282,
                   300, 303, 328
Mathew J., Jr.   111, 282, 283, 303
Mattie (Bennett)   93
Merle   93, 284, 285
Michael Christian 202, 285, 286
Miles Edwin   120, 121, 123, 135, 136,
                   155-158, 177, 210, 255,
                   281, 282, 300, 303, 309,
                   316, 319, 320, 325, 351

READER'S COMPILE

Those who wish can use the indicated pages to record information on your immediate family which was not available to the author.

414